W9-BRJ-730

IN THE COMPANY OF LEGENDS

Joan Kramer and **David Heeley**

BEAUFORT
BOOKS

IN THE COMPANY OF LEGENDS

Library of Congress Cataloging-in-Publication Data On File

For inquiries about volume orders, please contact:

Beaufort Books
27 West 20th Street, Suite 1102
New York, NY 10011
sales@beaufortbooks.com

Published in the United States by Beaufort Books
www.beaufortbooks.com

Distributed by Midpoint Trade Books
www.midpointtrade.com

Printed in the United States of America

Cover Design by Brian Whitehill
Interior Design by Mark Karis

Hardcover ISBN: 9780825307423

In memory of my parents, Eleanor Cohen Kramer and Milton S. Kramer, who believed that their daughter could accomplish anything.

—JOAN KRAMER

To the television pioneers, who inspired me, and on whose shoulders we stand. And to all those from whom I learned along the way.

—DAVID HEELEY

CONTENTS

FOREWORD

You don't spend fifty years of your life doing something you don't think highly of. Not if you're lucky, you don't. I have been able to spend fifty years of my life doing something I adored and was praised and paid. However, I did not endure fifty years of doing something stupid or dull for money. I did it because I loved it and honored it and knew its value. Joan and David are the only people I've ever met who have memorialized this experience, who have told the stories of actors on as high a level as they deserve.

Here's a secret: People come up to an actor on the street and say, "Thank you." They don't say that to their rabbis, their divorce lawyers or their neurosurgeons. They say it to actors because they are the ones who give them "surcease from sorrow." I do not take lightly the compliment and I am thrilled when it happens gracefully. Joan and David have a body of work that is simplified down to the words, "Thank you."

We walk around the world surrounded by loss, tragedy, anxiety, and stress. Then an actor makes you laugh or focuses you on some part of the human experience. It's known as a "mitzvah." It is a gift that actors give and actors get. Joan and David are the only ones I've ever met who understand that on the level it should be understood. So if they say they're going to tell you some stories, pay attention.

—RICHARD DREYFUSS

Beverly Sills on location in East Harlem for the *Salsa!* episode of *Skyline with Beverly Sills*. New York, 1979. Photograph by Brownie Harris.

CHAPTER ONE

Back Story

As with so many events in life, our meeting each other was a matter of chance. The fact that we then began working together was the luck of the draw.

JK David and I come from two different worlds, an ocean apart. I was a ballet dancer and assistant choreographer before starting to work in television production. From the age of seven I mingled with people from the worlds of music, dance, opera, and art, and always felt comfortable talking to anyone of any age. Part of that is due to the fact that I was an only child who was never asked to leave the room when my grandmothers and their siblings were talking. I was just part of the family discussions.

Born and raised in Chicago, I knew early on that I wanted to be a ballet dancer. But I eventually discovered that I preferred working behind-the-scenes instead of in front of the curtain, finding it more satisfying to help put the pieces together for a production than to actually perform in it.

After graduating from high school, I moved to New York to pursue a career in ballet. Within a few years, I was hired as the assistant to a choreographer, traveling to Philadelphia and San Francisco, dealing with contracts, rehearsal schedules, costume fittings, and stage props. It would all come in handy a few years later when I switched careers.

Today, getting a start in television or film seems a lot more complicated than the way I began. As a matter of fact, I was just plain lucky.

I'd had a disagreement with the choreographer for whom I'd been working. It happened to be when *The Mary Tyler Moore Show* was at the height of its popularity, and that series made an indelible impression on me, since Mary's character was a single career woman, working in the traditionally male business of television news. I thought, "I could do a job like hers. It's just an extension of what I've been doing all along."

I called all three major television networks in New York, asking, "Do you have any production jobs available?" CBS and NBC said all their programs were produced in California. ABC told me basically the same thing, but then added, "We do have one show that's done in New York, *The Dick Cavett Show*, and it's produced for ABC by Cavett's own company, *Daphne Productions*. Try calling their office. Here's the number."

Cavett's secretary at the time, Doris Mikesell, was the entire personnel department, and when I was put through to her line and heard, "Mr. Cavett's office," I thought, "Why am I talking to the host's assistant?"

My first words were a textbook example of what *not* to say. "You don't have any job openings, do you?" I asked.

"As a matter of fact, I do," said Doris. "I'm going on vacation at the end of next week and I need to hire a receptionist before I leave. When can you come in for an interview?"

Then, as if my opening line was not bad enough, I said, "What kind of receptionist? If it's working a switchboard, I don't know how to do that."

"No one who has ever come to work here knew how to work

our old-fashioned board, but it doesn't take long to learn. So please, come in to see me on Monday."

It was as though no blunders were enough to prevent me from getting that job. I met Doris just before Christmas, and began working the first week of the new year.

The switchboard was indeed a challenge that took me some time to master and, along the way, I accidently disconnected a few very important people, including Dick Cavett, himself. Fortunately for me—and everyone else who called that office—I was promoted to the position of assistant talent coordinator three months later.

It was the mid-seventies, and the *Cavett Show* was not just an entertainment talk show; it was a reflection of the times. More than once we had bomb scares and had to evacuate the office or the studio, usually because of controversial guests, such as Angela Davis and Philip Berrigan. Often there'd be lines stretching around the block when a big star was due to appear: Bette Davis, Anthony Quinn, Paul Newman, and Joanne Woodward, Rudolf Nureyev, the Muppets, Paul Simon, Ethel Merman, Lily Tomlin, the Harlem Globetrotters, to name just a few.

It was there that I earned a reputation for booking people who were hard to get. I rarely called their agents; instead I found ways to track them down and reach them directly.

DH To this day, Joan's contact book is probably worth a fortune. She's a phone person. I'm not. She can find almost anyone's home number and schmooze with them. More often than not, by the end of the conversation, she has gained their trust and co-operation for the project we're working on at the time. I use the telephone as a practical necessity instead of a tool for visiting with people. So my calls are usually short and to the point.

JK I've also always been a perfectionist, even as a child. I can glom on to one tiny thing and spend hours or days fiddling with it in order to make it better. I know there are times when David feels

I'm actually making it worse; more than once he's told me, "You've thrown out the baby with the bath water." But he, too, is no slouch when it comes to perfectionism. Fortunately for both of us, we usually don't obsess over the same things.

DH I'm from the north of England: born in Yorkshire, and raised in Lancashire. My parents were both schoolteachers, and I realize now that raising two children[1] had to be a struggle for them financially. Nevertheless, they were determined that we both get a good education, and I eventually secured a place at Brasenose College, Oxford, along with a scholarship to pay the way.

As a child I had been fascinated by the stories I read about this new medium, television, before there was even a transmitter in our area. All aspects of it interested me: how it worked, who was involved, and how the early live shows were produced.

Another key event of my childhood was my joining the Boy Scouts. At the age of ten or eleven I was somewhat timid, and not at all adventurous. But my cousin dragged me to a meeting, and I was hooked. Ironically, he attended just that once, and never returned; I went all the way, eventually becoming a Queen's Scout (the equivalent of Eagle Scout in the US).

It was as a Scout that I learned how to be a leader. And it was at Oxford that I learned not to be intimidated by others, whatever their rank or position in society (Britain had then, and still has now, the remains of a class system). I believe that both those experiences were invaluable when I started directing and had to deal with crews and on-camera talent.

I loved the sciences, and chose to study (or "read," as they say at Oxford and Cambridge) Physics. But, although I'd always been one of the top students at my high school, I found it tough at the

---

1   I am five years older than my sister, Marilyn. She remained in the UK, and is married with four—now adult—children.

4

university level, and wasn't sure what my career path would be when I finished. Then, by a stroke of luck, I stumbled across a talk being given by the chief engineer of ATV, London's big commercial television broadcaster. As I chatted with him afterwards, he offered me a six-week summer internship, and I was in heaven. All the things that had fascinated me from my childhood were there[2], giving me my first hands-on chance with cameras, lighting, etc. I knew I'd found what I wanted to do.

After I graduated from Oxford, I went to work in the engineering division of the BBC, starting in the telecine department, handling many miles of film. But a promotion that sent me even deeper into engineering led to the realization that I was moving in the wrong direction. Fortunately the BBC was about to start a second television network, BBC-2, and it gave me the opportunity to jump the barrier between engineering and production. I was able to get a "training attachment" to the Presentation Department, which needed to expand quickly. There I learned the director's craft, first with simple on-camera announcements, and later live talk shows and performance programs. Within a few years I was also making short filmed documentaries, mostly about luminaries in the performing and visual arts. It might seem a strange path for someone with a degree in Physics, but it fit right in with my many passions.

In 1969, I made one of those difficult life-changing choices many of us face at some point in our lives. I decided to resign from the BBC and move to New York. There was no job waiting, and there were lean times trying to find one. But eventually I was hired as an associate director at WNDT, the New York public television station, which would soon become WNET.

---

2   Four weeks were at ATV's Wood Green studio, where plays, musicals, and variety shows were produced. The last two weeks were at the Foley Street Network Control Centre.

Dick Cavett with Joan Kramer.
New York, 1998. Authors' collection.

JK I've maintained close contact with Dick Cavett. Even now, so many years later, I believe that working for his show was the best job in television, and the best training for what came later.

But good things don't last, and eventually *The Dick Cavett Show* was canceled. However, I'd caught the television "bug," and one of the jobs I landed afterwards was writing intermission segments for *Live from Lincoln Center*, at a time when Robert MacNeil was the host. When he learned of my background, he told me, "WNET is about to launch a new series about the arts. I think you'd be a good candidate to work on it."

I wasn't especially interested in working for public television, so when Robin (as most people call him) offered to pass along my résumé to the executive producer, I was not as enthusiastic as I should have been. "Let me think about it," I said. "I don't want to put you in an awkward position. Maybe I should just send it myself with a cover letter."

"No," he said. "It would be much better coming from me."

DH By the late seventies, I'd gone from associate director, to director, to managing station breaks and Pledge Weeks, and back again to directing, when it was announced that the station was developing a weekly arts show. In my opinion, it was long overdue; I'd already submitted a proposal for a similar series myself. So I was pleased to be chosen to join the staff as a producer/director.

The executive producer of the new program, *Skyline,* was Gail Jansen, who was impressed by Joan's résumé, which Robin had sent to her with a hand-written note, and she realized that the staff she was putting together didn't have anyone with a dance background. So after they met, Gail hired her as an associate producer. There were three teams of producers and associate producers, and everyone, except Joan, came from within the station.

My first program, which also launched the series, was a profile of flutist Jean-Pierre Rampal, with Linda Romano as my associate producer. It was nominated for an Emmy, but didn't win.

In the meantime, Joan had suggested to Gail a program about the set and costume designer, Rouben Ter-Arutunian, whom she had interviewed for the *Lincoln Center Library of Performing Arts Oral History Project.* Gail liked the idea, and assigned me to produce it with Joan as my associate producer. It was a nightmare.

JK Rouben was a wonderfully-talented man, and charming—until we came to the actual taping of the show in WNET's Studio 55, on 9ᵗʰ Avenue and 55ᵗʰ Street.

We had arranged for scale models and photos of many of his sets to be brought to the studio. But, when David tried to shoot them, Rouben came into the control room and stayed there, not hesitating to insist how each model should be lit and shot, and how each picture should be framed for the camera. It went on for hours.

DH Unfortunately, we didn't have hours. The same studio was used every weekday evening for the live broadcast of *The MacNeil/Lehrer Report,* so we had to be finished and out in time for that production to reset, rehearse, and go on the air. It was the first—and thankfully—the last time in my career that I thought I was going to leave a studio with nothing "in the can." But here was where my many years of working with the same crew paid off. They were terrific. They saw the problems I was having, and worked through required union breaks, and even shortened their official lunch hour until we got everything we needed on tape. I'll never forget that. In some ways it meant more than any of the awards I would receive in the future.

JK I felt terribly guilty, knowing that this was my idea to begin with, and seeing what a hard time David was having with it. He finally succeeded in getting the show recorded, including an excellent interview of Rouben by art critic, Grace Glueck. But the whole day was like pulling teeth. After the program was edited, Rouben went back to being a friend and gave each of us a signed original costume sketch in appreciation. Apparently, there had been very few, if any, programs devoted to a costume and set designer before this one.

However, I wondered if this would be the last time David would ever want to work with me again.

DH Together, Joan and I did profiles of Rudolf Nureyev, Lotte Lenya, Patricia Birch, John Curry, the ice dancer who'd won an Olympic gold medal, the Wagnerian opera soprano, Birgit Nilsson, and the musical genre, salsa. All of them received critical acclaim, and for the show about Patricia Birch, we received an Emmy nomination—although we didn't win.

JK My three months at WNET were extended when *Skyline* was renewed for a second season, and then for a third, when it became *Skyline with Beverly Sills*.

JK and DH However, it wasn't in the cards for the series to be renewed again. But by then it didn't matter to either of us because we had proposed an idea that would propel us from the local programming arena onto the national stage.

Olympic Gold Medalist John Curry with dancer/choreographer Peter Martins in the *Skyline* program *John Curry:Dance On Ice*. Curry told us, "Every choreographer says, 'I'd love to learn to skate.' That passes quickly."
Westchester, NY, 1978. Photograph by Ken Diego.

Authors' collection.

CHAPTER TWO

Fred Was First

"**M**r. Astaire is furious. He thought he made it clear to that man that he does not want a program done about him and will not co-operate."
The response from Fred Astaire's agent, Michael Black, was not a surprise. "That man" was Jac Venza, one of our executive producers, who'd recently been in Los Angeles, managed to meet with Astaire, and received a similar polite, but firm, reaction to his proposal. Even so, we knew we had to try again, and had written a letter of our own. It had done no good.

JK Previously, I had been responsible for booking Rudolf Nureyev twice on *The Dick Cavett Show,* and during one of his appearances he said, "So many people have taken Fred Astaire's dreams and put them in their own pockets." He confided in me that he hoped they could meet one day, and wondered if I might be able to come up with a plan to make it happen.

Joan Kramer escorting Rudolf Nureyev to taping of *The Dick Cavett Show*.
New York, 1974. Authors' collection.

By then, Joanne Woodward and I had become friends[1]. We shared a love of ballet, and a mutual admiration for Nureyev. And she knew Fred Astaire. So together we came up with the concept of a television special in which she would interview both of them. Nureyev leapt at the idea. Astaire turned it down flat.

DH That was before Joan and I met. However, when we produced *Nureyev on Nijinsky* for *Skyline*[2], she told me about the idea and I thought it was worth trying again. Once more, it never got off the ground. So we came up with a different approach: a documentary about Astaire and his career as a dancer. However, just as our boss, George Page, the head of *Arts and Sciences*, was about to submit the proposal to PBS for funding, a small turf war broke out. It turned

---

1   We first met when she and Paul Newman appeared together on *The Dick Cavett Show* in 1973.

2   He was in New York working with the Joffrey Ballet to recreate two of Nijinsky's famous performances in "Prélude à l'Après-Midi d'un Faune" and "Petrushka."

out that Jac Venza, head of *Great Performances*, was also about to submit a similar proposal. It was resolved by George and Jac agreeing to be co-executive producers of the project.

Amazingly, no program about Fred Astaire had ever been produced for American television. In fact, the biography/profile format was almost non-existent, with the exception of an occasional segment in news magazines such as *60 Minutes*.

However, many public television stations had had considerable success a few years earlier with a documentary devoted to Edith Piaf, originally made for British television. So PBS saw the potential in our show and agreed to finance it using a pool of money put aside for special programming during the two or three times a year when stations ask viewers to send in their pledges of financial support[3]. Most of the profiles we produced for PBS would be broadcast during these fund-raising periods.

JK and DH Unlike our own dismay over the "Astaire is furious" phone call, Jac Venza's attitude was, "He's a public figure; just go ahead and do the show."

What none of us knew was that he had the power to stop us. In the 1930s, when his lawyer negotiated his contracts with RKO, he inserted a clause giving Astaire approval of the use of excerpts from his films. This was very unusual at that time. To the best of our knowledge, the only other performers who had similar deals were Cary Grant and Myrna Loy. It's a good thing we didn't know, or we would almost certainly have given up. In our ignorance, we pressed on.

Our research had revealed that Astaire particularly disliked "tributes," of which there seemed to be a growing abundance; the format usually had the subject sitting either at a table or on stage while friends and colleagues lavished him or her with praise. We

---

3   The notorious Pledge Weeks are usually at least two weeks, and have been known to last even longer. They are unloved by both viewers and the stations, but do produce income for the always-strapped public television system and are not likely to disappear any time soon.

could understand why he might feel uncomfortable with that, but our program would be in the form of a documentary retrospective, which would have no resemblance to a tribute. So we felt we had a valid excuse to contact him one more time.

DH A few days later my phone rang. It was Michael Black.

"Mr. Astaire received your latest letter. Didn't I already tell you that he doesn't want a program done?"

We'd laid out all our arguments, and I couldn't think of any more. I had resigned myself to this being a "don't ever contact him again" phone call, when he said, "But because of your tenacity, he has agreed to let you proceed."

"Please thank him for me," I said in a low-key tone of voice, as I was thinking, "That's very nice, but we don't need his permission." I had no idea what a breakthrough this was.

Then he added, "And Fred owns his last television special and wonders whether you'd like to use a number from it." Then he added a rider, "And he's chosen the one he'd like you to consider. It's 'Oh, You Beautiful Doll,' a duet with Barrie Chase." She, of course, was his television partner in the 1960s.

JK and DH A few weeks later, we flew to Los Angeles to shoot interviews, and went to Michael Black's office to pick up the videotape. He was very cordial and wished us well with the production. Then, as we were about to leave: "One last thing. When you have a rough-cut, why don't you show it to Fred? He might have some useful suggestions for you. And who knows? At that point, he may even give you a short statement on camera."

So that was the quid pro quo, the bombshell after all the good news. Fred Astaire was known to be a perfectionist; he had once insisted that RKO pull back all prints of one of his films after he saw it in a theater and noticed something he did not like. We could not imagine that we'd come through a screening unscathed. This could be a terrible trap, but how could we say no?

JK However, there were other issues we had to deal with first.

Since it was becoming evident that Astaire would not appear in the program, we knew we had to have Ginger Rogers. Their partnership in the series of films they made together for RKO in the 1930s is perhaps the most famous in the history of motion pictures. The problem was that Ginger was fed up with talking about Fred. After she'd won her Best Actress Oscar for *Kitty Foyle,* she felt she'd proven she was a star in her own right; but every interviewer always wanted to ask about her work with Astaire.

I discovered that she spent much of her time at a ranch she owned on the Rogue River in Oregon. Rather than calling her "cold," I found the address of the ranch and wrote her a letter. An answer soon came back from her assistant: "No." I wrote again. A few days later, the same response. That's when I said, "David, this needs another voice. You should call her." While I usually acted as the talent booker, my instincts told me that his British accent—plus the fact that he's a man—might turn the tide.

DH I can make myself take on that role when I have to, but unlike Joan, it's not one I relish, and I know it's not one of my strong points. I took a deep breath and dialed the number. We spoke for about forty-five minutes, about what I cannot remember, but she made it very clear that she didn't want to be interviewed. Then she mentioned that she was being honored in a few weeks by the Masquers Club in Los Angeles. I didn't know what that was, although it obviously was important to her. So I said, "I'd like to film the event and perhaps we can use an excerpt in our show." Where we were going to get the money to shoot it, I had no idea; the budget was tight with no spare filming days. There was a pause. Then, "That sounds interesting," she said. "Let me think about it." I had a foot—actually just a toe—in the door, so I pushed further.

Joan and I had decided that the only way to persuade Ginger to co-operate would be to ask her to talk specifically about *her* experiences in the making of those famous films with Astaire.

"We want to know what it was like for you to make those pictures. How were you able to dance on the shiny floors? Can you tell us about the rehearsals? And how did you manage in those long gowns and high heels?" It was a barrage of questions.

Eventually I paused to catch my breath, when I heard, "Hmm. Let me think about it." Followed by, "Call me back in a few days."

JK At one point during that second call, I saw him blush. She had not only agreed to the interview, invited us to shoot it in her home just outside Palm Springs, and said she'd do her own hair and makeup, but somewhere in the middle of all this good news, she added, "You're British, aren't you? Quite charming."

DH We set the date and Ginger walked into the room spot on time at 2 pm. I'm sure that was a result of her Hollywood training; almost without exception we found that the actors and actresses who had been a part of the old studio contract system were very disciplined, and never late. Ginger Rogers was not only completely professional, but she was also friendly and easy to work with.

Ginger Rogers after being interviewed for *Fred Astaire: Puttin' On His Top Hat*. Palm Springs, CA, 1979. Authors' collection.

She did ask to see the questions ahead of time, and the only one she didn't want to answer was "Can you tell us what sort of formal dance training you had?" The truth was she didn't have any. She wasn't a formally trained dancer. Which makes it all the more remarkable that she more than held her own with Fred Astaire.

Of course we had to ask her about the often-reported rumor that the two of them didn't get along. "We *never* fought," she said. "But do you think I can get anyone to believe me?"

JK and DH It may be true that they never fought, but memos in the RKO files reveal that Fred was not happy with the partnership; he didn't want to make any more pictures with Ginger. It was not that he disliked her. It was that he did not want to be part of another team after so many years spent performing with his sister, Adele, prior to his career in the movies.

Pandro Berman, the RKO executive in charge of production, granted his request and put him in a film with Joan Fontaine, George Burns, and Gracie Allen, *A Damsel in Distress.* But the "distress" extended to the box-office returns, making it clear that it was the Astaire and Rogers team that brought audiences into the theaters. So they were reunited in *Shall We Dance, Carefree,* and *The Story of Vernon and Irene Castle,* their last three pictures together for RKO.

But, of course, there were some disagreements between them. The most famous was over the gown Ginger wore in "Cheek to Cheek." It was made almost entirely of feathers, which had a tendency to shed as the two of them danced, getting all over Fred, much to his annoyance. It's not difficult to see the flying feathers in good prints of the film, *Top Hat.* Another problem dress was created for "Let's Face the Music and Dance" in *Follow the Fleet.* She told us that it was made of hand-sewn bugle beads, and weighed close to forty pounds. Unfortunately, the loose sleeves, which looked so beautiful, slapped Astaire across the face when she did a turn near the beginning of the sequence. He later said to us, "I was groggy throughout the rest of the number. We did several re-takes. But the first was the best, and the one we used in the finished film." If you look carefully you can see him subtly flinching when the sleeve hits him.

DH We did keep our promise to Ginger Rogers. Her comments in the program are all about *her* pivotal contributions to the making of those iconic movies.

JK Another reluctant partner was Astaire's sister, Adele. They started out as children in vaudeville, and became stars when they performed in the 1923 production of *Stop Flirting* in London. She was the more famous of the two, until she retired in 1932 to marry a British Lord, leaving her brother to continue his career alone. Getting her to take part in the program would be a coup, since she never appeared on television and hated being interviewed.

After a bit of sleuthing, I learned that she had moved back to the United States following the death of her husband, and now lived in Arizona. It did not take too much more detective work to find her telephone number. But again, I knew that this was a job for David.

DH She must have retained a soft spot for the British, because she allowed me to make some small talk even though she stated from the beginning that she had no intention of appearing in the program. When I mentioned the dates we had put aside for filming, she said, "Well, that certainly counts me out; I won't be here. I'm planning to visit my brother." I told her that wouldn't be a problem because we'd be doing most of our interviews in Los Angeles, and would be there at the same time as she would. But as we continued to chat, I was beginning to sense that her biggest concern was appearing on-camera, so I said, "How about doing it just voice only?"

"You little devil; you're talking me into this, aren't you?" she said. "But you mustn't call me at my brother's house. He'll kill me if he finds out."

It dawned on me that she was probably enjoying the conspiracy.

"I'll call *you*," she said. "Give me the number of your hotel."

JK I was as amazed as David by her turn-around. However, the letdown came when we'd been in Los Angeles for three days and she had not called. It was an early December whirlwind trip, and there were only two days left before we had to return to New York. I knew that we had to take the initiative, and suggested that David take the plunge and call her again. Luckily Fred was out, and Adele picked up the phone.

"Okay," she said. "I'll do it. But remember, voice only. And tell Barrie to pick me up."

Of course, she meant Barrie Chase, whom we'd interviewed the day before.[4] Astaire had plucked her out of the chorus of one of his movies to be his co-star in the four television specials he made for NBC, and he clearly admired her as a dancer. In fact, the number he wanted us to use from the special he owned showcased her talents more than it did his own.

While Barrie had made us feel as though we'd known each other for years, it was a little embarrassing for me to ask her to play chauffeur for Adele. But when I did, she just laughed. "Leave it to Dellie," she said. "Okay. I'll pick her up and you can do the interview at the new house my husband and I just bought. It has a beautiful, quiet yard that should work for you."

What we didn't know at the time, and only learned much later, was that she and Adele hadn't been on speaking terms for a number of years. So Adele asking me to ask Barrie to pick her up was a test to see if she'd actually do it. Unwittingly, I had become the bridge to their reconciliation.

DH It's a shame that Adele Astaire wouldn't allow us to film her. She looked beautiful, was full of beans and very funny. She told us that Fred had been a perfectionist from the start, always wanting to rehearse, while she preferred to go to parties.

---

4 After Adele and Ginger, Barrie was the partner Fred danced with most often in his career.

"But a girl has to get married," she added. "My brother was very gracious about it. And I noticed he did better after I left him."

When the interview was over, I realized that sitting on the bench in front of us were Fred Astaire's first and last partners. And even though Adele had said, "If I see a camera anywhere, I'll strangle you," by then she was very comfortable and clearly having a good time. I told her I had a still camera in my bag and asked if she would mind my taking a picture of her and Barrie together.

"Oh yes. What a good idea!" she said.

As far as we know, that was not only the last photograph ever taken of Adele Astaire, but the audio interview is the only one of her extant.

Sadly, she died in January, 1981, just thirteen months after we met her.

Adele Astaire and Barrie Chase.
Sherman Oaks, CA, 1979. Authors' collection.

JK Among the other interviewees was Hermes Pan, the choreographer and dancer who'd worked with Astaire on almost every film he'd made. They were also very good friends. While David was setting up with the crew, Fred happened to call Hermes to confirm dinner with him the following evening. Of course, Hermes told him what he was doing at that moment, and also mentioned some of the other people who were participating in the program. Apparently Astaire said, "Maybe at the end I'll give them a sentence or two on camera, if they still want it." Hermes shared that with me in confidence, and said he thought that maybe Fred was beginning to feel a bit left out. But he also said he didn't envy us showing him a rough-cut because he could be devastating if he didn't like something.

Although I was never able to arrange for Rudolf Nureyev to meet Fred Astaire, we did fly to Paris to film Nureyev for the program. And while we were there, we also interviewed Leslie Caron and choreographer, Roland Petit.

JK and DH During one of our trips to Los Angeles, Joanne Woodward and Paul Newman invited us to a party at their home, and Joanne took us aside and said, "I want to be part of your show." We were stymied. She wasn't a dancer and, even though we'd originally wanted her to interview Astaire and Nureyev, our program had evolved into something quite different. All those taking part in it were Fred Astaire's partners, his choreographers, such as Hermes Pan, Roland Petit, and Eugene Loring, as well as luminaries in the dance world, including Jerome Robbins and Bob Fosse, who could analyze his technique, and dancers who were the top in their fields, like Nureyev, Honi Coles, and Gene Kelly. It was hard to see how Joanne could fit in.

Then we came up with a solution. We asked her to narrate the program and she immediately accepted.

DH The day we were dreading finally came in late January, 1980. We'd completed our rough-cut and rented a screening room in Los Angeles to show it to Astaire. What we had was *extremely* rough technically. It had my voice-over as a scratch track, temporary film clips that were not very good quality, black holes where still photos would eventually be, and only the crudest sound mix. Looking back on it now, I wonder how we had the guts to let him see it.

In addition, I wasn't feeling too well when I left New York, and by the time we landed in California, I had either the flu or a very bad cold and was barely functioning.

So when he walked in that morning with Michael Black, I was already feeling dreadful, and I remember thinking to myself, "If he gives us a hard time, I don't know how I'll be able to deal with him."

JK He was as debonair as I expected him to be; about five feet eight inches, wearing a sport jacket, a tie, and plaid pants, with burgundy leather shoes. I remember he said, "I'm not going to say too much. I'm just interested in seeing how you're coming along."

I thought, "Really? Not based on what Hermes Pan told us."

He took a seat just a few feet away from the screen, and we were careful to position ourselves just behind, where we could see him without turning around. And we braced ourselves for the worst.

DH The first number was "Top Hat, White Tie and Tails" from the film, *Top Hat*. We'd been told that brief excerpts of his dances irritated him, so throughout the program we tried wherever possible to show complete performances, and this was one of them.

About a minute in, I could hear him humming along to the music and then noticed he was tapping his feet, completely glued to the screen. I must have been holding my breath up to that point, because I suddenly realized I was breathing again.

Near the end of the sequence, when the chorus of male dancers is lined up behind him and he starts "shooting" them with his cane, he half-turned to us and said, "Remind me to tell you a story about that last guy." A few seconds later, he said, "He wound up as the head fireman on the Warner Brothers lot."

It wasn't much of a story, but it was music to our ears at the time.

JK and DH We knew that among his many solos, he was especially proud of "Bojangles of Harlem" from *Swing Time*. However he had also become somewhat embarrassed by it; this performance from 1936—a tribute to the legendary tap dancer, Bill "Bojangles" Robinson—although brilliant, was in "blackface."[5] We had decided to take a risk and include it, and both of us were expecting a reaction from Astaire when the sequence started. He had been making comments on almost all the numbers, but he was silent during "Bojangles." We took his silence as approval and to the best of our knowledge, there were no negative calls or letters from viewers when the show aired.

JK During "I'm Old Fashioned" from the film, *You Were Never Lovelier*, he said, "Look how much better I'm dancing with her." The "her" was Rita Hayworth. I was particularly struck by that remark because up to that point, all the film clips in the program had him dancing only with Ginger Rogers. Anyone who has done any research into Fred Astaire knows that he always avoided answering the question, "Who was your favorite dance partner?" Yet, here he was, giving us a very broad hint that Rita was probably one of them. Was he also saying that he felt his own dancing changed from partner to partner? It's quite possible, since I know from my own days as a dancer that a good partner can make a significant difference in your own performance.

---

5   The number is shown in the film as a part of a nightclub performance. However, within a few decades, portrayals of African Americans by Caucasians in motion pictures, and especially "blackface" performances (although Astaire did not wear the exaggerated "Minstrel Show" style of make-up), were virtually non-existent, considered offensive.

DH With the screening over, it looked as though we'd come through it without any scars. And, miraculously, my cold felt a lot better! Now was my last chance to ask Astaire if he'd agree to a brief interview we could put into the show.

"The film is perfectly good as it is," he said. "You've done a wonderful job. And you don't need me."

It was a much-appreciated compliment, but not the answer we wanted.

JK *Fred Astaire: Puttin' On His Top Hat* and *Fred Astaire: Change Partners and Dance* premiered on PBS in March, 1980. Both programs were nominated for Emmy Awards, and *Change Partners* won.

However there is another postscript to these shows. During our interview with Jerome Robbins, he said about Astaire: "He infused our souls with the visions that he made." It was a reflection by one of America's great choreographers on the work of another. And although Robbins was talking about Fred Astaire's work as a whole, we decided to use that comment to lead into the film clip, "I'm Old Fashioned."

Soon after the programs aired, Jerome Robbins' assistant at New York City Ballet called. "Could Mr. Robbins borrow a cassette?" "Of course," I told her, and immediately called a messenger to have it delivered the few blocks from WNET to Lincoln Center. In less than a week, the cassette was returned. Then, within a few days I heard from Robbins himself, asking to borrow the cassette again. And again it came back promptly. Two days later, another call from him, and another request for the cassette. By then I couldn't contain my curiosity.

"I'm honored that you like the program, but have to ask why you want to keep borrowing it?"

"Oh, I'm sorry. I didn't mean to be secretive," he said. "I'm creating a piece for New York City Ballet based on "I'm Old Fashioned." Every time I watch your show I see more details in it, and I've been calling Astaire to ask questions. He's been very helpful and supportive."

"Variations on 'I'm Old Fashioned,'" with a score by Morton Gould and based on the Johnny Mercer song, premiered at the New York State Theater, Lincoln Center on June 16th, 1983. David and I were invited to the opening night and were given seats next to Joanne Woodward, Paul Newman, and Morton Gould. All of us went backstage afterwards, where Robbins greeted everyone with handshakes and then said to us, "See what you've done. It's all because of where you placed me in the program. You're responsible."

I remember saying, "Thanks for the compliment, but we didn't do anything. *You* did. Congratulations. It's a masterpiece."

JK and DH In a *New York Times* interview the previous Sunday, Jerome Robbins was asked what ballet dancers could learn from Fred Astaire. He replied, "Everything."

Jerome Robbins and David Heeley after filming interview for *Fred Astaire: Change Partners and Dance.*
New York, 1979. Photograph by Brownie Harris.

Katharine Hepburn.
Old Saybrook, CT, 1980. Photograph by Len Tavares.

CHAPTER THREE

"That Won't Work—
They're All Dead"

Hers was a carefully constructed public image and, by her own admission, the "creature" she created needed a great deal of attention. Smart and intuitive, Katharine Hepburn knew what was right for her down to the socks she wore under what she called her "rags." Near the beginning of our 1993 program, *Katharine Hepburn: All About Me,* she says, "It's my job to keep her fascinating. Have I succeeded? Who knows? Who knows?" The question may have sounded like an admission of self-doubt. In fact, it was the opposite. She was aware that, just by asking, she was nurturing her creature and, indeed, adding to its fascination.

That she chose to include us among the few people she trusted is still gratifying. Throughout our eighteen-year professional and personal relationship with her, she enriched our lives. And it all started almost by accident.

DH The two programs about Fred Astaire had not only been well received, but also brought in a bundle of money for the stations across the country. Soon after, my phone rang.

"Congratulations on the Astaire shows," said Ron Devillier, an executive at PBS in Washington. "So, who are you going to do next?"

We hadn't thought about a "next," and I said so, which in retrospect wasn't too bright. However, our boss at WNET, George Page, had more sense. Maybe another star profile wasn't such a bad idea, especially since PBS was prepared to put up the money.

It didn't take long to come up with the perfect subject: Katharine Hepburn, a woman who lived by her own rules, was strong-willed and well known for protecting her privacy. She never went to premieres, parties, or awards ceremonies, and seldom appeared on television.

The response from Devillier was immediate. "Great. Why don't you call her?"

JK I was never a shrinking violet when it came to contacting celebrities. But, even though I already had Katharine Hepburn's number in my phone book, my instincts told me not to use it. Instead I called Pandro Berman, whom we'd met in connection with the Astaire profile. He'd also been Hepburn's boss at RKO during the early years of her film career, and the two of them often butted heads over scripts, directors, co-stars—in other words, just about everything.

However, when I asked for his help, he said, "I'm not the right person to talk to her. We were never really friends and I haven't seen or spoken to her in years. You need (director) George Cukor. They've made a lot of films together, are very close, and she respects him. I'll get in touch with him and tell him to expect your call."

DH Unlike Joan, I am definitely *not* a phone person. But I knew that it made most sense for me to be the one to approach Cukor, director to director, and a few days later I reached him at his home in Los Angeles.

"I think it's a splendid idea," he said. "As it happens, I'm going to be in New York next week and I'll be having dinner with Kate. Let me discuss it with her, and I'll get back to you." It seemed that we were in luck.

Two weeks went by without any word from George Cukor. Eventually I knew I had to contact him again. "Oh," he said. "She told me she's not interested. But I think she should do it. Why don't you call her yourself? Here's her number."

This was not going to be easy, and I had to steel myself before picking up the phone and dialing. After two rings:

"Yes. Who's this?"

That unmistakable voice. I hadn't expected her to answer the phone herself.

"Miss Hepburn, this is David Heeley. I'm calling from Channel Thirteen[1]. I think George Cukor mentioned to you recently that PBS wants us to produce a profile of you."

"Can't do that. Much too busy. I'm going on the road with *West Side Waltz*[2]. Won't be back until the end of the year."

"That's not a problem," I said. "We could film you wherever you are in the country."

"No, no. There won't be any time."

The "No" was hardly a surprise. But she hadn't yet told me to get lost. So I took that as an opportunity to keep talking and try to change her mind.

"I understand, Miss Hepburn. But there might still be a way to do this. For the programs we just produced about Fred Astaire, he gave us his co-operation, but didn't appear in them. We told his story by talking to the people around him. We could do a program about you the same way, interviewing people who know you and have worked with you."

"That won't work. They're all dead."

For a moment I was thrown. Until I realized she'd given me an opening.

---

1 New York's public television station, WNET, has always been known by its channel number.

2 *The West Side Waltz*, a play by Ernest Thompson, went on tour before opening in New York on November 19th, 1981, at the Ethel Barrymore Theatre.

"No, they're not," I countered. "There's George Cukor, Lauren Bacall, Sir Ralph Richardson, Peter O'Toole, and Henry Fonda, whom you've just worked with, and of course your friend Laura Harding, who I know went to Hollywood with you in the thirties."

I hadn't reached the end of my list when she interrupted me.

"You mustn't forget Tony Harvey. He directed me in *The Lion in Winter*. Did a great job, and he lives here in New York. And is Pandro Berman still alive?"

I felt a sudden rush of excitement. Did she realize that she had effectively said "Yes"?

"Pandro is definitely alive," I responded. "We interviewed him about Fred Astaire. He's a nice man."

She laughed. "Nice? I'm not sure I'd say that. He was tough as nails when he ran RKO. Now he probably walks around with a halo over his head. But I'm sure he'd have a lot to say about me."

I knew I needed some sort of confirmation that she was really giving her consent.

"Do you have any photographs or other memorabilia we could use?" I asked.

"When you're ready, call this number and arrange with Norah, my housekeeper, to come over and take a look at what I have here."

I couldn't quite believe what had just happened. She'd gone from a "No" to giving us her blessing in the space of a few minutes. My heart was racing, but I tried to sound calm.

"Would you like to see cassettes of the Astaire programs?" I asked.

"Do you mean I'd have to put them in a machine and watch them on television?"

"Yes, exactly," I replied.

"No thanks. Much too busy. And I don't even know how to turn on the set. Never look at it."

I called George Cukor to thank him, and also to ask if he'd give us an on-camera interview.

"Leave it to Kate," he said. "Everyone else has to put themselves out while she's off on tour. But that's her. We've been friends for almost forty years, and made a lot of films together—and somehow we've managed not to kill each other."

JK and DH Licensing clips was a constant struggle, especially the ones we needed from MGM. We'd asked for excerpts from five of Hepburn's films. The studio sent word that they wouldn't allow us to use anything from either *The Philadelphia Story* or *Adam's Rib*. While we could have made do without the latter, we couldn't live without *The Philadelphia Story*, which had been a major turning point in Kate's career. After making a number of unsuccessful pictures in the late 1930s, she was labeled "*Box Office Poison.*" However, just about that time, writer Philip Barry approached her with a play he'd written about a divorced socialite on the brink of getting remarried. It was tailor-made for her—a starring vehicle that brought her back to the stage for the first time in many years. She was then dating Howard Hughes, who bought the movie rights to the play and gave them to her as a gift. She sold the rights to MGM with a few strings attached: that she'd have the starring role in the film, that George Cukor would be the director, and that she'd have approval of her co-stars[3]. *The Philadelphia Story,* released in 1940, was a big hit; Hepburn was nominated for an Oscar as Best Actress, and her career was back on track.

DH I found an excuse to call her. And during the conversation, I asked if she still owned any rights in *The Philadelphia Story.*

"No. I sold them all to Metro at the time. Why?"

"Well, MGM is allowing us to use excerpts from three of your films, but they've told us we can't have any from *Adam's Rib* or, worse, *The Philadelphia Story*, which, as you know, will be a glaring omission in the program since it was so important in your career."

---

3   She asked for Spencer Tracy, whom she didn't yet know, and Clark Gable, but neither of them was available. So Louis B. Mayer, the head of the studio, hired freelance actor, Cary Grant, and assigned the other male lead to one of MGM's own contract players, James Stewart.

"Hmm," she said. Then after a moment of silence, she asked, "Who's the head of Metro these days? Is it that man who got himself in trouble?" She was, of course, referring to David Begelman, who despite the fact that he was caught forging Cliff Robertson's name to a check for $10,000, was now, indeed, the President of MGM. "Why don't I try reaching him?" she said. "But I'm not sure he'll take my call."

"I have a strong feeling he will," I told her.

The next day, she tracked us down in an edit room.

"Well, I've spoken to Begelman. I told him, 'These nice people are doing a program about me for PBS and you've said they can't use any film from *Adam's Rib* or *The Philadelphia Story*.

"'Of course, they can,' he replied."

It had taken her less than one minute. We then called Peter Kane, an MGM lawyer who'd become our friend through the Astaire programs. He laughed and said, "Great news. And you should know that the person who originally said "No" was the Chairman of the Board. So David Begelman was going over his own boss's head by giving Hepburn permission to use clips from those movies."

JK and DH We soon discovered exactly how important her stamp of approval was. Every person we asked to do an interview called her before saying "Yes." No one was going to risk ruining their relationship with her by participating in an unauthorized program.

DH Our first interviews were in Los Angeles with Jane Fonda, Henry Fonda,[4] Mark Rydell, Pandro Berman, and John Houseman, among others. George Cukor was working on what turned out to be his last picture, *Rich and Famous*, so we had to plan a separate trip later to film him.

---

4   Details of the Henry Fonda interview are in "Henry and Jane and Ted and Peter."

I'd met Jane Fonda briefly in the early seventies when she and her then-fiancé, Tom Hayden, appeared on a late night TV show in New York called *Free Time,* which I directed. Produced by Fern McBride, it was a radical and outspoken series, which tried to expand the boundaries of conventional television, and that particular edition was devoted entirely to the Vietnam War. When I reminded Jane of it she told me, "That program was what really cemented my relationship with Tom." They married soon after.

JK Jane Fonda both produced and starred in *On Golden Pond,* and she and director, Mark Rydell, were in the midst of post-production. It was clear that she relished having worked with Hepburn, who plays her mother in the film. They sparred a little at first, but soon developed a very close relationship. The script called for some very emotional scenes between Jane and her father, in which she had to say words that she'd never said to him in real life. As she told us, "It was a terrifying, getting-up-in-the-morning, wanting-to-throw-up, kind of experience." And although Kate was not needed on the set when those scenes were being shot, she agreed to be there in order to give Jane moral support.

DH The next day we interviewed John Houseman, who lived in the hills above Malibu. I have never before, or since, seen a swimming pool in the middle of someone's living room. It was beautiful and impressive, but I noticed that there was no protective rail or fence around it to prevent unplanned dips. I wondered how often that must have happened.

He was his usual erudite self, very much like the professor he played in *The Paper Chase.* In the fifties, he'd been the artistic director of the American Shakespeare Festival in Stratford, Connecticut, when Katharine Hepburn starred in several productions there. He talked about how brave it was for an actress of her fame to open herself up to criticism by taking on "the classics." As she told us years later, she had to prove to herself that she could play more than just "Katharine Hepburn." She knew the material would test her, and wanted to know that she was up to it.

JK Leaving Malibu, we headed to Pandro Berman's home on Roxbury Drive in Beverly Hills. It was comfortable, but relatively modest. He was already an ally, and soon became a friend. In subsequent years, David and I would visit him and his wife, Kathryn, whenever we were in LA. That day he welcomed us warmly and led the crew to set up in his back yard near the pool. He had a deadpan way of talking in real life, and even more so on camera, seldom smiling. But that demeanor belied an intelligent wit.

He said, "It was one thing to deal with Wallace Beery and even Fred Astaire. But Katharine Hepburn was much different—much more difficult."

David Heeley, Pandro Berman, and Joan Kramer.
Beverly Hills, CA, 1980. Photograph by John Haggerty.

DH It was an exhausting day. We had booked four interviews, at four different locations. By the time we left Pandro's home, it was about 4 pm, and we still had one more to go: Walter Plunkett, the famed costume designer, who created Hepburn's wardrobe in several of her films[5].

After I'd discussed with our cameraman where to set up, I joined Joan who was chatting with Plunkett and his son, Lee. I said, "We've been asking everyone if they know about any behind-the-scenes footage of Katharine Hepburn. So far, we haven't found any. She was obviously very good at avoiding home movie cameras." I was simply making conversation to fill time while our crew got ready. But to my surprise he thought for a second and then replied, "When I was at RKO in the thirties, I'd sometimes bring my camera to the set. I wonder if I have any footage of Kate in the closet upstairs?"

JK It was as if David had taken a pep pill. Suddenly he perked up, and I saw him try to contain his excitement.

He said, "Mr. Plunkett, would you be kind enough to see if you can find the film?"

"Do you have the time?" he asked. "It looks as if you're almost ready for the interview."

"Don't worry," said David. "We can wait."

DH He went up to the second floor and we heard him rummaging around. When he returned about ten minutes later, he was carrying several small cans and a projector. He didn't have a movie screen, so he showed the film on a white wall. And there she was: the elusive Katharine Hepburn playing ball with the crew between takes during production of *Quality Street*, practicing a formal dance sequence with her co-star, Franchot Tone, and talking with a young Walter

---

5   A few years later he designed the costumes for *Gone With The Wind*, and won a "Best Costume Design" Oscar for *An American In Paris*.

Plunkett. On the same reel, there was also *color* footage of Charles Laughton in *The Hunchback of Notre Dame*, which RKO had shot in black and white. Yet here he was on that famous set in color. I could hardly believe what I was seeing.

"Mr. Plunkett, can we borrow your film and have it transferred?" I asked him. "I'll take it to New York and then send back the original and a copy on tape."

He said, "Of course," and also signed a release, which gave us permission to use it in our program.

We learned an important lesson that day. People forget what they have tucked away in closets and garages until you ask. If you're lucky and push the right button at the right time, it can lead to pay dirt.

JK A few weeks later, we returned to Los Angeles to interview George Cukor. He was somewhat frail at the time and noticeably tired. But his sense of humor was intact.

"I directed her first picture[6]," he said. "And even then she tried to give orders. Sometimes she has good ideas—but she's not always right. *I*, on the other hand, am always right."

His house was beautiful. He was clearly proud of it, and gave us a tour. I wondered if parts of it had been the inspiration for the set of *The Philadelphia Story*. There was a slightly sunken but very large guest room where Greta Garbo and many other legends had stayed. And Spencer Tracy had lived with Katharine Hepburn in another house on the property until Tracy's death in 1967.

JK and DH Back in New York, we filmed Lauren Bacall who'd been on location with her husband, Humphrey Bogart, and Katharine Hepburn during the filming of *The African Queen*.

---

6   *A Bill of Divorcement* in 1931.

Lauren Bacall.
New York, 1980. Photograph by Brownie Harris.

We also interviewed Kate's old friend, Laura Harding. They'd met in 1929 at The Berkshire Theatre Playhouse where both of them were aspiring actresses and were cast in the same play. After Hepburn was offered a contract with RKO, they both went to Hollywood and shared a house together. When Cukor chose Kate for *A Bill of Divorcement*, he gave Laura a cameo role; she appears at the top of the stairs in the opening scene.

Rumor always had it that John Barrymore, the star of the picture and a well-known womanizer, tried to seduce Hepburn during production. Over fifty years later, she told us over lunch,

"Never, never. He was sweet and helpful. A generous actor. No one ever made a pass at me like that. Never was subjected to the fabled 'casting couch' by producers or directors or male stars. No, no. Never. Never."

DH In our first conversation, she had said, "And don't forget Tony Harvey."

He'd been the editor for Stanley Kubrick on *Lolita* and *Dr. Strangelove,* but by 1967 had directed only one short film of his own, *Dutchman.* Peter O'Toole had seen it and, having been asked to star in *The Lion in Winter,* took an enormous leap of faith and recommended that Anthony Harvey be hired to direct. O'Toole also felt that there was only one actress to play Queen Eleanor of Aquitaine opposite his King Henry II in James Goldman's epic story about a dysfunctional royal family in twelfth century England. He sent Kate the script and a few days later, she called him.

"Do it before I die," she said.

Despite his inexperience, Tony knew he could not be cowed by the star power of his leading actors. In one crucial scene where Queen Eleanor is examining herself a mirror, he wanted Hepburn's hair to fall loosely around her face.

She reacted immediately: "No. No. Never wear my hair down."

Tony insisted. She refused. The test of wills spilled over to the next day, and Tony shut down production. Two days later they were still at a stand-off.

Having a cast and crew on location and on salary for three days without working is almost unheard of, and Peter O'Toole decided he had to step in.

"I think you'd better give in to her," he warned, "or you're going to be replaced."

Tony was adamant. "No. I'm going to damn well hold out for this."

Years later, Ray Gow, the hairdresser that Hepburn requested we hire for *The Spencer Tracy Legacy: A Tribute by Katharine Hepburn,* told us that the first time he worked with her was on *The Lion in Winter*. On the third day of Kate's stand-off with Tony Harvey, Gow said to her, "Let's just see how you'd look with your hair down." He took out the pins that held it up and created a style which made it seem as though it had fallen naturally.

"Now *that* is how Eleanor of Aquitaine would look at the end of a tough day dealing with her husband and three grown sons," he said.

Hepburn looked at herself in the mirror, carefully analyzing the effect from every angle.

"Hmm," she said, and then turned to Gow who was standing behind her. "You know," she said to him, "you're more than just a pretty face."

"That night," Tony Harvey told us, "she sent me a bottle of champagne with a card that said, '*I hope the moon and stars will be with you for the rest of this film.*'"

The next day, she was back on the set and they shot the scene with her hair down.

It was only a few weeks after we'd interviewed Tony that we heard through our Hepburn grapevine that he felt uneasy about his on-camera performance and was considering asking if we would film him again. Apparently, he shared his feelings with Kate over dinner one evening.

"Idiotic," she told him. "Don't be an ass. You're not that important."

He never did request the re-shoot.

DH We'd been trying for some time to line up interviews with Peter O'Toole, Ralph Richardson, and Laurence Olivier, and knew we'd have to travel to England to shoot them. PBS agreed to give us the additional funds we'd need on the condition that Peter O'Toole would film an on-camera introduction to *The Lion in Winter*, which the network was planning to show directly after the premiere of our documentary. His agent confirmed that he'd do it, so we sent him the short script about ten days before we left New York.

We weren't able to get Olivier, but succeeded in scheduling both O'Toole and Richardson for the same day during the week before Christmas, 1980.

JK I'd never been to England before and was looking forward to the trip. But at the airport in New York, I felt the beginnings of a cold. On the plane, I started to have chills, and by the time we landed at London's Heathrow that evening, every part of my body ached. I took a hot shower as soon as we arrived at the Gloucester Hotel in South Kensington, met David for dinner downstairs (a few spoonfuls of chicken broth was all I could manage), then went straight to bed, hoping I'd feel better for the interviews the next day.

O'Toole's home was in Hampstead, in the north of London. There was no heat in the house and, to my horror, the plumbing wasn't working, so the toilet wouldn't flush. I was freezing and my stomach was upset. But there was no way I was going to miss this.

DH Peter O'Toole told us, "The first time Kate walked into my dressing room, I was pissing in the sink. Of course, I then had to pretend I wasn't. And *she* pretended she didn't notice." And he said, on another visit, Hepburn hit him. "She punched me. Never knew why."

There is a somewhat different version of the story. In it there appears to be a motive for the punch, although whether O'Toole deserved it is up for debate. He and Hepburn both shared Ray Gow as their hairdresser, and Gow was chatting with O'Toole in his dressing room on the lower level while Kate was shooting one of her scenes on the stage above. Between takes, Hepburn needed Gow, and sent a production assistant to find him, but he didn't show up. She tried again. When he still didn't appear, she marched downstairs into O'Toole's dressing room and slapped him. "You're not working at the moment. I am. The next time I send for the hairdresser, make sure he comes." She turned around and left with Ray Gow in tow, leaving behind a stunned Peter O'Toole.

"I only hit the people I love," she later told him.

To which he replied, "Maybe you should start hating me for awhile!"

After the interview, I handed him the script for the introduction to *The Lion in Winter*.

"No, I don't want to do that," he said firmly.

I was astonished. But no amount of coaxing would change his mind. He was unyielding. How was I going to explain to PBS that he refused at the last minute?

Then, suddenly, he said, "But come into the den. I'd like to show you some photos." He led me to the cluttered front room of his house and took some pictures out of a desk. They were photographs of his children, including his daughter, Kate, who was named after Katharine Hepburn. As he shared his feelings about his family, I found it hard to believe this was the same person who, just moments ago, had adamantly refused to read our script.

JK We headed back to central London to film Ralph Richardson. He'd agreed to let us shoot in the dressing room of the Comedy Theatre, where he was appearing in the play, *Early Days*. By now, I knew I had the flu, and even though I hadn't eaten anything all day, the urge to throw up caused me to spend some time in the theatre's bathroom.

I made it out by the time David and the crew were ready and, a few minutes later, Richardson arrived. I was amazed to see how tall he was. Somehow I hadn't expected the height. And he was sweet. He offered to arrange tickets for that evening's performance, but David told him, "Joan's not well, so I think she needs to go to bed as soon as we've finished filming." He put his hand on my cheek and said, "Would you like me to call my doctor for you?"

I managed a weak smile and replied, "No, I think I'll be okay. But thank you for the offer."

DH Despite my asking him not to look into the camera, he did, and parts of his interview felt too much like a performance. But he was insightful, describing Hepburn's role in the one picture they made together, *Long Day's Journey Into Night,* as "a deep part that should be played as though on a cello."

She told us years later that she felt that movie was a real departure for her. She said to herself, "Don't act. Don't do anything. Just stay out of the way of that poor, lonely, drug-addicted woman and let her carry me along."

JK We'd written a letter to Cary Grant, asking him to take part in the program. He and Hepburn had made four films together and, even though we knew the chances of him agreeing were next to zero, we felt there was no harm in trying. We received a call from Barbara Harris, who would later become his wife, telling us that he wouldn't participate. A few days later, I wrote to him again, asking him to sign the release form I'd enclosed[7], giving us permission to use film clips in which he appeared. Barbara Harris called again, but this time she said, "Hold on please. Mr. Grant would like to speak with you."

Suddenly, I heard that voice, and I must admit I was excited. He sounded exactly as he did on screen, with the same clipped accent.

"I'm signing the release you sent me, but please use excerpts that make Kate look good."

"Mr. Grant, thank you. However, we want to show clips in which *both* of you look good."

"No. It's her show. So it's important that *she's* the one that looks good."

While I had him, I couldn't pass up the chance to say, "And Mr. Grant, we'd love to do a similar program about you."

"Darling, I never do television. If I said 'Yes' to one project, I'd

---

7   As with Fred Astaire, he controlled the use of clips from his films.

be playing favorites, so I just refuse all of them."

"Well, we may not go away so quickly. You might hear from us again one of these days."

"Okay. But my answer will be the same[8]."

My signature below signifies approval of your request to be granted permission to use certain R.K.O. excerpts from films in which I appeared with Miss Katherine Hepburn. The afore-mentioned film clips can only be used in connection with your proposed Katherine Hepburn documentary.

Cary Grant

Cary Grant's permission.
1980. Authors' collection.

DH We had to decide soon who should narrate the program. We wanted someone with a connection to Hepburn, and decided to ask Douglas Fairbanks, Jr. He had starred with her in *Morning Glory*—her first Oscar win—back in 1933, and they were still friends. He agreed to do the narration, but, although he lived in New York, he was making a movie in Vermont (*Ghost Story*, which also starred Fred Astaire and John Houseman). So I'd have to go there.

The day before leaving, I called him to confirm when and where we would do the recording session, but I could barely hear the person who picked up the phone. It was unsettling to discover that the weak, hoarse voice at the other end was his. He explained he'd been sick with laryngitis, but assured me that he would be fine in a couple of days, and not to worry. Of course, I did.

It was late January, and Vermont, living up to its reputation, was blanketed with snow. However, the tiny commuter aircraft

---

8   See "A Few That Got Away."

had no trouble landing, and after a short drive I was in Woodstock, VT. We recorded Douglas Fairbanks the next day in a conference room at his hotel, and he must have been nursing his vocal chords because he sounded much stronger than when I spoke to him from New York. However there's still an undeniable rasp to that famous voice on the soundtrack of our program. I'm very aware of it, but most people seem not to notice.

JK and DH   With post-production completed, and the show ready to deliver to PBS, it looked as though the end was in sight. But there was one last stumbling block.

The previous year, WNET had launched a new magazine, *The Dial*, to replace the small, brochure-like monthly program guides that most public television stations sent out to their viewers. *The Dial* was large format, glossy, and needed to make an impact. For the issue that coincided with our airdate, the editor decided to commission Helen Lawrenson to write an article about Katharine Hepburn, which became the cover story. Entitled "Hepburn Reconsidered," it was an unflattering evaluation of her talent as an actress. *The New York Post* picked it up and wrote gleefully, "*We can't wait for Kate the Great to strike back.*" Since WNET was the source of both *The Dial* and our program, it wouldn't be too much of a stretch to assume that our show, which wouldn't air for another couple of weeks, was a similar hatchet job. We needed to move quickly to contain the damage, to reassure Hepburn, her family, and friends, and everyone who had participated in the program that we hadn't betrayed them.

By then, Laura Harding had already reached Jay Iselin, the president of WNET, to complain. Jane Fonda's office called to say she wanted nothing to do with a project that treated Hepburn in this way, and asked for her interview to be removed from the show. Cary Grant contacted KCET in Los Angeles to protest and also wrote an angry letter to the editor of *The Dial*. Fortunately, we were able to convince all of them that our program had nothing to do with the Helen Lawrenson article, and that we were as shocked by it as they were.

Not long after the show aired, we received a letter from San Francisco, where Kate was still on tour with *The West Side Waltz*. She told us not to worry about the article, as she had learned long ago that such criticism came with being in the public eye. *"I'm sorry your spirits were hurt,"* she wrote. *"Really it's so quickly yesterday's sour jibe. And of course I knew you people had nothing to do with it."*

Then she commented on the program, stating that she hadn't seen it and wouldn't until she was back in New York, when we'd watch it together. But she'd had reports from those who had: *"Family and friends all thrilled, even the most critical ones. Many, many thanks for making me seem so fascinating... You obviously did me proud."*

In accordance with the rules of the Screen Actors Guild, she was entitled to residual payments for several of the film clips we'd used. Our colleague in the legal department, Lynne Autman, sent Hepburn a letter asking for her social security number so that WNET could issue a check for the total amount: $1,100. Kate wrote back immediately and Lynne shared a copy of the note: *"Here's my social security number. You keep the money."* Essentially, Katharine Hepburn was making a donation to public television, and when we told Jay Iselin, he sent her a Channel 13 tote bag and umbrella, along with a letter of thanks.

True to her word, she called us not long after returning from the tour. "Hello. It's Kate. Come for tea."

We arrived at her town house on East 49th Street a few days later. She opened the door herself and said, "So you're the ones that did it."

"Guilty as charged," we replied.

"Come on upstairs."

The house had an immediate feeling of comfort, of being lived in, with wonderful aromas coming from the kitchen. The second floor living room was furnished with a white sofa, several chairs, a coffee table, buffet table and a slightly worn rug. And there was a fire burning in the fireplace even though it was the beginning of July. On the mantle were two candlesticks that had belonged to

Hepburn's mother. There was nothing pretentious about the room or about the big star who lived there. She was wearing white pants, a navy shirt with the collar turned up, sandals, no makeup, and her mostly gray hair, still with a touch of auburn here and there, was loosely pinned up. She sat on what was obviously her favorite chair near the window, with her feet propped up on an ottoman. Hanging from the ceiling above her was an enormous carved wooden bird that had belonged to Spencer Tracy.

She mentioned that she'd just come back from having her driver's license renewed that afternoon, and laughed as she said, "I was whisked to the front of the line. It sometimes pays to be a movie queen."

That was the first of our many teas and lunches there. And it was also our first taste of Norah's delicious brownies and lace cookies, with Hepburn's favorite ice cream, Sedutto's mocha chip.

And while we never watched the program with her, we were told by her friends that she had indeed seen it. And she inadvertently confirmed it when she said, "George Cukor looked relaxed and much younger in the interview. He must have really liked the two of you." However, in the years that followed, she claimed that she hadn't ever seen the show herself.

"But my spies saw it and told me how good it was."

When it was nominated for an Emmy, she said, "It deserves to be nominated, and it should win." It didn't, but knowing she was pleased was enough.

Most importantly—and we didn't realize it at the time—by producing *Starring Katharine Hepburn*, we'd passed the obstacle course through which she puts people before deciding whether or not to trust them.

And if we still needed proof, we called her the day after we went to a performance of *The West Side Waltz*.

"Why didn't you come backstage?" she asked.

"It was late and we didn't want to bother you."

"You two never bother me," she said.

1980. Authors' collection.

Joanne Woodward and Paul Newman during interview for *20/20*.
Beverly Hills, CA, 1984. Authors' collection.

CHAPTER FOUR

Joanne, Paul, and Hugh

JK By 1983, I'd known Joanne Woodward for ten years and we'd become good friends. Not long after David and I started working together, that friendship extended to him, too. At WNET, we'd completed programs about Fred Astaire and Katharine Hepburn, which had aired to considerable success. We had proposed profiles of Henry Fonda and Cary Grant, each of whom had agreed to co-operate. To our amazement, PBS had turned down both of them. Now we were thinking about who and when our "next" could be.

Joanne and her husband, Paul Newman, had already made nine films together and were about to make their tenth. It was *Harry and Son*, based on the novel, *A Lost King*, by Raymond DeCapite. Paul would play the lead, with Joanne as his co-star. He would also direct, and co-produce, and had co-written the script with Ronald Buck. It was to be filmed in and around Ft. Lauderdale, Florida.

DH Our boss, George Page, told us he could find a small amount of seed money for us to go to Florida to shoot footage of the Newmans at work, assuming they would agree. After that we would have to secure a commitment from PBS to do a complete profile of them.

JK Once we knew we had the funds, I called Joanne and asked to meet with her and Paul. At the time, they were living temporarily at the Carlyle Hotel on Madison Avenue in New York while the apartment they'd just bought was being renovated.

My timing couldn't have been worse. Their dog had died the day before at their home in Connecticut, having fallen into the river that ran through their property. (Soon after, they installed an invisible perimeter that prevented any accidents of this sort from happening again; their dogs now wore collars with built-in sensors that stopped them from going beyond the boundary.)

Joanne told me that she and Paul were both still very upset, but agreed to meet us for tea in the hotel's coffee shop. When we arrived at about 4 pm, she came down wearing dark glasses; Paul joined us a few minutes later, also wearing sunglasses.

We reminded them that she had narrated our first two shows on Fred Astaire, and I remember Paul saying, "Yes, and they were terrific."

I said, "Now we're being asked to produce another profile and we'd love it to be about the two of you. If we start right away, it should be possible to have it air around the premiere of your new film."

Without further argument, they said, "Okay, let's do it."

DH A few weeks later, we were on our way to Ft. Lauderdale. Their assistant, Marcia Franklin, booked us into the Marina Bay Resort, where the cast and the crew were staying. It was a beautiful and unusual complex consisting of houseboats in a sheltered harbor. Joan was worried that she'd be seasick, since the boats undulated with the movement of the water, but her stomach and brain adapted, and she was fine.

We were able to capture scenes of Paul directing, as well as interview the Newmans' daughter, Nell, who was visiting the set.

JK and DH Meanwhile, there had been some changes in Washington. Unbeknown to us, our ally at PBS, Ron Devillier, who had given the

Paul on location for *Harry and Son*.
Ft. Lauderdale, FL, 1983. Authors' collection.

green light to both the Astaire and Hepburn projects, had moved on, and his replacement was not as confident in us as Ron had been—or maybe wanted to make his own mark. For whatever the reason, we were not getting the go-ahead we needed, and an opportunity was slipping away.

Since we had virtually made a concrete promise to Joanne and Paul that our show would air at a time to help promote their film, we felt an obligation to do our best to make that happen. We recalled that ABC's weekly prime time news magazine, *20/20,* had recently devoted an entire program to a profile of Barbra Streisand. It had generated a great deal of publicity and a huge audience. We decided to find out whether they would do it again if we offered them the Newmans.

JK I made a cold call to *20/20* and was connected to the program's executive producer, Av Westin. As luck would have it, he had seen—and enjoyed—our Fred Astaire shows and asked us to come to the ABC offices, just a few blocks away, to meet him. He had decided before we got there that he wanted the project, but explained that he couldn't give us the entire hour because after the Streisand piece, some critics accused *20/20*, which fell under the ABC News umbrella, of abandoning important national and international stories so that it would get higher ratings with a big name entertainer. Therefore, he'd like the Newman/Woodward profile to comprise two-thirds of the show, which would be thirty-three minutes. We were a bit disappointed, but accepted his offer, and then it was just a matter of working out a start date.

JK and DH   Now we had to tell Joanne and Paul that we had set up the project at ABC for *20/20*, which would provide a much larger audience, and therefore, more publicity for their film than PBS could. Fortunately, they were enthusiastic; their only condition was that, of the two *20/20* hosts, Hugh Downs and Barbara Walters, Hugh be the correspondent for their piece. WNET gave us a three-month leave-of-absence to work at ABC, and a deal was struck for *20/20* to buy the footage we'd already shot in Florida.

We were assigned to one of the show's senior producers, Karen Lerner, and an ace associate producer, Rosanne Zoccoli, who could guide us through the *20/20* machine.

JK   The first snag came when the Newmans' press agent, Warren Cowan, learned that they had agreed to a profile without us going through him. He called me and said, "I'm going to do everything I can to stop this project." I remember saying, "Warren, you know that Joanne and Paul are friends of ours, so we called them directly." That just made him even more furious and he repeated the threat. I spoke with Joanne, who was surprised that Warren's ego was getting in the way. After all, our piece would make his job as their publicist easier. She said, "Don't worry. We'll deal with him."

DH   Time was of the essence. We were producing a portrait of two stars, each with a very large body of work[1]. We had to watch almost all of their films, find some of the television programs in which they'd appeared early in their careers, and cull all of it down to thirty-three minutes. That's a long time by news standards. But for us, it presented a real challenge: doing justice to the Newmans without using such short clips that the audience would never have the chance to appreciate any of them.

The solution was "less is more." We'd have to choose sparingly, both in the number of clips and in the number of people we'd interview.

Locating feature films isn't hard. But finding television shows from the 1950s is a tedious, time-consuming job that's similar to looking for the lost treasures of the Incas. Back when Joanne and Paul started their careers, most of their work was in live television dramas, which aired in prime time on the East Coast. But on the West Coast, with the three-hour difference in time, those shows would either have had to be seen at 5 or 6 pm, or else the networks had to come up with a way to copy the live shows, in order to play them during prime time on the West Coast. Thus the kinescope, a relatively crude way of recording live broadcasts by pointing a film camera at a television monitor. The quality was not great, but kinescopes were certainly better than nothing. And once they served their intended purpose, most of them were then destroyed or thrown into a dumpster, since no one thought they would ever be of any future value. Fortunately for us, some were saved, or salvaged, by producers, directors, stars, or crew members. Now these kines are considered collectors' items, with archives all over the world actively trying to find and preserve them.

JK Joanne suggested that we look for a program she'd done in 1953. It was called *A Young Lady of Property*, written by Horton Foote.

---

1   At that point, Paul had made over forty films, and Joanne more than twenty, in addition to their TV work.

And she also asked us to find one of Paul's best performances—as a punch-drunk fighter in a live television show called *The Battler*, directed by Arthur Penn.

I called everyone I could think of to search for those two programs. The original broadcast networks didn't have them. Arthur Penn said, "I've been trying to get a copy of *The Battler* for years, and so has Paul." Horton Foote hadn't seen *A Young Lady of Property* since it was first shown, but during our conversation he mentioned that his agent, Lucy Kroll, was "a real pack rat" with a good memory. I telephoned her on a Friday afternoon. She called me back on Monday morning.

"You completely blew my weekend. I spent the whole time digging in my closet. And I found it! It's a kinescope in an old dented can, so I can't open it."

I said, "Lucy, first, let me tell you how impressed I am that you have a closet big enough in which to spend a weekend. Second, let's get that kine transferred to tape immediately."

"Fine," she said. "But I'm not letting it out of my hands. I'll bring it wherever you tell me and you can use it if you make cassettes for me and Horton."

"Done deal," I replied.

That same afternoon, I was talking to Joanne, whom I'd asked to see whether she could find film of her wedding. She had good news.

"I found the footage in the barn yesterday. It was in a stack of films in the projection room." (The Newmans' guest house was formerly a barn, and is outfitted with a screening room which has professional 35 and 16 millimeter projection equipment.)

I said, "Joanne, will you please go to the barn and I'll call you there in a few minutes? I want to know what else is in that stack of films."

Five minutes later I could hear the sound of cans being moved around. "I'm looking at all the labels," she told me. And then after a few seconds, "Oh, look at this. I think I just found *The Battler*."

I tried to stay calm. "Joanne, how long has that can been in the barn?"

"I have no idea. Probably many years. I didn't even know we had it. Wait until I tell Paul. He's not going to believe it."

"Tell him to join the group. I've just spent weeks talking to dozens of people, including Arthur Penn, trying to find it. It's going to be a race to see which one of us strangles you first. Don't open the can. We have to get that kine transferred right away. We'll make you a cassette of it along with the one I promised Arthur Penn. And by the way, Horton Foote's agent, Lucy Kroll, found *A Young Lady of Property* in her closet over the weekend. This is turning out to be a very good day."

DH We were able to track down several more kinescopes of Joanne's and Paul's early television careers, including episodes of *Tales of Tomorrow*, *Playhouse 90*, *Goodyear Playhouse*, *The Alcoa Hour* and *GE Theater*. And in order to speed up the process of getting clips from their feature films, we asked them to sign a letter saying that we were producing an authorized biography of them, in which they were fully co-operating, and requesting that the studios make available excerpts from their films.

In the meantime, we had decided to interview only four key people: directors George Roy Hill, Arthur Penn, and Sidney Lumet, and the Newmans' long time friend, Gore Vidal, who was also the godfather of their eldest daughter, Nell. (As he said to them, "Always the godfather, never the God.")

Gore was the only one who spoke about the Paul/Joanne marriage. "It works so well because they have nothing in common," he said, with a touch of hyperbole. "She likes ballet; he likes racing. They don't get in each other's way."

We asked Arthur Penn to come to our office and watch clips from several of the kinescopes to analyze Joanne's and Paul's early performances. Much of what he told us was worked into our final script. For example, he pointed out that Joanne showed a relaxed assurance from the beginning of her career. But Paul didn't until he did a television program called *Guilty Is the Stranger*. Penn told us, "He's allowing his emotions to carry him, and we can see the actor developing right before our eyes."

JK The Newmans had to be in Los Angeles, where Joanne was making a movie for television. And the only day available for us to film an interview with them turned out to be Super Bowl Sunday. By then, their publicist, Warren Cowan, had calmed down and accepted that this profile was indeed going forward. He suggested we shoot at the home of his ex-wife, Barbara Rush, with whom he still had a very good relationship. He ordered flowers for the room where we'd be filming—and for every other room in the house, too; then he sent us the bill. I had to tell him that our budget couldn't cope with the hundreds of dollars of floral displays, and in the end we paid only a portion of the total amount.

Two days before the shoot, we heard that Paul's lawyer wanted to sit in on it, as did his agent, Michael Ovitz—an audience with the potential for causing trouble, even if only to justify their presence. I told Joanne's and Paul's assistant, Marcia, that David and I didn't want any spectators.

She called me back and said, "Don't worry. No one will be there. I told them both not to come." We didn't particularly want Warren Cowan there either, but since we were using his ex-wife's house, we couldn't bring ourselves to ask him to leave. Fortunately, he and Barbara had plans to watch the Super Bowl at a friend's house, so soon after we arrived, they disappeared.

DH The original plan was for Hugh Downs to talk with Joanne first, then Paul, and then both of them together. But Paul also wanted to watch the game, so he said to Joanne, "Darling, what would happen if I went first?" Without missing a beat, she replied, "Darling, I would mourn you." It was just banter at the time, but now that Paul has died, it takes on a completely different meaning. He also placed a quarter bet with each of the crew members on who would win the game. He lost—and he paid up.

Paul and Hugh Downs.
Beverly Hills, CA, 1984. Authors' collection.

Joan and Joanne.
Beverly Hills, CA, 1984. Authors' collection.

Rosanne had filled the refrigerator with cans of Budweiser, so that Paul could help himself, which he did. He and Joanne had brought their small dog, Harry (named after the film they'd just completed, *Harry and Son*), and Paul was teaching it to jump higher and higher, saying, "He thinks he's Baryshnikov."

JK and DH So by the time the camera rolled, the interview with Hugh became an easygoing conversation.

Paul told us that, in his early days as an actor, he used to go to the bus station just to watch people. But that became impossible with fame.

"You can't watch people if they're watching you. It's a shame because I miss that."

Joanne admitted that while she considers Paul a "star," she thinks of herself as "a character actress" and that no one recognizes her when she walks down the street. "I even have trouble getting checks cashed," she said with a laugh.

They also talked about each other's performances, as well as their own, in some of their most famous films.

At the end of the afternoon, they asked the two of us and Rosanne to join them for dinner and a movie. We went back to our hotel to freshen up and then met them at the restaurant. It was about 7:30 when Paul said, "Joanne, what time does the movie start?" She said, "At 8, so we'd better leave or we'll be late."

"Where is the theater?" he asked.

"Oh, it's not far—on Santa Monica."

"Where on Santa Monica²?"

"I just told you. It's not far from here."

"Joanne, that doesn't give me a clue where it is. It could be in Denver for all I know."

"Don't worry. I know where it is. Let's go."

Turning to me, Paul said, "Why don't you just follow me in your car?"

It was not "far from here," maybe only a couple of miles, but I had to try to keep up with a Formula One racecar driver. I think he took pity on me, always slowing down just as I was about to lose sight of him.

---

2   Santa Monica Boulevard is over eighty-seven miles long.

JK We finally arrived at the theater, and Paul made a beeline for the refreshments' counter and asked if he could taste the popcorn. The vendor recognized him, of course, and gave him a free sample. He then bought the largest size available to share with Joanne. The movie was *Carmen*, a Spanish language film based on the Bizet opera and Mérimée's novella—with a large dash of flamenco.

Joanne told me that she and Paul always preferred to sit in the back row. So David went in first, followed by me, Rosanne, Joanne, and Paul, who was on the aisle. To our astonishment, they whispered to each other during the movie, and the people in front kept asking them to be quiet, completely unaware that two famous stars were the source of the noise.

DH A few weeks later, we filmed them in Connecticut. Joanne had told us that in a future life she will return as prima ballerina, Anna Pavlova, so we shot her taking one of her frequent ballet classes.

We also interviewed them both again, this time in their barn. I had wanted to film additional footage of them walking in the yard together, but Paul nixed that idea because he felt that it might breach their security by showing too much of the property's location. I don't think he was too happy to have us shoot there at all, but once on camera, he relaxed, joking about the fake Oscar that director, Robert Wise, gave him after they completed *Somebody Up There Likes Me*. And Joanne told us how she prepared for her (real) Oscar-winning role as a multiple-personality in *The Three Faces of Eve*. "The voices were different, but it was as if each of the characters resided in a different place in my head."

Then came the hardest part: the editing. And in the midst of it all, ABC decided to move the *20/20* offices to another building about a block away. Since we were knee-deep in the project, we and our editors were allowed to stay in the old space while everyone else packed up and left.

We'd been warned that Av Westin could be very tough during screenings of rough-cuts. But he approved our piece with only a few minor suggestions.

JK It was during this final stage that we had to deal with two bomb-shells. The Screen Actors Guild required us to get permissions from actors who appeared in the clips we planned to use. One of Paul's important films was *The Hustler*, and in his interview, he analyzed his own performance in a pivotal scene with his co-star, Jackie Gleason. But Gleason refused to give his consent, and no amount of coaxing by us, or a direct appeal by Hugh Downs, could change his mind. Unfortunately, we had to remove that section entirely.

Worse, Dewey Martin, who had co-starred with Paul in *The Battler* (the kine that turned up in the Newmans' barn) was also refusing to allow us to show a crucial scene of them together, one which both Paul and director, Arthur Penn, had talked about in their interviews. This time we won the stand-off by offering Martin a fee above the standard residual rate.

That should have been the end of our problems. But there was one more.

DH Barbara Walters, who had to have been miffed that she did not get to do the portrait of Paul and Joanne, had the other third of the program—an interview with Ursula Meese (the wife of Edwin Meese, the United States Attorney General, who was embroiled in a political scandal). The day before *20/20*'s Friday night broadcast, Barbara told Av Westin that her piece was five minutes longer than had been allocated, and she couldn't cut it. He pointed out that the profile of the Newmans was finished and in the can, so she had to find a way to bring in her segment to time. She refused. The argument went all the way to the President of ABC News, Roone Arledge, who had created *20/20* back in 1978.

At about 6 that Thursday evening, we were sent back to the editing room to cut out five minutes. These were painful choices, which included a wonderful sequence of Joanne in various wigs and costumes from the film, *A New Kind of Love*, and a portion of Paul's interview in which he talked about how and why he was often compared to Marlon Brando. It was exhausting, frustrating, and infuriating, and it took almost all night. Of course, it also showed where much of the power was at *20/20*.

The uncut version had been sent to a number of newspaper reviewers, and on the morning of the broadcast, more than one of them referred to the Paul Newman/Marlon Brando comparison. Surprisingly, there were no viewer complaints about the missing section.

JK and DH We watched the show air from the control room of the studio. By then, we were just happy that we'd finished the project and hoped that the deletions hadn't ruined it. We needn't have worried. Everyone was pleased. Joanne called the next morning to congratulate us and tell us how happy she and Paul were. And Hugh Downs said it was the best experience he'd had with any segment he'd ever done. But we knew what was missing and even now, thirty years later, wish we hadn't had to cut those five minutes.

JK That program was something of a milestone for me. It marked the first time I shared a producer's credit with David. And after we returned to our jobs at WNET, I received a note from our boss that said I'd been officially promoted from associate producer, and that my credit on future shows would be producer. When I thanked him, he said, "You're welcome. But you should thank David. He's the one that requested—actually, *insisted* on it." Of course, I'd been completely unaware that he'd done that, but did know it was almost unheard of for anyone to voluntarily arrange for another person to share his or her title, not just in the entertainment business, but in every other business as well.

JK and DH The friendship with Paul continued until his death in 2008, and our relationship with Joanne continues to this day. We've had many wonderful times with both of them together and with her separately: dinners at David's loft, at Joan's apartment, at restaurants, invitations to join them at the ballet, premiere screenings of their films, memorable days at the house in Connecticut, delicious egg rolls made by their housekeeper, Cora.

The Newmans at a dinner party in David's loft.
New York, 2005. Authors' collection.

JK I thought I was used to being teased unmercifully by David, but he met his match with Paul Newman.

I don't know what it is about me that leads people to making me the victim of their humor and practical jokes. And not only do I realize that I encourage it, but also that unwittingly I bring it on myself.

Through the years, I've often called the Newmans at their homes in Connecticut and New York. Unlike so many big stars, they usually answered their own phone. Frequently, the first voice I'd hear would be Paul's. I'd say, "Hi. It's Joan." He'd say, "Hiya," and then sometimes tell me that Joanne wasn't there. Once, before I'd caught on to his deviousness, he said, "Joanne's not here. She's in Calcutta—playing in summer stock."

"But I just spoke with her a week ago," I said, surprised. "She didn't mention that she was going to India. When did she leave?"

"A few days ago."

"How did she get there? I know she doesn't like to fly."

"She will if I'm with her. So I took her on my plane and I'll pick her up in about three weeks and bring her home."

"Paul, this is July. Isn't it very hot in Calcutta now?"

"Remember, she grew up in the South, in Georgia, so she's used to hot weather."

I remember thinking, "Joanne gets involved with causes she believes in, so this must be one of them."

I said, "Well, if she won't be back for a few weeks, I won't leave a message. I'll just call back later."

"No, don't hang up. She's walking into the room right now."

"What?" I screamed. "I don't believe I fell for that craziness. Please stay on the line and ask her to pick up an extension."

"Why?"

"You'll see in a second."

"Darling, pick up the other phone."

Joanne came on the line. "Hi. Who's this and what's going on?"

"It's Joan," I said. "And I just heard from your husband that you weren't home. Paul, why don't you tell her where you told me she was?"

"Uh, oh, I think I'm in trouble."

She said, "I'm not surprised. What did you do this time?"

"I told her you were in Calcutta for three weeks doing summer stock."

"Paul, hang up the phone," she said. "We'll talk about this later."

The joke was on me, but I was laughing so hard that tears were rolling down my cheeks.

Each time after that, Paul came up with a different tale. But by then I was on high alert. During the Iran-Contra scandal, he answered the phone with, "Ollie North here."

I replied, "This is Queen Victoria. Where's Mrs. North?"

When they were in Kansas filming *Mr. and Mrs. Bridge*, I called the house where they were living, and as soon as he heard my voice, he said through clenched teeth, "I told you never to call me at this number. She's home. Meet me on Route 6, motel room number five. The key'll be under the mat."

I said, "Paul, if anyone is listening in on this call, we'll be arrested. And I wish I were recording this. One of the world's sex symbols is making a pass at me, and I'd like to have a tape of it."

In the background, I heard Joanne laughing, "Is that Joan you're driving crazy again? Give me the phone."

Many years later, after Paul had died, I told some of those stories to Joanne's assistant, Darice Wirth (who had replaced Marcia). She pointed out something that hadn't occurred to me.

"The fact that he joked around with you that way showed how much he trusted you. After all, if you wanted to cause trouble, you could have created a scandal by telling the press that he propositioned you, and it would have been your word against his. As a matter of fact, when I started working for him and Joanne, I made it a habit to sit in whenever either one of them was being interviewed. I thought it safer to have a third person in the room in case anyone had it in mind to accuse them of some wrongdoing. They both thought I was being over-protective. But better safe than sorry."

JK and DH   Over six years after Paul's death, Joanne is still reeling from it. They had been married for over fifty years, yet whenever we saw them together, he would stroke her hair or tickle her neck and hold her hand, as though they were still newlyweds.

A few weeks after Paul died, Joanne's aunt, Mary Jane, came for a visit. When she said she wasn't feeling well, Joanne thought it would be best for her to return home to Florida where she could be tested by her own doctor. She flew back in Paul's private jet, but the following day, she had a massive stroke and died soon after. The two of them had been very close, almost like sisters. Joanne was devastated by her death.

Then came news that one of Joanne's cousins had died in Georgia. A few months earlier, the Newmans' publicist, Warren Cowan, had died. Paul's agent, Sam Cohn, passed away in 2009. And soon after that, so did their long-time lawyer, Leo Nevas.

We tried to call Joanne and left several messages, but, understandably, we didn't hear from her for about six months. After she had recovered enough to come into the city, we all went to the opening night gala of American Ballet Theater. Now we frequently have dinner with her in New York, and often visit her beautiful home in Connecticut.

JK Her friendship means a great deal to me. We share so many common interests; in addition to ballet, both of us love theater, knitting, antiques, and so much more. With just one word, we can start laughing at something silly, or singing the title song from *Anything Goes.* If prompted and encouraged, she'll even perform the bump-and-grind she did in the film, *The Stripper.* On a moment's notice, she'll revert to the thick southern accent of her childhood in Georgia. And she's taught me a few of her favorite expressions, such as "hissy fit," and "tough as a west Texas boot." She still says, "y'all," and "bacawse" instead of "because." She loves to laugh, she loves the arts, relishes good food, and she has a sweet tooth that has to be satisfied, always insisting that we have dessert.

JK and DH As Paul used to say, "I'm married to one of the last of the great broads." He adored her. So do we.

David, Joanne, and Joan.
Westport, CT, 2005. Authors' collection

Spencer Tracy.
Collection of Susie Tracy.

CHAPTER FIVE

"Now That I Have Friends"

JK "Hello Joan. It's Kate."

It was August 18, 1982, and even though David and I had spoken with Katharine Hepburn many times by then, and had been invited by her for afternoon teas and lunches, it was still a jolt to pick up the phone and hear that voice when I didn't expect it.

"Good morning. How are you today?"

It was a mundane question, just to give myself a few seconds to tune in. And then, without telling me how she was, her next comment made my mouth drop open.

"Now that I have friends in public television, why don't we do a show about Spence together?"

That was the last thing I ever expected to hear from her. I think I uttered something appropriate, but I knew I needed time to gather my thoughts. Somehow I found the nerve to say, "Miss Hepburn, I have someone on my other line. Would you please hold on a second?"

I pushed the "hold" button and called across the hall for David.

Katharine Hepburn had never before spoken publicly about her twenty-seven-year relationship with Spencer Tracy, and no one had ever even dared to bring it up when she occasionally granted an interview.

David said, "Ask her if she'll host it."

I picked up the phone again. "Miss Hepburn, I have a loaded question."

"Go ahead. What is it?"

"Would you be willing to host the program?"

"What the hell do you think I was talking about? Of course, I should host it. Come for tea tomorrow afternoon."

We didn't know then that we wouldn't begin production for over three years.

JK and DH It was obvious that this could be an exceptional show. It also dawned on us that it could be our ticket to bigger things. So, instead of offering it immediately to WNET, we decided to test the commercial television waters.

We heard every excuse one can imagine, including, "No one will know who Spencer Tracy was." We were amazed; we couldn't believe that anyone would turn down the chance to support a program that Katharine Hepburn had not only suggested, but had agreed to host.

At some point during those frustrating three years, we offered it to HBO: no interest. We contacted Dick Clark, who had a long relationship with the commercial networks. He was excited by the project and we went to several meetings with him to pitch it. ABC, CBS, and NBC all passed on it.

By then, it was 1984 and we were worried about Hepburn getting older. She was in her late seventies, and had had several operations: one on her shoulder, another for a hip replacement, and she almost lost a foot when she ran her car into a telephone pole near her home in Connecticut.

There was another big obstacle: getting the excerpts from Tracy's films. Our first thought was to contact MGM, which owned the bulk of his movies, and ask them to co-produce the program. To our surprise, they also turned us down.

It was time to use our trump card: Katharine Hepburn herself. We asked her if she would send a letter, and she came up with a "beaut." It ended with: *"You should be an important part of this venture, with David Heeley, Joan Kramer and myself."*

DH I had read in the trade press that Frank Yablans, the new Chief Operating Officer of MGM, was known for returning every phone call that he received. So I decided to find out whether he'd return mine.

What happened next was that we almost got caught red-handed. At this time, I was also the executive producer of *Nature,* and was on location in Puerto Rico for a shoot with the host of the series, George Page, who was also Joan's and my boss at WNET, and who knew nothing about the Tracy project. We were in my room at the DuPont Plaza Hotel going over the script for the next day's filming when my phone rang.

"Hello. This is Frank Yablans at MGM. Is this David Heeley?"

I panicked, but tried not to show it.

"Speaking," I said.

"I received a letter from Katharine Hepburn, and I don't know who told you that we are not interested in a program about Spencer Tracy, because we are."

"Oh, thank you. I'm very pleased to hear that. I'm on location now. Can I call you when I get back to my office at the end of the week?"

"Of course, call any time."

Somehow I'd pulled it off. George didn't even ask what the call was about.

Eventually, our sad tale of futile deception ended, and I told George Page that Hepburn had suggested a show about Tracy. He immediately picked up the phone and called his PBS contact. A few minutes later we had a green light.

JK and DH We spent many hours with Kate, during which she painted a picture of a complex man: "Spencer had eyes like an old, wild animal; he had a soul that had no release; you were not looking into an empty room. He found acting easy and life difficult. He was like a baked potato. I, on the other hand, am more like an ice cream sundae with whipped cream."

She also told us why she decided now was the time to do this program. "Recently I was asked to do a picture about Rose Kennedy. But I know that family, and I feel I cannot do it while she is still alive. This situation is similar; I couldn't speak publicly about Spence out of respect for Mrs. Tracy, but she died last year. And Spencer's daughter, Susie, is a friend of mine; I'll call her and ask if she'll help us."

At one point she said, "I have to go upstairs. I'll be right back." She came down holding a painting and a small bronze sculpture. "I did this bust of his head a long time ago," she said. "Regal, isn't it? But never could paint his face," as she showed us a portrait of Tracy reading a newspaper which partially obscured his features. "You can use these in the show, if you want. But that's up to you." Needless to say, we did.

When we pointed out that our legal department would be sending her a contract, she said, "You already have a contract with me."

We discussed who should be interviewed, and she was full of suggestions. As we were to discover, everyone we invited to participate accepted, and in the end, we had an illustrious roster of actors, directors, and Tracy admirers: Joan Bennett, Joanne Woodward, Burt Reynolds, Lee Marvin, John Sturges, Joseph L. Mankiewicz, Richard Widmark, Robert Wagner, Garson Kanin, Sidney Poitier, Frank Sinatra, Mickey Rooney, and Elizabeth Taylor[1]. It was a surplus of riches, more than we had had for any other program. They were all surprised to hear that Hepburn was doing the show and many of them called her to confirm that it was true.

---

1   See "Frank, Paper Towels, and Mickey" and "At Last, Elizabeth Taylor."

JK A few were even more surprised when I told them that she had suggested we contact them. Among them were Joseph L. Mankiewicz and Garson Kanin, each of whom had had a falling out with her years earlier.

Mankiewicz had not only produced Hepburn's comeback film, *The Philadelphia Story*, but also *Woman of the Year*, her first film with Spencer Tracy. Then in 1959, he directed her in *Suddenly Last Summer*, co-starring Montgomery Clift, who was recovering from a car accident. She thought Mankiewicz was unreasonably harsh in his treatment of Clift, not showing any consideration for the fact that he wasn't well. After the last shot, when she was assured that she was no longer needed for any pick-ups or dubbing, she spat in Mankiewicz's face, saying, "That's for being so cruel to Monty." They never spoke again. Not surprisingly, he asked me more than once whether Hepburn knew and approved of my calling him. When he arrived for the interview, he said, "I'm so happy that Kate wants me to be a part of this show." There were tears rolling down his cheeks.

Garson Kanin and his wife, Ruth Gordon, had been close friends of Spencer Tracy and Katharine Hepburn for many years. Their town house was next door to hers in New York, and they often had dinner and even went on vacations together. After Tracy's death, Kanin wrote a book called *Tracy and Hepburn*, based on the copious notes he took of their most intimate conversations. Hepburn was furious, feeling that he'd betrayed her trust, and she banished him from her life.

DH We knew how important Kanin had been in Tracy's career, and decided to ask Kate how she would feel about his participation. She said, "Spencer and Garson were great friends and he wrote some of our best pictures. He should be on the show."

When I first reached him, he turned me down. But he called back a few days later, saying he'd changed his mind. We told Hepburn, and after the program aired, she invited him for dinner, mending their relationship. However, she confided, "I've decided we can be friends again, but I still don't trust him. I'll always be wondering if he's writing down everything I say."

JK Our executive producer at MGM, George Paris, was also concerned about Kate's advanced age, and asked us to shoot an on-camera interview, so that we would have her thoughts and stories about Spencer Tracy on tape. That interview would serve as an insurance policy in case anything happened to her before we finished the program. She was familiar with "test shoots" for movies, and so never questioned the need for this one. Of course, she was no fool, and might well have known what it was really about, but if so, she never let on.

The interview also had another important purpose—giving our writer, John Miller, Hepburn's own words with which to write her scripted pieces. She would later say to him, "You write quite well for my kind of lingo."

DH It was the Tuesday after Labor Day, and the temperature and humidity were both in the nineties. Then, with our added lighting equipment, it got even hotter, exacerbated further by the fact that we had to turn off the air conditioning while we were shooting because it caused too much background noise.

As the crew was setting up, Hepburn said, "I've been thinking about it, and I really don't have too much to say about Spencer. No one really knew him. Not even me."

"Don't worry," I replied. "Whatever you have to say will be helpful." Little did she know that Joan and I had a list of over a hundred questions, and hoped that once we got going she wouldn't realize how many there were.

About an hour after we began, we heard children laughing outside. I said, "Cut," and our production manager went to see where the noise was coming from. Hepburn said, "Tell them to go inside because we're making a movie here and need them to be quiet." A few minutes later, the noise stopped and we picked up where we'd left off.

"Roll tape and tell me when you have speed," I said to the crew.

Then again, the sound of children playing.

"Cut!" I said.

This time, Hepburn got up from her chair, navigated her way across our cables, and said, "Let me go. I think it's the kids next door; the Brazilian Consul lives there with his family. I know them and I think they'll pay attention to me if I tell them to stay inside."

Sure enough, no more noise.

JK We had ordered a catered lunch. But Kate had asked her housekeeper, Norah, to prepare soup and sandwiches for all of us, so there were two lunches. And for dessert, she served vanilla ice cream with fresh raspberries. Hepburn insisted that all of us have a comfortable place to sit. She sat on the floor.

DH Following the break, we taped for several more hours, and for someone who had claimed she didn't have much to say about Tracy, she'd answered every one of our questions by the time we finished at around 4:30. As the crew was breaking down, Hepburn started to help them. She said, "Don't report me, guys. I've been around so long, I've got a waiver from all the unions." Then suddenly she stopped what she was doing. "I'd better go tell the children that they can come outside now," she said, as she headed downstairs. When she came back, she was laughing. "I thought I'd ordered the nanny to keep them quiet earlier, but I just discovered that it was actually Mrs. Brazil."

The day had gone very well. She was comfortable, and certainly gave us an excellent back-up should we ever have needed it. Fortunately, we didn't.

JK We had a summer intern that year, Blaine Smith, a young woman almost nineteen years old and about to enter her second year at Amherst. She mainly did research for the program, but we instantly recognized her potential. She was so bright and enthusiastic that, even though she had no hands-on television experience, we asked her if she'd like to serve as our production assistant on the shoot at Hepburn's house, where she'd take notes of time code readings and help the crew. She was thrilled. In preparation, she asked to look at files of some of our previous shows, staying in the office after-hours and coming in on weekends to learn the mechanics of doing notes herself. She understood the responsibility we were giving her and embraced it wholeheartedly, knowing that there was a bonus: meeting Katharine Hepburn. Understandably, she was both exhilarated and terrified.

On the morning of the shoot, we introduced her to Hepburn. That was the extent of their interaction for most of the day. Our associate producer, Cindy Mitchell, had brought packages of plastic sheets and asked Blaine to cover the sofa and all the chairs in the living room where the crew was beginning to set up the camera and lights. The rest of the equipment was being put into an adjacent room where Blaine would spend the majority of her time.

At the end of the day, David and I were downstairs as the crew was about to leave, and Cindy asked Blaine to remove the plastic from the furniture. She was alone in the living room when Katharine Hepburn walked in. Blaine was facing the opposite direction at that moment, but she felt Kate's presence and heard her mutter under her breath, "Boy, it's hot."

Blaine was about to say something, when she lifted the plastic from a chair and saw a huge red stain—the sign of fresh raspberries—right in the middle of the white upholstered seat cushion. She froze, horrified, not wanting to believe what she'd just discovered. But there it was, and she didn't know what to do next.

She thought: "Oh, God. There's this big spot and I'm alone in the room with Hepburn; if I show it to her, I'll probably get killed. But if I don't, she'll think everyone had known about it and nobody had the nerve to own up, and that would look terrible for Joan and David." So she took a deep breath and turned around, hiding the view of the chair by standing directly in front of it. And this young woman who'd only said "Good morning, Miss Hepburn," when she had arrived some eight hours before, suddenly began to talk in a nervous babble, moving her arms up and down at the same time:

"Oh my gosh, Miss Hepburn, I don't know how it happened. I'm so sorry, but I'm sure our insurance will take care of it…It was obviously an accident, and I don't know how it happened because there was plastic all over everything…I'm sooooo sorry."

Kate interrupted her: "What is the problem, young lady? I don't know what you're talking about."

Blaine started again, "Well, you see, I covered everything with plastic, but there was an accident and I don't know how it could have happened, but look…there's this big red raspberry stain on this chair. I'm so sorry." And she moved aside, pointing at it.

Hepburn glanced at the cushion and saw not only the stain, but also the very real agony that Blaine was experiencing. She walked over to the chair, and then turned to Blaine. "Is that the problem? Is that what you're so upset about? Well, watch this." She picked up the cushion, flipped it over, fluffed it up a bit and put it back in place, clean side up, sat down on it, and said, "You see, there's no longer a problem. Now no one will ever know, will they?"

Blaine was speechless. And when she recovered her composure, she began to laugh. So did Katharine Hepburn.

JK and DH We didn't know anything about that story until we were back in our office, because Blaine felt that Hepburn had not wanted her to make a big deal over it. However, we called Kate and offered to have the chair cleaned. She refused. She said, "It's seen worse. Forget about it. Did you get what you wanted on film?"

Ever the pro, she was worried about whether she'd performed well. We told her that indeed she had. But what she did best that day was not captured on camera.

For all we know, throughout years, that stain was still on the underside of her white cushion. Each time we went to the house for tea or lunch, we wondered about it. But it would have been rude to ask. Wouldn't it?

DH Two months later, in December, 1985, we were all in Los Angeles for the location shoots[2]. MGM gave us an office in the Thalberg building, where many of the studio's legendary leaders had wielded their power. However, we rarely used it, operating most often from our rooms at the Beverly Hilton Hotel. Hepburn stayed at the home of Hal Wallis and his wife, actress Martha Hyer, who were out of town at the time. Wallis had not only produced dozens of great Warner Bros. pictures in the thirties and forties, but also had been responsible for Kate's only film with John Wayne, *Rooster Cogburn.*

One afternoon, she invited us to the Wallis house for a drink, a visit that I knew would eventually include a discussion of the plans for the shoot a few days later. The house was large, light and airy, and filled with original paintings, including some by Monet and Renoir, as well as several bronze sculptures on tables and pedestals.

We chatted for a few minutes, and suddenly she said, "Is that a Giacometti?" pointing to one of the pieces.

"I don't know," I answered, "but it looks like his style."

I went over to it and bent down, searching for any clues.

"I can't see a signature anywhere."

"Well, pick it up and bring it over here into the light. Now turn it over and see if it's signed on the bottom."

Sure enough, under the base was the signature, which made it very clear that I was holding in my hands a genuine, and possibly priceless, Giacometti.

Of course, the house had an intricate security system, which Kate never was quite able to master. So when she went out, she would often ask her assistant, Phyllis Wilbourn, to stay and guard the place—not very practical, since Phyllis was in her eighties, frail, and hardly capable of deterring thieves.

---

2   See "Directing Kate."

JK   Shortly after she arrived in Los Angeles, Hepburn took her hairdresser, Ray Gow; makeup artist, Michal Bigger; Phyllis; and driver, Hilly, on a tour of the various homes she had lived in during her years in Hollywood. According to Gow, she gave second-by-second directions to Hilly as she pointed out who had lived where: "Turn left here; now turn right; go straight up this road; Bogie and Betty lived here; Leland Hayward owned the one over there; that one was mine." They stopped to take closer looks at a few others. At one, Hepburn jumped over a fence and was chased by a barking dog. At another, she told a gardener, "Yes, you did see me in *On Golden Pond.*" She talked her way past a Spanish-speaking housekeeper and, as she was showing Ray, Michal, and Phyllis around the house, the woman who lived there returned home, carrying several bags filled with groceries. She was so astonished to find Katharine Hepburn standing in her living room that she dropped the bags. Oranges, apples, potatoes, and other vegetables rolled out onto the floor. Kate got down on her knees and helped pick them up, thanked the owner for letting them see the place, and left. We wonder whether the woman's friends ever believed her story of finding that Katharine Hepburn had broken into her house.

JK and DH   While she was playing tour guide, we and our cinematographer went to survey The Riviera Country Club's golf course, and MGM, to determine the exact locations we'd want to shoot later in the week. The following day, we were in the midst of taping an interview with Richard Widmark when Hepburn called.

"I've been waiting for Michal Bigger to come and practice my makeup for the filming, but she hasn't shown up, so why don't we go and look at the locations you've chosen?"

We explained that we'd already checked them out the day before, and that we couldn't meet her for awhile because we were taping Widmark.

"Call me as soon as you're done."

We weren't "done" until just before 3 pm.

"Meet me at Metro as soon as you can," she said. "And hurry because we're going to lose the light."

We rushed to the lobby of the hotel and asked the valet for our car. But some sort of event was in progress there and, after what seemed like an eternity, but was actually only about ten minutes, the valet reported that he couldn't find our car in the garage. Panicked, we got into a taxi and headed for MGM in Culver City.

JK Hepburn had arrived some twenty minutes before us, sending everyone at the studio into a tailspin. All rules suddenly were broken. The guard at the front gate had not only allowed Hilly to drive her onto the lot, against union regulations, but then told our taxi driver to do the same.

"Just go straight ahead," he said. "They're at Stage 10."

We found Kate talking with George Paris, and as soon as she saw us, she said, "Let's go; we don't have much time," as she put her arm through his and started walking. Over her shoulder, she said to us, "You go in the car with Hilly; I want to walk with him [George]." It was quite a trek to the next location, and when we met them there, David said, "Something's not quite right here. The star shouldn't walk while we ride."

DH Each building on the lot was named after an MGM star, producer or director. The one that housed all the actors' dressing rooms was now called the Stallone building. When Hepburn saw the sign, she said with a laugh, "Maybe some day I should play 'Rocky's' grandmother."

Phyllis, always prim and proper, said in her most British schoolteacher tone of voice, "No, no, no. This is serious. You must refrain from trying to make it funny."

Kate then pointed to the windows where Tracy's, Robert Montgomery's, and Robert Taylor's dressing rooms had been, and added, "Mine was at the far end on the second floor." However, just as she was about to walk away, she looked up at the sign again and said, "Obviously times have changed."

JK   I noticed Sylvester Stallone's reserved parking space with his name printed in big white letters on the ground at the front, and thought, "What would be really funny is if he arrived right now and saw Katharine Hepburn staring at 'his' building. I wonder what they would say to each other."

A bit further on, we approached a rather drab-looking, small structure, which was the Tracy building.

Kate stood there quietly for a moment and then said, "Not very interesting. Doesn't do him proud. I wonder what goes on in there. I hope it's respectable for Spence's sake."

JK and DH   We finished the tour and were heading for the car as the sun was setting. Shadows played across the windows of the buildings and Hepburn turned around and stopped again, staring into the distance. We were moved by the silence, and realized that she was absorbing the ambiance, thinking back to the days when she and Spencer Tracy made some of their best movies there. And that she wasn't just being sentimental. It was her way of preparing for the shoot over the next two days when, for the first time publicly, she'd be telling stories about Tracy, the actor and the man.

Page from Spencer Tracy's diary, noting the first day he and Hepburn worked together. Collection of Susie Tracy.

Authors' collection.

CHAPTER SIX

Frank, Paper Towels, and Mickey

"You should definitely ask Frank. He adored Spence," Katharine Hepburn told us when we were planning the show about Spencer Tracy.

JK However, getting to Frank Sinatra was like breaching Fort Knox. Protected by security and close friends, he was just about impossible to contact directly. There were official representatives, but calling any of them would lead to a quick brush-off. Nevertheless, I felt I had to try going by the book, so my first call was to his lawyer, Milton (Mickey) Rudin. The predictable answer came back the next morning: "Not available." Then, buried in my address book I came across an old listing—*Sinatra, Frank*—complete with a home number. I had no idea where it came from, but it was worth a try. A man answered and said he'd take a message. After a few days, I tried again, with the same results. I wasn't getting anywhere.

Then I remembered that, many years back, my father once told me he'd met Frank Sinatra at an event in California, and that among his entourage was a man named Jilly. Jilly Rizzo at one time owned a bar in New York, appropriately called Jilly's, where Sinatra and his friends would often hang out. I was grasping at straws, but it occurred to me that maybe Jilly would be willing to give Sinatra a message. The trick was to find him.

My next call was to one of the Palm Springs country clubs where Sinatra was known to play golf and I asked the receptionist if anyone there knew how I might reach Jilly Rizzo. I was transferred to someone who said, "Call him after 4 pm at the jewelry store in the Waldorf Astoria Hotel in New York. He's a friend of the owner and he's there most afternoons."

Now, I've used some unusual means to find celebrities, but calling a jewelry store was a first. I dialed the number at 4 o'clock sharp. The man who answered the phone sounded as though he were auditioning for a 1930s Warner Bros. movie.

"Yeah?"

"Hello, is Mr. Rizzo there?"

"Who's looking for him?"

"I'm producing a program about Spencer Tracy for public television, and I've been told that Mr. Rizzo might be able to help us get a message to Frank Sinatra. We'd like to invite Mr. Sinatra to appear in the program, since he and Tracy were friends."

"Yeah. Yeah. Just a minute. Hold on."

A few moments later, a hoarse voice that could have been in the same movie: "Yeah, Jilly here. Who's this?"

Once again, I explained who I was and why I was calling.

"OK. Send me a letter by messenger and I'll get it to Frank."

"Where should I send it?"

"Here, at the jewelry store."

That afternoon a messenger took a letter addressed to "*Mr. Jilly Rizzo,*" in care of the jewelry store on the Lexington Avenue side of the Waldorf Astoria. I followed up the next day with another phone call.

"Yeah, I got it. I'll get it to Frank."

"When?"

"In the next day or so."

I waited a couple of days before calling again.

"Frank got the letter. If he's interested, you'll hear from someone."

I never received a reply, and worse, I lost contact with Jilly. He suddenly "wasn't in" when I called. What had sounded promising turned out to be a dead-end. I still wonder if Sinatra actually saw that letter. My guess is that Jilly gave it to someone else in his circle and that was the end of the line.

When we told Katharine Hepburn about our plight, she said, "That's odd. Frank and Spencer were really good friends. I'll find him."

JK and DH Several weeks later, in December, 1985, we flew to Los Angeles to shoot interviews for the program. Almost every big name we asked to talk about Tracy had agreed, and we found ourselves filming as many as four a day. Our schedule was tight and we knew that our shooting budget would be depleted by the end of the trip.

JK Katharine Hepburn called me at the hotel.

"I've spoken to Frank and you're going to interview him at his house in Rancho Mirage on Thursday. Here's the number of the phone in his kitchen. You'll speak to a woman named Dorothy. Call and set it up. And by the way, Thursday is his birthday. I also called Mickey Rooney and he's waiting to hear from you too. Here's his number."

"Miss Hepburn," I said, "would you like to come and work for us? How did you do that?"

She replied with a laugh, "I knew I'd find Frank. And Mickey would rue the day if he didn't do this for Spence."

DH When Joan told me that Kate had booked Sinatra and Rooney, I remember saying, "We'd better stop her. If she calls any more people, we can't tell her we don't have the time or money to interview them. She's on a roll and this could get out of hand."

We didn't have a crew booked for that Thursday; nor did we have the budget for an additional day of shooting. I called our boss, George Page, in New York and asked if we could have some additional money to interview Frank Sinatra. It was a no-brainer. The answer was an immediate "Yes."

JK A woman in Sinatra's kitchen answered the phone.

"Is this Dorothy?" I asked.

"Yes, speaking."

When I told her who I was and that Sinatra had told Katharine Hepburn that I should call her, she said, "Mr. Sinatra will do the interview at 2 o'clock Thursday afternoon, the 12th, so why don't you and your crew get here about 1 to set up." She then gave me the exact address which made me smile. The man who was so hard to find lived on Frank Sinatra Drive.

Rancho Mirage, CA, 1985. Authors' collection.

JK and DH We reached the gate to the estate·and were greeted by a man in a security uniform, complete with a gun and holster. He had a pleasant smile, but was clearly a no-nonsense type. He told us where to park, and led us to his office, which was actually the size of a small house. It had wall-to-wall television monitors, showing every angle of the compound, inside and out. He gave us directions to the pool area and said, "Just point your camera at Mr. Sinatra. Don't shoot the house or any scenery. We don't allow that for security reasons."

DH I thought, "Uh, oh. Joan and I both have still cameras in our bags, and this is definitely not a place to take beauty shots."

JK David whispered to me, "No pictures. Don't even take out your camera unless you want it confiscated."

The pool itself was beautiful. All the tiles depicted playing cards: ace of spades, queen of hearts, etc. While David was setting up with the crew, I saw a housekeeper walking nearby, and asked if I could use a bathroom.

She said, "Certainly, follow me."

David told me later that at one point, he looked around and didn't see me. The thought crossed his mind that I might have wandered into the house just to see what it was like.

I had indeed gone into the house, and at the entrance I'd noticed a door mat that read, *"Blue Eyes and Barbara[1]."* The housekeeper led me to a bathroom nearby, and after I closed the door, I realized that the walls were decorated with framed cartoons, several of which depicted Sinatra and the Mafia. I couldn't resist. I pulled out my camera and took pictures of the pictures. Then in somewhat of a panic I thought, "I wonder if there's a security camera in this bathroom." But it was too late to worry. I'd already taken the pictures, and so far, no alarms had gone off.

On the counter near the sink, there were brightly colored paper towels. "These are pretty," I thought. "If they're meant to be used and then thrown in the waste basket, I'm sure it won't hurt to take one for David and one for me as souvenirs. After all, when will we ever be at Frank Sinatra's again?" So I put two paper towels in my

---

1   Barbara Blakely Marx was Frank Sinatra's fourth wife. They married in 1976.

bag and went back outside. David saw me coming out of the house and shot me a look as if to say, "Where were you?" He seemed relieved when I told him that I'd just been to the ladies' room.

JK and DH At exactly 2 pm, Frank Sinatra came to the pool and shook hands with all of us. He was wearing a navy blazer that had a gold medallion insignia on one breast pocket, gray pants and a shirt and tie. He looked tanned and relaxed and was friendly, but somehow there was a slight tension in the air—almost a sense of danger about him. Maybe that was just us, having dealt with his notoriously tough lawyer, then his friend, Jilly, and now the security guard with the gun. And, of course, here he was in person, the embodiment of so many stories through the years.

He told us how happy he was to have heard from "Katie" and that he was pleased to be part of the show. His stories were as revealing about himself as they were about Tracy. When he was a young actor at MGM, he'd sneak onto the soundstage where Tracy was filming, and climb up a ladder behind the set so he could peek over to watch him at work. And years later, when they co-starred in their one film together, *The Devil at Four O'Clock*, he spent every free moment standing just out of camera range, still watching Tracy.

"One day I asked him how he makes it all look so easy. I said, 'Spence, what's the trick?' Tracy said, 'Just learn the lines and hit the mark. And don't act...*re*act.'"

In one scene, the script had Sinatra being beaten up. Tracy was watching from a short distance away. When the take was over, he took Frank aside and said, "What did I tell you about reacting? Those guys are punching you and you're just standing there and taking it. What would you do in real life?"

Sinatra said, "I'd fight back."

"Exactly," said Tracy. "Defend yourself. React as you would if these guys jumped you on the street."

JK After the interview, I asked Sinatra to autograph the book, *The Films of Spencer Tracy,* on the page that related to *The Devil at Four O'Clock.* We gave him a bottle of champagne and wished him a happy birthday (it was his seventieth), which seemed to take him by surprise. Then he shook hands with all of us again and went into the house. We packed up and drove back to Los Angeles.

Earlier that day, I'd felt the beginnings of a sore throat. By the time we got into the car at about 4:30, it was much worse and accompanied by a headache. I slept most of the way back to LA, and when we reached the hotel David said, "Why don't you order some soup and tea and take a rest? I'll come by later to write questions with you for tomorrow's interviews."

That evening we put in a few hours of work before both of us were ready to collapse. But just as David was about to leave, I remembered the paper towels in my bag.

"Oh, wait a second. I have to give you something I stole from Frank Sinatra's house." I was trying to be funny, but David heard the words "stole from Frank Sinatra's house," and suddenly turned pale. Usually calm under any circumstances, he said in a voice that increased in a crescendo of both volume and pitch with each word: "Joan, what did you take from that house? Are you crazy? We'll get our knees broken!"

"Calm down," I told him. "They're just paper towels from the bathroom. So relax." Then I also admitted shooting pictures of the cartoons on the wall. I said, "Since nobody took my camera away, I guess that guy's not monitoring people in the bathroom."

A few weeks later, back in New York, I asked David's partner, Don, if he'd seen "what I stole from Frank Sinatra's house." He said, "What was it?" And I told him the story of the paper towel and David's reaction.

"Oh no," he said. "I saw a colored paper towel on the counter the other day and used it as a napkin when I ate a piece of chocolate cake. Then I threw it away."

I confronted David. "How could you just leave that lying around?"

He replied innocently, "What did you expect me to do with it?"

Over the years, I took some pretty famous paper towels. In addition to the one from Sinatra's bathroom, I have a Gene Kelly, and a Barbra Streisand, among others, including one from the Reagan White House. Mine are in scrapbooks that I put together after each program was finished. Obviously, the ones I gave David met a completely different fate: they ended up in a garbage dump.

DH I never quite cottoned on to Joan's fascination with paper towels—even though she likes to tell people that she "risked her life" to get some of them.

JK and DH As for Mickey Rooney, he was something of a disappointment. The original plan was to tape him in his home. But he called two days before and said, "I have to cancel. I've got a job so I'll be working. And you're not paying me anything for this, are you?" We were rather shocked by his matter-of-fact attitude, especially since Hepburn had called him personally. Because she did, we knew we had to try our best to accommodate him. We suggested that we might be able to interview him several days later at Universal where we'd be taping Angela Lansbury on the set of her series, *Murder She Wrote*. We asked the production manager if he could help, and he arranged for us to use an adjoining soundstage to shoot Mickey Rooney.

While we were setting up, he began letting off steam, talking about how badly Hollywood and the old studio system had treated him. He came across as bitter and angry. But when our camera rolled, he changed radically, becoming almost too sweet. Unfortunately his statements tended to be mostly platitudes and generalities, with very little substance about Tracy and how they worked together. He repeatedly told us how much he loved Spencer Tracy and how much he loved Katharine Hepburn. It didn't work, and we were able to use only very little of what he said. But what struck us most was the instant change of personality—a very different image for the public.

JK While Hepburn knew about all the people we had interviewed, the only ones she asked about were the ones she'd contacted herself.

"How was Frank? Did he have anything fascinating to say? And how was Mickey? Was he good?"

Having worked on *The Dick Cavett Show*, I knew where she was coming from. She was exhibiting a typical talent coordinator's instinct—to be most interested in those guests *she* had booked.

JK and DH And then there was Elizabeth Taylor. But that's worth a chapter of its own.

Paper towel from Frank Sinatra's bathroom.
Rancho Mirage, CA, 1985. Authors' collection.

Father of the Bride

1950

Elizabeth Taylor gave us her autograph.
Bel Air, CA, 1985. Authors' collection.

CHAPTER SEVEN

At Last, Elizabeth Taylor

She'd co-starred in two films with Spencer Tracy: *Father of the Bride* and *Father's Little Dividend*, and was high on our wish-list of interviews for our profile of him.

Her press agent replied to our letter. "She's interested. When do you need her?" We explained that we'd be in Los Angeles for two weeks in December, and had a chocker-block schedule, but would like to give her preference.

"What days would be best for her?"

"I'll get back to you," was the response.

Not a bad start.

JK Soon after, I received a message to call Roger Wall, Elizabeth Taylor's personal assistant, who worked from an office in her home.

He said, "She definitely wants to do this, but she's put her back out. So right now, she has to stay in bed. Call me when you get to Los Angeles, and we'll take it from there."

That was all rather inconclusive and not at all helpful in trying to prepare a shooting schedule. We had to confirm dates and times for Angela Lansbury, Richard Widmark, Robert Wagner, Lee Marvin, and Mickey Rooney, among others, or run the risk of losing them. Our days were filling up quickly and our crew budget was already stretched to the limit.

Once we arrived in LA, I called Roger. He said, "She's still suffering with her back. Call me tomorrow."

I said, "Roger, please understand that we're on a tight schedule and budget, so if Ms. Taylor is feeling better tomorrow, we can't just come over and do the interview; we'll need some notice. Do you think maybe we should plan to do it the day after tomorrow?"

"We can aim for that, but I can't promise," he said. "I'll give you an update tomorrow. And here's my home number in case you miss me at work."

It was encouraging, but disconcerting at the same time. There was a sort-of commitment, but it was flimsy at best.

The next day, during a break in shooting, I called Roger again. A housekeeper named Liz answered. "He's not in. Can you call back in an hour?"

JK and DH It was a similar routine every day of the first week and into the second. By then, Katharine Hepburn had arrived in Los Angeles for the filming of her host sequences. We told her of our daily pursuit of Elizabeth Taylor, and that we were running out of time. Our plan had been to leave LA on Friday of that week, but to give ourselves an extra day, we changed our flight to Saturday.

And then we had an idea. We suggested to Hepburn that she send flowers to Elizabeth with a note. Kate agreed, but said, "You arrange for the flowers and here's what the note should say: "*Dear Elizabeth, Sorry you're having trouble with your back. Spencer's daughter, Susie, and I are so pleased that you have agreed to do an interview for the program we're doing about him. Fondly, Kate.*"

JK The phone rang the next day. It was Roger.

"Elizabeth received some beautiful flowers and a note from Katharine Hepburn and would like to call her. Can you give me the number?"

"I'll have to get back to you because she's staying in someone's home and I don't have the number yet," I told him.

Hepburn said, "No, no. I'd rather call her. And if she asks me to appear at one of her benefit fundraisers, I'll strangle the two of you." Kate told us later, "Elizabeth is sweet. But she sounds like a little girl. It was obviously such a thrill for her to hear from me. Call her tomorrow. I think she's ready to set a date."

The next morning Roger confirmed it. "I think she might be ready to do it later today. Will that work for you?"

"Yes, we have a crew on hold and can be there around 4. But we do need to give them a definite call time. When will you know for sure?"

"In a couple of hours." By then it was already noon.

Two hours later: "Elizabeth would rather do it tomorrow about 5 in the afternoon. Can you be here at 4 for set-up?"

I said, "Roger, tomorrow is Friday. We've spoken every day for the past two weeks and I appreciate all your efforts. But we're leaving LA on Saturday. Is this for real?"

I was only half-surprised to hear: "I think so, but let's confirm tomorrow morning."

We booked the crew and crossed our fingers.

Friday morning's call was predictable: "Elizabeth would like one more day. She promises she'll do it tomorrow."

I said, "Roger, we have a crew available today. And as I told you, we have to fly back to New York tomorrow. So this is our last chance. Can you please push her to do it this afternoon? Otherwise, we're out of luck." It was an ultimatum, but this routine had to end and it was time to say, "Now or never." We banked on her not wanting to disappoint Katharine Hepburn. And we were right.

Roger called back within minutes. "Okay, come at 4 for a 5 o'clock shoot." And he gave us directions to the house.

DH The housekeeper, Liz, let us in and took us to the living room. I'd expected a fluffy, touch-me-not kind of house. It wasn't. It looked very comfortable and lived-in. The furniture was white, with overstuffed chairs and pillows, and there were some impressive pieces of art. Family photos were everywhere, and Liz showed us the kitchen, which had on the refrigerator a photo of Elizabeth at her heaviest weight.

"She keeps it there as a reminder," she explained.

JK There were pictures of Richard Burton, but none of her other husbands. Liz told me that Elizabeth's grandchildren are frequent visitors and the public would be amused to see them rough-housing with their grandmother, smudging chocolate on her face.

The clock ticked away. We knew her makeup artist and hairdresser were upstairs with her. They were both superstars in their fields, and each charged $1,500 a day. We'd already said politely that we didn't have that kind of money in our budget and would appreciate some relief. In the end, we never got any invoices. She obviously paid them herself.

DH Roger had gone upstairs to speak with Elizabeth and when he came down, he said she would like to ask a favor. Since she'll already be on camera, she wondered if I'd mind shooting a Public Service Announcement she'd promised to do on behalf of AIDS research. I said I'd be happy to do it. He made a call to get the script sent by messenger.

It was now 6 pm. Jose Eber, her hairdresser, came down and told us she was now getting made up.

7 pm: No sign of her.

8 pm: We were still waiting.

9 pm: Elizabeth Taylor came downstairs.

Her entrance was breathtaking; it felt like a scene from a movie. She was dazzling. Her eyes were indeed violet, and she was wearing a dark purple blouse that offset them perfectly. We were all surprised to see how short she was; she appeared to be no taller than five feet.

JK and DH   The messenger with the AIDS copy never arrived, which was a shame.

But Elizabeth was eager to talk about Spencer Tracy, and she was still full of admiration for him. It was worth waiting all those days—plus an extra four hours.

She recalled that in the films they made together, in which she played his daughter, Tracy called her "Kitten" and she called him "Pops."

"And we kept those names until the day he died," she said. "If I was ever in trouble—or happy times—he would sense that I needed his big bear-like arms around me, and he would send me the most wonderful telegrams: always '*to Kitten*,' and always signed '*Pops*.'"

When we told Katharine Hepburn about that story, she said, "Hmph. 'Pops and Kitten.' Who do you think sent those telegrams?"

Elizabeth Taylor during interview for *The Spencer Tracy Legacy: A Tribute by Katharine Hepburn.*
Bel Air, CA, 1985. Authors' collection.

Cinematographer John Sharaf, David Heeley, Mary Bell Painten, and Joan Kramer with Katharine Hepburn and Susie Tracy preparing to shoot items from Spencer Tracy's scrapbooks.
Los Angeles, CA, 1985. Photograph by John Bryson, courtesy Bryson Photo.

CHAPTER EIGHT

Directing Kate

DH That night in early December, as I lay in my bed at the Beverly Hilton Hotel, I was not sure that I'd be able to get any sleep. I'd been a television director for over twenty years, having started back when I worked for the BBC in London, but the next morning was to be my first time directing Katharine Hepburn, and I didn't expect to get through it unscathed.

It could be argued that my debut had come three months earlier in New York at her 49th Street townhouse, when we had taped a protection interview[1]. But that could hardly count as "directing Katharine Hepburn." That test was to come early tomorrow at The Riviera Country Club, where MGM had once filmed scenes for the Tracy/Hepburn comedy, *Pat and Mike*.

Our writer, John Miller, had adapted easily to Kate's style, and we had gone over the script many times with her in New York before we left for Los Angeles. She always had some comments and suggestions—never anything major, and always improvements. It had been at one of our script meetings that she and I had our first

---

1   See "Now That I Have Friends."

difference of opinion. I knew this was going to be a new experience for her, and therefore possibly a challenge. Despite her more than sixty years as an actress, she had never hosted a television program, so I tried to make it seem as easy as possible. I reassured her that she would not have to memorize her lines.

"Do you need glasses to see at a distance?" I asked.

"No. I may be falling apart, but so far my eyes are fine. Why?"

"There'll be a teleprompter on the camera, so that when you look into the lens you'll see the script right there, and it will run at whatever pace works for you."

"Hmmm," she said. "Why don't you stand next to the camera, and I'll just talk to you?"

"No, Miss Hepburn. It's important that the viewers feel that you are speaking directly to them. You have to talk to the camera." I felt very strongly about this, and would have fought her hard if she had resisted.

"Oh," she said. And that was that. Or so it seemed.

Somehow I did get some sleep that night in Los Angeles, and was up well before dawn for our shoot on the golf course at The Riviera Country Club. There had been storms the previous couple of days, and we'd seen reports on television of high winds knocking down trees and power lines. Fortunately the weather had calmed down somewhat overnight and the sun was trying to peek through as we drove to the location, but it was a brisk, chilly morning.

Kate knew her golf, and had already warned me that we had to get our shot before the first player of the day teed off. "It's dangerous out there, and we'll be like sitting ducks," she said, referring to some of the less than expert golfers who might be up early. "If a ball comes our way, we'll all get killed."

We had a small crew: our cameraman, John Sharaf, and his assistant, who also helped with the lights; a soundman, John Vincent, who had worked with us many times before; a prompter operator; and our production team: Cindy Mitchell, our associate producer; Mary Bell Painten, our West Coast co-ordinator; and Don Shump, who had been hired by Cindy as a runner/production aide. We all met at the clubhouse, and then made our way to the spot a few hundred yards away where we could get the shot we needed, planned to match a scene in *Pat and Mike.*

David Heeley and crew setting up on The Riviera Country Club golf course. Los Angeles, CA, 1985. Authors' collection.

JK The first thing that comes to mind when I remember that day is how cold and windy it was. Both of us hate the cold, though I think that I'm even more sensitive to it than David is. But serious golfers don't seem to mind it. In fact, as we were setting up, I noticed Dean Martin, one of the club's many famous members, walking towards the main building. It wouldn't be long before he appeared on the course, ready to play eighteen holes with some friends.

Soon after we arrived, Cindy and I went back to the clubhouse to wait for Hepburn. Only a few minutes later, she came through the door of the lobby, followed by her makeup artist Michal Bigger; Ray Gow, her hairdresser; and her driver, Hilly.

As I greeted them, Michal said to me, "The family always travels together." However, Phyllis Wilbourn, Hepburn's assistant, had been left behind to "guard" Hal Wallis' house and art collection.

Kate was wearing the tan raincoat, red scarf, black sweater and beige slacks that would be her outfit for all the exterior shots. She said "Hello" to everyone, and then turned to her makeup artist.

"I need a mirror, Michal," she said. "You only have a small one, don't you? I need something bigger."

Cindy and Michal and Ray ran into the ladies' room, the men's room, the locker room, frantically searching for a large, yet portable mirror. In the meantime, Hepburn noticed the round marble table in the center of the lobby, holding a very big vase filled with fresh flowers. Under it was a circular mirrored top. Before anyone could blink, she began to try moving the vase in order to get to the mirror.

"This'll be fine," she said.

"Miss Hepburn, you can't take that," said the flustered receptionist.

"Don't worry. I'll bring it back when we're finished."

At that moment, the Riviera Golf Club manager suddenly appeared carrying a large mirror.

Kate yelled, "Bravo. Bravo! I'll use that one instead."

She took the mirror from the manager, and walked through the back door of the clubhouse, down the steps, and onto the golf course. Cindy ran after her and offered to carry it.

"No, no. I can do it myself. Don't worry. I've got a good grip," she insisted.

It was reminiscent of when she was filming *The African Queen* in the Belgian Congo. She wore a period costume for that picture and knew she had to have a way of seeing how she looked before the camera rolled. So she found a full-length mirror, and carried it with her throughout the entire location shoot. When it broke, she kept what was left of it, propping it up against the nearest tree.

DH We'd been setting up for about forty-five minutes when I saw Kate heading towards us. I was to discover that whatever time she was scheduled to start, she'd be there early, wondering why everyone else was not ready yet. I went over to say "Good morning," and told her we only needed a few more minutes, then excused myself to go back and work with the crew.

I'd just finished lining up the first shot, when I saw Joan walking towards me. And she had a very worried look on her face.

"David, we have a problem. You've got to come and talk to Hepburn. She's very upset."

I found Kate haranguing poor John Vincent.

"If I'd known I had to wear one of these I would never have agreed to do this."

"OK, this is it," I thought to myself. "The first test."

"What's wrong, Miss Hepburn?" I asked.

"It's this," she said, holding up the wireless microphone that John was trying to put on her. "They work in Spain, but they're no good here. Never work. I don't know why. They're just useless."

It wasn't the time to ask what was special about the microphones in Spain, but I've always wondered.

"Unfortunately we have to use the radio mic to get the shot we need here," I told her. "Can you just try it? If it doesn't work, we'll find some other way." I had no idea what that other way would be, but I knew the most important thing was to bring some calm to the situation.

"Well, just this once. But I don't like it."

She then let John fit the battery pack and transmitter around her waist and hide the small microphone just inside her raincoat. She probably was also upset that the battery would protrude and make her look bulky, but I knew we could frame the shot in a way that it would not be seen.

Moments later she was ready.

"Where do you want me?"

"Over here," I told her, as we walked together towards her opening position. "You'll start with the golf course in the background and then walk over here so that we can see the clubhouse behind you, just like the shot in *Pat and Mike*."

She seemed a bit more relaxed. But it was to be only a brief respite.

"Before we try a run-through, let's make sure that you can read the prompter from this position," I told her.

"Are you set?" I shouted to the prompter operator.

"Ready when you are," he replied.

"OK, let's go," I said, and threw a cue to Katharine Hepburn.

She peered at the camera which had the prompter screen mounted in front of the lens, paused and then peered again, this time with her hand extended above her eyes as though shielding them from the sun.

"I can't see a thing."

I knew I couldn't move the camera, or I'd lose the shot of the clubhouse I needed. The only choice was to move her.

"Try a few steps closer," I said.

"How many?"

"You can come a good six feet; it'll still work."

"Okay."

She walked a couple of paces forward, and I told the prompter operator to reset to the top of the script. She squinted towards the camera again. A pause.

"It's hopeless. I still can't see a thing." And this was the same person who had told me back in New York that she had no problem with her eyesight.

It was the first set-up of our first day of shooting, and she couldn't read the script. I was standing next to her, rather than at my usual position by the camera, and I knew I had only seconds to find a solution. We had spent much of the last three years trying to raise several hundred thousand dollars to make this program, and PBS had finally come through. Now it was looking as though everything could fall apart—including our careers. I had to get that, and other thoughts racing through my mind, out of the way, calm down Kate, and come up with something that was going to work. Frankly, there weren't too many choices, and it was the most obvious one—perhaps the only one—that came to mind first.

"Miss Hepburn, we can do this without the prompter. We've

Directing Kate

been through this part of the script many times already, and it doesn't have to be word perfect. You are making two points here: this is the Riviera Country Club, where you and Spencer shot scenes for *Pat and Mike*, and you need to describe the characters the two of you played, so that we can get into a clip from the film. Just tell the story to the camera. You start here and walk over to the spot over there," I told her, indicating her finishing mark.

"Yes, but when I talk about what he and I played, you want me to say 'You know the old cliché about opposites attracting.' Now, is that meant to be a 'double entendre?'"

"No," I said. "I just need enough words for the shot to reveal the clubhouse behind you. But if you're not comfortable with the line, we can change it."

"OK," she said. "Let's try it."

"Quiet, everyone. Ready for rehearsal." I said.

I didn't tell John Sharaf to roll tape, as this was to see if Kate could hit her marks as well as tell the story, and had only just reached my spot next to the camera when I realized that she had already started—without waiting for a cue from me. I turned to see her walking and talking, her stride deliberate and her voice strong.

"This is the Riviera Country Club," she said, pointing to the golf course. "It's where Spence and I shot the picture, *Pat and Mike*..."

She was full of confidence. And I noticed she used the line about opposites attracting, but changed the word "cliché" to "adage." I wished we'd taped the rehearsal, not knowing that John Sharaf had indeed done so.

"Cut!" I said. "That was great. Let's do one more rehearsal,"

"Go ahead and waste the film," she said. "Why not just shoot it?"

"Fine," I said. "Let's do it. Everyone set? Roll tape and... Cue!"

She reached her final spot about halfway through, so I asked her to walk more slowly.

"Why don't you just make me walk further?" she said. She finished three takes, getting better each time. We completed the last one just as the golf balls started whizzing by.

103

Now she was in great spirits. And the mood on the set had definitely changed.

"How was it?" she asked me.

"It was excellent," I assured her. "We can do all the scenes like this. You did a terrific job."

It was only later that I realized what had gone on that morning. Hepburn was very nervous, probably even more than I was. She was doing something she had never done before: host a show. I was also asking her to break one of the golden rules she had learned early in her career; I wanted her to look directly into the lens of the camera, something she'd been taught *never* to do. Then add the teleprompter, which was something else new. Too many "firsts" all at once. In trying to overcome her nerves, she was giving everyone around her a hard time. Once she regained her confidence, we never looked back.

We'd escaped death by flying golf balls, so we packed up, returned the borrowed mirror, and headed to our next location, which was outside Susie Tracy's house, not very far from the Riviera Country Club.

As we were unloading the equipment, I noticed that John Vincent had commandeered our production aide, Don Shump, to work as his assistant. John had found a broom handle and taped a microphone to the end, improvising a boom. Don was going to be his boom operator. Now there was no need for Hepburn to wear a wireless mic.

By this time in the morning the sun was shining brightly, but there was still a chill in the air. Don was wearing a shirt and jeans, holding the new makeshift boom, just a few feet away from Kate, waiting for the shot to be lined up.

"Young man, aren't you cold?" she asked.

"I'm really OK, thank you Miss Hepburn."

"No, you must be freezing," she said. "Give me that thing," as she grabbed the broom handle. "Go and get yourself a jacket. It's awful to be cold."

JK It was a moment that few people noticed, but I had seen this aspect of her character previously in New York. We had brought a crew to survey her house in preparation for taping there, and were all crowded into her second floor living room to discuss the practical aspects of the lighting, loading in equipment, etc. Everyone had found a seat except for one of the stagehands, who was standing near the door.

Kate noticed, and said, "Just a minute." She went to the next room, and a few seconds later, came back carrying an upholstered chair, which she placed within the circle among the rest of us, motioning to him to sit down.

He said, "Thank you, Miss Hepburn, but you didn't have to do that."

"Yes, I did," she said. "No one should ever be uncomfortable in this house."

DH Once we had overcome the problems at the Riviera Country Club, Kate was nothing but supportive and helpful. She never balked at doing multiple takes. If a member of the crew said something to me that she couldn't hear, she'd say, "What's wrong? If something didn't work, let's do it again." And when we were shooting a sequence that included both her and Susie Tracy, Susie asked if she could watch a playback of it.

"No, Susie. Don't do that," Kate said. "They have to be ruthless. They're looking for things you and I won't see. You must trust them."

She had told us that early in her career, she always went to the "dailies" (the ritual screening of the previous day's filming) until she realized that she was concentrating on such things as whether her collar was high enough to hide signs of her own aging, rather than looking at the bigger picture of whether the scene was working as a whole. From that point on she decided not to watch herself, and trust the director.

David Heeley and Katharine Hepburn discussing her first scene on the MGM lot. Culver City, CA, 1985. Photograph by John Bryson, courtesy Bryson Photo.

JK The second day of taping was at MGM in Culver City. The studio gave her a dressing room, just one floor below the one she'd had back in the 1940s. We decorated it with red roses, a bottle of champagne, fresh fruit and Godiva chocolates.

The crew met us shortly after dawn, and we were setting up in front of the famous Thalberg building when Hepburn arrived— early again, of course.

"What are you going to do when it rains?" she asked.

Unlike the day before, there was no blue sky to be seen, and the weather forecast promised showers.

"It wouldn't dare rain on you, Ms. Hepburn," I said. I hoped I was right, since all the shots we had planned were exteriors.

"I wouldn't bet on it," she said. "So let's get going."

As it turned out, there was only one brief shower in Culver City that day, and it happened while we were all inside having lunch.

DH She went off to her dressing room, and ten minutes later, was back and ready to shoot. But then John Vincent told me, "David, I can't use the boom mic here. You're taking such a wide shot there's nowhere I can hide it. I don't see any way around using the wireless mic again."

"OK, John. I'll tell her," thinking to myself that I wanted to get over this hurdle as quickly as possible.

"Ms. Hepburn, we have a problem with this first shot."

"Yes, what is it?"

"Well, it's so wide that we can't use the boom. The only way I can get it is with a radio mic."

She looked at me, but didn't reply. Instead she walked over to John Vincent, who was standing just a few paces away.

"Young man, you didn't have the courage to tell me yourself, did you?" she said with a laugh. "If it's better with that other microphone, you have to be mean to me."

We got the shot in two takes, just before the office workday started. Moments later, it would have been impossible to stop the traffic of executives and others entering the building.

JK People at the major Hollywood studios are used to seeing actors—big stars, television series cast members, character actors, and extras galore; it comes with the job. But when word spread that Katharine Hepburn was shooting on the lot, many of them found a reason to come by our set; we even noticed that some were hanging out of windows to try to catch a glimpse of her. To ensure there were as few interruptions as possible, the studio assigned two security guards to be with us at all times.

Around 10 am, not long after we had the first shot in the can, crews from *Entertainment Tonight* and CNN showed up. Suddenly there was a battery of lights, cameras, and microphones aimed at Hepburn, reminding me of old Hollywood. She had agreed to give them a brief statement about Spencer Tracy, but then the reporters started asking questions, and she was answering them. I was getting concerned that the questions could become too personal, and she might get upset.

So was the MGM publicist, who told them, "OK. That's it. We have to go now."

"Go where?" asked an annoyed Kate. I didn't realize that she would have preferred to keep talking to them. But by now the publicist had already begun to usher them all away.

Katharine Hepburn being interviewed by news crews.
Culver City, CA, 1985. Photograph by John Bryson, courtesy Bryson Photo.

Soon after the press had left, I received a message from our office in NY; a vice president of programming at HBO had called and left her number. I found a phone and returned the call.

"Oh, Joan. Thank you for getting back to me. I know you pitched a show about Spencer Tracy to my head of programming here, and that we passed on the idea. I'd like to revisit it now. I assume Katharine Hepburn is still planning to host it."

I know I took perhaps an unreasonable amount of pleasure in telling her that it was now too late. "The ship has sailed," I said. "We're doing the program for PBS and Hepburn is indeed hosting it."

DH While the crew and I were moving to the next location, I saw Kate with Joan and about six others disappear through the big glass doors of the Thalberg building. It was only later that I found out where they were going.

JK "I want to see L.B. Mayer's office. C'mon," said Hepburn.

Like a mother duck leading her ducklings, we followed her inside and into the elevator. When it stopped on the executive floor, she marched into what used to be Louis B. Mayer's office, now occupied by Frank Rothman, the Chairman and CEO of MGM. What happened next sounds like a scene from an old movie. As she continued to lead the charge, we passed Rothman's secretary, whose mouth dropped open at the sight of this sudden invasion. Valiantly she tried to play gatekeeper, jumping to her feet, one arm outstretched, following the flow of the parade, as her voice faded while saying, "Oh, Miss Hepburn. I'm sorry but you can't go in there."

It was too late. Kate had already burst through the door of Frank Rothman's office, arm extended to shake his hand. "Hi, I'm Kate Hepburn. Where's the table—the mahogany table that L.B. had in his office?"

Understandably, he was startled, but quickly recovered his composure as he stood up behind his desk, shook her hand, and said, "Welcome back to MGM, Miss Hepburn. The table is right over there in the conference room." He led us all in and asked us to sit down.

She began to reminisce: "I remember four of us sitting around this table. Greta"—(I realized she had to be talking about Greta Garbo)—"sat there; I sat here; George Cukor sat next to me; and L.B. sat at that end. We were trying to sell him on the idea of letting Greta and me star in *Mourning Becomes Electra*[2], which George

---

2   Eugene O'Neill's play had a short but successful run on Broadway in 1931-32. It was eventually made into a movie, starring Rosalind Russell, by RKO in 1947.

would direct. Well, we didn't get very far. We could tell right away that we were not heating up the room. So George nodded to me and Greta, and we got up and left. That was the end of that idea." Katharine Hepburn and Greta Garbo in a movie together? Not the only time a studio head would miss a golden opportunity.

Then, turning to me, she said, "Do you think David is ready? We'd better get back down there." She shook hands with Rothman and his still-shell-shocked secretary, and back we all went into the elevator.

DH She came down, but had to go right back up again, because our next shot was on the roof of the Thalberg building, where the only access was through an office on the top floor. When we did our technical survey, the office was empty. However, on this day, we discovered that it was occupied. And the occupant was another high-level executive, David Gerber, the head of MGM Television, who hadn't been warned that we were about to invade his space. We and our crew, all the equipment, Hepburn, her assistant, Phyllis (who'd been temporarily allowed to abandon her post as guard of Hal Wallis's art collection), her makeup and hair artists, and our MGM executive producer, George Paris, had to walk through David Gerber's office, past his desk and out of his window as he was trying to conduct business as usual.

JK Each time, Gerber was on the telephone, and each time he saw Hepburn, he said to the person he was talking to, "Please hold on a moment," and then politely stood up to greet her as she walked by. It was almost a comedy routine, but he didn't seem at all surprised or annoyed by the scene playing out in front of him. Then, about forty-five minutes later, after we finished shooting, the same thing happened all over again, as our small caravan walked past him on the way out.

Months later, I asked George Paris if he ever talked to Gerber about that day and what he'd said to the people he'd put on hold.

George said, "Oh yes. I saw him at the studio's Christmas party and when I asked him that very question, he said, 'I told them all the truth…Katharine Hepburn was climbing through my window.'

"So I said, 'What was their reaction?'

"And he said, 'No one believed me. They all thought I was pulling their legs.'"

DH The shot I'd planned from the Thalberg building's roof gave us a view of 20ᵗʰ Century Fox, where Spencer Tracy had been a contract player before he was hired by MGM. However, there was no fence or guardrail at the roof's edge, just a low wall. And, not having a very good head for heights myself, I wasn't going to ask Hepburn to get any closer to it than was comfortable for me, so I suggested she stand about three feet in. But as we were setting up, she said, "Wouldn't it be better if I sat on the ledge?"

"Possibly," I said. "But I don't want to risk losing the star."

"Oh, nonsense," she replied dismissively, perching herself on the narrow parapet. "I can see tomorrow's headlines: '*Star Falls Off Roof of Thalberg Building—Or Was Pushed!*'" she laughed.

Katharine Hepburn on the roof of the Thalberg building.
Culver City, CA, 1985. Photograph by John Bryson, courtesy Bryson Photo.

JK Phyllis didn't see any humor in the situation or in Kate's cavalier attitude. She reacted with alarm: "Miss Hepburn, that's dangerous. Be careful!"

In fact, it was Katharine Hepburn who was concerned for the safety of Phyllis.

"She's got tunnel vision," she told us. "We have to make sure she doesn't fall over the cables."

DH There were two more set-ups before we broke for lunch. The first was a tracking shot along the side of the Thalberg building, leading into the second set-up, at a side entrance where Kate first met Spencer Tracy in 1941. She had requested him as her co-star in the movie, *Woman of the Year*, but had never actually met him until that day. She spotted him leaving the commissary with producer Joseph L. Mankiewicz, and made sure she ran into them. It's a famous story that has been mis-told many times. This was her chance to set the record straight.

Mankiewicz introduced them to each other, and the exchange that followed was about her height. She was about five-feet-seven inches, but appeared even taller because she was very slim and was wearing shoes with heels. Tracy was actually about five-ten and a bit stocky.

"Sorry, I've got these high heels on," she said. "But when we do the movie I'll be careful about what I wear."

Tracy said nothing, just looking at her.

It was Mankiewicz who responded: "Don't worry, Kate. He'll cut you down to his size."

"I didn't know what to say," Hepburn told us. "I just stood there like a goof."

She then walked out of the frame. But she had forgotten to tell the final part of the story. Instead of stopping the camera and asking for another take, I motioned for her to go back, silently mouthing to her the words "dirty nails."

"Oh, I forgot to tell you," she improvised, popping back into the frame. "When they had departed, I rushed to Mankiewicz's office." She was eager to hear what Tracy had thought of her. Mankiewicz told her that Spencer's only comment was, "Kate Hepburn has dirty finger nails." She then held up her hands in front of the camera and said, "I still have." It was typical of her to make fun of herself. But what I liked most was the way she turned a mistake into a moment that felt so natural and genuine. We did, of course, use that take in the show.

JK The Directors Guild had contacted David to ask if he could persuade Hepburn to tape a brief statement for a tribute to the late Dorothy Arzner, one of the few women directors in the Hollywood of the 1930s, who'd directed Hepburn's second film, *Christopher Strong*. Both of them raised eyebrows back then by wearing slacks instead of dresses.

Kate told us, "I don't want to disappoint the Directors Guild, so I'll say something I hope they can use." She ad-libbed the piece, praising Arzner, and did it in one take, ending with, "So you see that women weren't always considered to be silly."

DH PBS also had a request: for Hepburn to do a Pledge spot, urging viewers to send donations to their local public television stations. I was reluctant to ask her, but she willingly agreed.

Again ad-libbing most of it, during a rehearsal, she said, "It's been my privilege and honor to do this program."

"Miss Hepburn," I said to her. "That was very nice, but I don't think it's appropriate for you to say, 'It's a privilege and honor.' *We're* the ones who are privileged and honored that you're doing this show."

"No, no," she replied. "I want to say that because I really *am* privileged and honored, and the people watching should help support more programs like this."

We then rolled tape, and she used exactly the same words.

That was the end of the day, and the end of our California shoot.

I said, "Cut. That's a wrap, everyone. Thank you very much."

JK Before the crew started packing up the equipment, we all gathered around her for a photograph, which we call the "graduation shot." I gave her a red sweatshirt that had the MGM lion logo printed on the front, and she shook hands with each crew member, as we began a spontaneous round of applause.

She did a curtsy and said, "You've all been very sweet to me. Thank you."

"Graduation photo" after shoot with Katharine Hepburn on the MGM lot. Culver City, CA, 1985. Photograph by John Bryson, courtesy Bryson Photo.

The following morning, Hepburn called George Paris and asked if she could bring her friend, Cynthia McFadden, onto the lot to show her around. (At the time, McFadden was still a budding journalist; now she is the Senior Legal & Investigative Correspondent for NBC News, and also a co-executor of Katharine Hepburn's Estate.) George Paris told us that he accompanied them to each location we'd used, and that Kate relived the previous day saying, "Here's where I said...." and then recited portions of the script. We didn't meet Cindy until some three months later, when she gave us her own recollections of that day, and told us that Kate had clearly enjoyed every minute of the shoot at MGM.

JK and DH Soon after we returned to New York, Hepburn called and said, "Come to lunch." While we were there, we asked her if she'd be willing to do some more publicity for the program.

"I'm not dumb," she said. "Of course, I'll do press. I want people to watch."

What we didn't know then was how cleverly she was already hatching her own plans for the publicity campaign.

She said, "Even though Spencer's been gone for almost nineteen years, I've recently written a letter to him and wonder if you think it might be interesting enough to use at the end of the show. Here it is. I'll read it to you."

We sat there silently. It was so personal, so moving that by the end, we could hardly speak.

"What do you think?" she asked. "Does it work for you?"

"It's wonderful. And yes, we'd very much like you to read it as the finale to the program."

"Good," she said, matter-of-factly. "And I've already read it to the editor of *TV Guide*, who's a friend of mine. He wants to use it as the cover story the week of the show's premiere."

We were stunned, but had to think clearly. We knew how valuable it would be to have the cover of a national magazine, and certainly a major coup for any public television show. But there was a downside to it: by publishing the letter a few days prior to our airdate, *TV Guide* would steal the thunder from the end of the program.

As we shared our thoughts with her, she said, "Hmm. You're right. It'll take the surprise out of it. So I'll call the editor and tell him I'll write a different piece about Spence."

We realized that it would be like pulling candy away from a child. Anything else would pale in comparison. And we were right. She did write another piece, the title of which appeared as a blurb on the *TV Guide* cover that week, but it was *not* the cover story itself. [3]

DH The material we'd shot in Los Angeles was inserted into the rough-cut, and now we needed one more day of taping with Hepburn doing scripted, timed links to camera. I explained to her that, unlike the shoot in California, where she often ad-libbed and the timings weren't all that critical, the sequences she was about to do now *had* to be exact or they wouldn't fit into the spaces we had allowed for them.

She thought for a moment and then said, "What was that contraption you wanted me to use in California?"

"Do you mean the teleprompter?"

"Don't know what it's called, but why don't we try it again?"

I realized that this was now an opportunity for her to master a leftover challenge from California. And I was ready to give her advice on how to do it. But it turned out to be completely unnecessary. So often, people unused to a prompter are afraid to look away; their eyes are glued to the script, moving left to right—a dead give-away that they are reading. But Kate took to it like a fish to water—looking down from time to time, as though gathering her thoughts—using the prompter as a tool, rather than as a crutch.

JK While the crew was setting up, Phyllis came into the room and sat on a chair not far from the camera.

Kate said, "Go away from there. You're in my eye-line."

I happened to be on the floor below at that moment, so when I came back upstairs and saw that nobody was using that chair, I sat down, waiting for the taping to start. A few seconds later, Hepburn noticed me and said, "You'll have to move; you're in my eye-line." As I was standing up, she said, "Oh, wait a minute; you can stay where you are. I know *you* have to be there."

---

3   The only *TV Guide* cover any of our shows had was six years later, in 1992, for *Fonda on Fonda.* It was also TNT's first-ever *TV Guide* cover story.

After about twenty minutes, the camera needed re-loading. During the break, she said, "David, why don't you just say 'revolve?'"

I stared at her, not having a clue what she was talking about. And I was even more confused when he, without missing a beat, replied, "Oh, I realize that you're used to film. So I'll just say 'Action.'"

Clearly, I was missing something here, or else both of them had suddenly gone insane at the same time. Her question made no sense and neither did his answer. A few minutes later, when the camera was ready again, David indeed said, "Action," and she did the next piece.

During another break, I said to him quietly, "Will you please explain that crazy exchange you had with her earlier?"

"Well," he said, "when she asked me why I don't just say 'revolve,' it hit me that over the past few months, in all our previous tapings with her, she thought I was saying 'rotate,' when in fact I was saying 'roll tape.' And I also realized that she wasn't familiar with the terms often used for television productions, so instead of 'Cue,' I should have said 'Action' when I wanted her to start talking."

I still laugh whenever I think of that story. And I'm still flabbergasted that David, under fire, came up with the right answer in less time than it takes to blink.

DH Her reading of the letter had to be the final shot of the day. Just before I asked the camera to roll, she said to me, "If something goes wrong before the end, stop me."

"Okay," I said, knowing exactly what she meant: she didn't want to use up her well of emotions if there was a technical glitch. Fortunately, there wasn't, and by the time she'd finished, everyone in the room, including the crew, was so overwhelmed by its intensity that nobody moved for several minutes after I said, "Cut."

I then asked her if she could do another take, just for protection. She said, "Okay." It was good, but I felt that her second reading was a bit more like a performance. She thought so too. At the end, she said, "I think the first one was more interesting, but use whichever you want."

JK When the show was completed and delivered to PBS, David went on a trip to England. Publicity cassettes had been sent to newspapers and magazines and full-page ads appeared in various publications. A few days after I sent Hepburn one of the press kits, my phone rang.

"It's Kate. Where did you get that title? I never approved it. *The Spencer Tracy Legacy*? It sounds like he left me money."

I couldn't believe my ears. We'd spent hours going through title choices with her long before and she had, indeed, approved this one.

"We never would have used a title we hadn't discussed with you and that you didn't like," I replied.

"Never. Never heard it before. You have to change it."

"Miss Hepburn, we can't do that. The master tapes have been duplicated and distributed to every public television station in the PBS network."

"Well, get them back. I'll pay whatever it costs."

"I'm sorry, but it's impossible to do that."

"So I'm done in. Is that what you're telling me? You've driven a nail into my coffin."

"Miss Hepburn, you have no idea how upset I am that you feel that way. I have tears rolling down my face."

"Stop trying to convince me you're noble," she retorted. "Tears are easy."

"Maybe for you, but not for me," I said in a choked voice.

"Well, this whole thing is shocking," she said. "And why am I listed as the 'host' who 'remembers' Spencer Tracy? It should be 'narrator.' And it all sounds sentimental."

It was going from bad to worse by the minute. But I knew I had to stand my ground.

"You *are* the 'host' because you're seen on camera. If we only heard your voice, you'd be credited as 'narrator.' And you're 'remembering' Tracy by talking about him to the viewers."

"Idiotic. 'Host' sounds wrong. Find another word and change it on the show," she said in her most commanding tone of voice. "And if you don't think the word 'remembers' sounds overly sentimental, you're naïve."

"I'm really sorry but there isn't another word for 'host' and we can't change anything even if there was," I said, now shaking.

"Well, if you can't find another word, then I will," she said, and hung up abruptly.

I was a basket case of nerves by then, and David was on his way to England.

Two minutes later, Hepburn called back.

"I just checked the thesaurus and you're right. There isn't another goddamn word for 'host,' except 'master of ceremonies,' and that certainly won't work. So I guess I'm stuck with 'host,'" she said—and hung up again. But this time, she said, "Goodbye."

I then composed a letter to her and sent it immediately by messenger. In it, I told her how badly I felt—that after all this time, she obviously didn't trust David and me, that we were honored that she'd asked us to produce the program, and were convinced that it would bring a new audience to Tracy's movies.

An hour later, she called me again. Furious.

"Never, never write a letter like that to me. If I didn't trust you, do you think the two of you would have ever made it through the front door of this house?"—and hung up.

Moments later, my phone rang yet again.

"I'm going to send this goddamn thing back to you right now."

"No, please don't do that," I replied. "Just tear it up and throw it away, and this whole episode will become ancient history."

"Deal," she said. "Call me tomorrow."

Then, even though I knew I'd received what amounted to a "Hepburn apology," I called David.

DH It was after midnight; I'd just checked into my hotel in Bristol, when the phone rang. Needless to say, I was upset by the story Joan told me, and knew that I had to speak directly to Kate. When she heard my voice, and I said I was calling from Britain, she said, "You didn't have to call me and spend all that money on long distance." Sweet as pie, she listened patiently as I reiterated that the title of the program was made with her input and final approval, and that she'd done an incredible job as its "host."

"Thank you. I'm glad you're happy with the result. Let's hope everyone else is too," she said. "And by the way, I've decided to throw a small cocktail party at my house next week and, of course, you and Joan are invited. Let me know who else should be asked. And now you should go to sleep. It must be the middle of the night where you are."

JK When David called me to report on his conversation with her, I had to laugh. First, she was impressed by him calling her from England; then she willingly and calmly accepted the same explanation I had given her during her tirade; and now she was inviting us to her party.

The next day, I called her—hesitantly—to suggest who else should be included on the guest list. She said, "Sounds fine. You and David can ask them for me." She was back to her old self, without any lingering hint of the anger I had experienced less than twenty-four hours earlier.

Katharine Hepburn preparing to read her letter to Spencer.
New York, 1986. Photograph by Len Tavares.

The Board of Trustees
of
The American Academy of Dramatic Arts

invites you to

A TRIBUTE TO SPENCER TRACY

with appearances by

MISS KATHARINE HEPBURN

*and other distinguished co-stars
and friends of Mr. Tracy*

&

The World Premiere of the feature documentary
"Spencer Tracy, the Actor: Hosted by Katharine Hepburn"

*Monday, March 3, 1986
The Majestic Theatre
245 West 44th Street
Curtain 8:15 P.M.*

*Informal Dress
Reply Card Enclosed*

*Pre-Theatre Champagne Buffet/
Cocktail Reception — 6 P.M.*

AADA invitation (note the incorrect title for the documentary).
New York, 1986. Authors' collection.

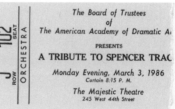

Our tickets.
New York, 1986. Authors' collection.

CHAPTER NINE

A Broadway Premiere

It was March 3rd, 1986. The tickets for *A Tribute to Spencer Tracy* were sold out. A one-night-only performance, it had all the glamour of a Broadway premiere, complete with police barricades which had been in place outside the Majestic Theatre on 46th Street since early morning. Fans were waiting behind the velvet ropes hoping to catch a glimpse of Katharine Hepburn, Robert Wagner, Sidney Poitier, and Frank Sinatra. But very few people knew about the chain of events which had led up to this evening, or the ones still unfolding behind the scenes even as the curtain went up. There was drama all around, and it wasn't just on the stage that night.

DH It all began some four years earlier when Katharine Hepburn received a phone call from the president of the American Academy of Dramatic Arts asking her to appear at a benefit honoring Spencer Tracy. Tracy had graduated from the Academy in 1923, and had always credited his training there as the foundation for his success as an actor. Hepburn had previously been told that the AADA was planning to build a theater in his name, but that wasn't even mentioned as the president described the event they had in mind now.

He said, "We've decided to set up an annual Spencer Tracy Scholarship, and we'll launch it at a dinner in the ballroom of a hotel here in New York. Of course, we'd like you to sit on the dais and be the keynote speaker."

She listened politely and then said, "It all sounds fascinating, but I don't sit on daises. I'm not like a bowl of sugar where you spoon me out and then put the lid back on. Two friends of mine are producing a documentary about Spencer, which I'm going to narrate. Everything I have to say about him will be in it. So wait until we finish and then you can show it at your event."

It was a clever ploy. If the Academy used the program, she wouldn't have to appear at a benefit. That was her plan. It didn't quite work out that way.

At the time of that phone call, we were, indeed, hoping to produce a profile of Tracy, which Hepburn would host. But she had no idea when—or if—we'd ever find the financing for it, a fact which she forgot to mention to the president of the AADA. So little did he know just how long the wait would be. It actually took over three years to raise the funds before we could even start production, and we wonder to this day what ruses she used each time she was asked, "When will the show be ready?"

There was one other significant hole in her plan. She never mentioned anything about it to us.

JK In the many conversations we had with her during those years, only twice did we ever discuss the Academy wanting to honor Tracy. In August, 1982, she told me: "The American Academy of Dramatic Arts is building a theater to be named after Spencer." Then a month later, when I asked her if the theater was still in the works, she said, "Yes. They're trying to raise the money for it, and I think the publicity for the show we're going to do will be a great help to them."

That was all we knew until four years later. By then, our program was completed and we'd delivered it to PBS for a March 10th,

1986, broadcast premiere. I was across the hall talking with David when I heard my phone ring.

"Hello, Joan. It's Kate."

Even though I always enjoyed talking with her, I still felt a twinge of nervousness whenever she called me.

I said, "Hi. How are you today?"

"Fine," she said. "But I must be getting feeble-minded because I can't remember if I ever told you that the American Academy of Dramatic Arts is going to honor Spencer."

"Yes, you did," I said. "But you haven't mentioned it for a long time. Have they started building the theater yet?"

"The theater? What theater?" Then before I could respond, she continued. "Oh that's right. They *were* talking about a Spencer Tracy Theater, weren't they? But they must have given up on that idea a long time ago because I haven't heard a word about it in years. Now they're doing a benefit at a Broadway theater and I told them they could show your documentary. You'll be getting a call from the president of the Academy any minute."

This was straight out of left field. I felt as if I'd been hit in the stomach by a fast ball. What on earth was she talking about? My mind began to race, but somehow it went blank at the same time. I thought, "Okay, Joan. Take it easy and try not to sound panic-stricken." But it didn't take long to realize that what she thought would be simple would, in fact, be very complicated.

"When is their event?" I asked. "And I need to check with the legal department to find out whether we have the rights for the program to be shown in a theater."

She said, "If you don't have those rights, get them. I've already promised the Academy."

I wanted to say, "What do you *mean* you already promised? When did all this happen?" But I already knew that engaging in a confrontation with Katharine Hepburn would not be a good idea.

However, she must have sensed how taken aback I was because, instead of waiting for me to say something, she continued. "It's just plain idiotic that I haven't told you about this before, but I can hear it in your voice that it's all news to you. So here's the story." And that's when I learned that she didn't sit on daises, give keynote speeches, wasn't a sugar bowl, and had decided our show should be the centerpiece of the AADA's benefit.

And as I listened, it began to dawn on me what a huge compliment this was. Obviously, she'd never doubted for a moment that the program eventually would get made, or that it would turn out to be worthy of representing her at a tribute to Tracy. And while her primary goal in all this was her own self-preservation, it also reflected the trust she'd placed in us years before.

My indignation vanished completely, and I finally said, "It would really be exciting to see the show on a big screen with a live audience."

"I think so too. It'll be thrilling—and very good for your careers," she said. "And it'll help them do Spencer proud."

Indeed, the president of the Academy called a few minutes later, his voice full of enthusiasm. I decided not to beat around the bush. "I have to be honest with you. None of us knew anything about this until Miss Hepburn called five minutes ago. It's a wonderful idea, but we may not have the rights for this sort of a screening. I need to get a reading from our lawyers." There was a dead silence on the other end and then, in an urgent tone, he said, "But she *promised,* and our benefit committee has already lined up the Majestic Theatre on 46th Street and sent a notice to all our members. We've waited almost four years for your show. *Please* work it out."

DH After months of twelve to fourteen-hour days, Joan and I were looking forward to a vacation. This should have been a period of winding down to the sound of gentle ocean breezes. But the call from Katharine Hepburn and then from the president of the Academy threw us right back into a maelstrom of activity.

There was a flurry of phone calls to lawyers at WNET, PBS, and MGM (which was supplying most of the films clips in the program), to the publicists at all three companies, and of course, to our two executive producers, George Page at WNET and George Paris at MGM. The questions were obvious: Would the AADA's use of the program cause a violation of any of the contracts which excluded theatrical exhibition of the show? Would the press coverage for this event steal the thunder from the publicity campaign for the program and therefore diminish its impact as a television special?

JK While executives were conferring, I was hearing almost daily from various people at the AADA, and from Katharine Hepburn. "What's the problem? Why is this such a big deal?" Their frustration was building. No, make that anxiety. I understood it because I felt it too. But all I could say was, "It isn't up to us. Please be patient. The powers-that-be are on the case and we should have an answer very soon."

Now I was the one having to come up with ruses to avoid an uprising.

Hepburn said, "Maybe I should call all these people myself. I can be pretty persuasive and quite adorable."

"Yes, we know how persuasive and adorable you are." I said. "Thank you for the offer, but let's keep it up our sleeve in case we need a last round of ammunition. Right now, everyone realizes how important this is and I think it's better to let it play out on its own."

She laughed and said, "Okay. But make sure I jump in if it looks as though the ship is sinking."

I knew the impact of hearing directly from Katharine Hepburn. And she knew it too. One call from her usually did the trick. But I was reluctant to turn her loose on people who'd never talked to her before, knowing that she can be both charming and intimidating. I also wanted to protect *her* from the risk of failing. She'd likely insist that she'd made a promise and was honor-bound to keep it, an argument which might just fall like a lead balloon on some executive trying to prove how unimpressed he was by saying, "With all due respect, Miss Hepburn, you never should have done that without clearing it first with us." My goal was to avoid any more tension than there already was.

DH Finally, there was a decision. The program could be used as part of the benefit only if it took place before the television premiere. It would then fall under the category of "advance publicity" for which we, indeed, did have the rights. And the press coverage it received in connection with the event would obviously enhance the publicity for the broadcast.

Everyone breathed a sigh of relief, and the date was set for Monday, March 3rd, 1986, exactly one week prior to the airdate of the program.

The Academy hired an experienced events producer, Inez Weinstein, who had chosen a very difficult career. Benefits involve influential people—often celebrities—volunteering their time and participation. The organization which is presenting the benefit has its own cast of characters, perhaps not well-known personalities, but with egos just the same. The producer has to treat all of them with the utmost finesse, inspiring confidence and respect, while getting the job done on time and on budget. It's a tough balance. And even though Inez was a seasoned professional, strong-willed and thick-skinned, this event turned into a wild ride not unlike a roller coaster on the brink of falling off its rails.

Right from the start, she told Katharine Hepburn that the gala needed top-flight, big name personalities to appear on stage telling stories of their professional and personal relationships with Tracy. It also needed his daughter, Susie, to accept the Spencer Tracy Award as the Academy launched the scholarship in his name. And it needed Hepburn *live* on stage to introduce the documentary.

Needless to say, Kate protested, but Inez stood firm. Apparently there were heated discussions. But Katharine Hepburn was, above all, a pragmatist. And she knew, despite her plan to avoid it, that she *had* to be there in person. So she reluctantly agreed and then became the talent coordinator. She called Robert Wagner to host the evening, and asked Frank Sinatra, Sidney Poitier, and Stanley Kramer to take part. All of them immediately accepted her invitation. They hadn't received a fee for appearing in the documentary and wouldn't be paid to participate in this event either. Susie Tracy agreed to travel to New York even though she was very nervous about speaking in front of a live audience. While she and Hepburn had become good friends in the years since Tracy's death in 1967, this would mark the first time they'd be seen in public together.

The writing team was just as distinguished: Betty Comden and Adolph Green, who interviewed each of the participants so that the script would be based on their own words. Susie Tracy was the only one who declined to have her comments scripted. She explained that, not being an actress, it would be easier for her to speak extemporaneously.

In the meantime, I was investigating what kind of equipment could project a television program on a big screen. No one at the AADA had any technical experience, and their original idea was to place television monitors in the aisles of the theater, which I felt would give the Majestic the aura of a school auditorium. Fortunately, I was able to convince them that seeing the show on a large movie screen would add to the impact of the entire evening. They were on a tight budget, but they found the funds for the projector.

JK Inez had every reason to believe that she'd covered all her bases. There was to be a 6 pm champagne buffet at the Marriott Marquis Hotel just a few blocks away from the theater. The script had been completed and sent to all those involved, and the tickets had been distributed.

But the closer it got to March 3rd, the more nervous Katharine Hepburn became. The woman who had insisted she wasn't "a bowl of sugar" was about to be spooned out onto the stage of the Majestic Theatre on Broadway. She had appeared live many times throughout her career, but always as a character in a play. This would be much different. Here she would have to play herself, standing at a microphone and facing the audience.

Her housekeeper, Norah, told us the tension in the house was building by the day. And it was during that period that Inez received a phone call from Hepburn.

"I have a great idea," she said. "Let Susie Tracy introduce the documentary."

"No. It has to be you," said Inez.

Kate said, "Just think about it," and hung up.

The next day, she called Inez again.

"Did you give my suggestion any thought?"

"No," said Inez, firmly.

"You're a very determined woman, aren't you?"

"I'll take that as a compliment, Miss Hepburn," said Inez.

We thanked our lucky stars that we weren't producing this benefit. Inez wasn't having it easy, and she didn't know it was about to get worse.

The following Monday, another call from Katharine Hepburn.

"Where are you putting my friend, Irene Selznick?" she asked.

"I've given her sixth row center seats, Miss Hepburn."

"No, no. She has to sit in the back row. She gets sick."

"What do you mean, 'she gets sick?' Do I need to have oxygen standing by for her? Does she throw up? What do you mean?"

"No, no, nothing like that. But she gets sick. Move her to the back row."

"Miss Hepburn, she already has her tickets. I don't know if I can get them back and move her."

Inez knew that making any switch meant re-juggling her jigsaw-puzzle of an audience seating plan, which had been carefully put together to accommodate the guests of the participants, the Board of the Academy, MGM and PBS brass, as well as those who paid full benefit prices for their tickets.

Kate insisted: "Just call Irene and tell her you're moving her."

Inez called Irene Selznick, who said, "No. I want to keep my sixth row seats. I don't want to sit in the back row."

(A brief note here about Mrs. Selznick: As the daughter of Louis

B. Mayer and ex-wife of producer, David O. Selznick, she was used to the perks that come to the privileged. She was also an outspoken personality with her own set of eccentricities. And she and Hepburn had been friends for many years.)

Inez Weinstein found herself in a no-win situation with Irene Selznick. And before it was resolved, she received another call from Hepburn.

"Where are you putting my housekeeper, Norah? And my niece, Kathy Houghton?" she asked, and without stopping for the answers, went on to list several others on her personal guest list.

"They're all in the center section in the sixth, seventh and eighth rows."

"No, no," said Hepburn. "They all have to sit in the back. They get sick too."

Now Inez herself felt sick. Her seating plan was about to be thrown into complete disarray. Not only did all these people already have their tickets, but so did those who were about to be displaced from their seats in the back few rows of the theater. It added up to about twenty pairs of tickets—forty people—from all over the country.

She said, "Miss Hepburn, all the tickets were sent out weeks ago and I haven't received any complaints."

"Call them all. You have to move them."

At that point, Inez Weinstein called me. When I heard what was going on I said, "Don't you find it peculiar that suddenly everyone in Hepburn's private circle gets sick? Unless they're all afflicted with some epidemic we haven't heard about."

"I know. But what can I do?" she said. "This is a mess. Am I going to need an ambulance standing by outside the Majestic?"

"Something's very odd here," I said. "Why don't I call her and try to find out what this is all about?"

Kate answered the phone in her typical way. "Yes? What?"

"Well, Miss Hepburn, Inez Weinstein is about to have a heart attack."

"Why? What's the matter with her?"

"Apparently you've told her all your guests get sick and have to sit in the back rows. It's not easy to redo her entire seating plan, let alone retrieve and then redistribute all the tickets from everyone involved. Also, she now thinks she's going to need medical equipment and personnel on hand."

She was silent for a few seconds, and then said, "I lied. None of them gets sick. I just realized that I'll be able to see them if they're that close to the stage. They'll be in my eye-line, and I don't want to see anyone I know. Better to see strangers than friends and family."

I said, "Do you want me to call Inez?"

"No, no. I'm the one who lied. I have to own up."

True to her word, she confessed to Inez. But she still insisted that everyone she knew had to be moved to the back of the theater, and she agreed to call all of them herself. This still left Inez with the task of getting back the tickets and rearranging who was to sit where. By the time she'd finished that chore she thought the worst was over. Now the evening itself would be smooth-sailing.

DH It should have been. By Sunday, March 2nd, Susie Tracy, Robert Wagner, Sidney Poitier, Stanley Kramer, and Frank Sinatra had arrived in New York with the scripts sent to them by Comden and Green. They were all in good spirits and seemingly well-prepared.

On Monday, the day of the event, I visited the theater during the afternoon to make sure that the projector was in place and working properly. Then I went home to change clothes.

Joan and I and our guests met at the Marriott Marquis Hotel for the champagne buffet and then made our way to the Majestic.

For us, this was an evening in which to revel. We'd never before seen one of our documentaries on a movie screen. And certainly never had one premiere on Broadway. We were invited members of the audience, so we could just relax and enjoy the show. Sitting a few rows behind us were Joan's former employer, Dick Cavett and his wife, Carrie Nye, and nearby were Leonard Bernstein, Christopher

Sidney Poitier, Robert Wagner, and Stanley Kramer backstage at the Majestic Theatre. New York, 1986. Authors' collection.

Betty Comden and Leonard Bernstein at the Majestic Theatre for *A Tribute to Spencer Tracy*.
New York, 1986. Authors' collection.

Reeve, and Phyllis Newman, who was married to Adolph Green, Claire Trevor, and many other "bold face names."

We had no idea what was going on backstage.

JK All the participants were due at the theater no later than 7:45 pm, the customary half-hour before curtain. Katharine Hepburn and Susie Tracy had arrived much earlier. Kate paced back and forth from one side of the stage to the other. Susie stood quietly by herself, trying to stay calm. Robert Wagner, Sidney Poitier, and Stanley Kramer, wearing tuxedos despite the "business attire" dress code for the audience, all arrived on time. No Frank Sinatra.

7:55 pm: Still no sign of Sinatra.

8:00 pm: No Sinatra and no way to find out where he was. Remember, this was before cell phones. Since it was getting ominously close to the curtain going up, Inez Weinstein, Betty Comden and Adolph Green were huddling together, trying to delete Sinatra's portion of the script and re-write the rest accordingly.

8:05 pm: The stage door opened and in walked three bodyguards with a drunken Frank Sinatra. He was dressed in his tux, but it was instantly clear to Inez that he was in no shape to go on stage.

She went into immediate action. Grabbing him by the arm, she said, "You're coming with me. If Katharine Hepburn sees you in this state, you and I are both going to be in serious trouble. Fortunately, she's on the opposite side of the stage right now."

The three bodyguards began closing in, but Inez brushed them off. She said in a no-nonsense tone of voice, "I'm not going to hurt him. I'm just going to sober him up as fast as I can. Come on, Frank. Remember me? We met last month at that benefit in LA. Let's go." Then she asked an assistant to bring her a pot of coffee immediately. She took Sinatra into a nearby bathroom and locked the door behind them, loosened his bow tie, took out the studs from his shirt, and removed his cummerbund. Then she force-fed him glass after glass of water, then coffee, and then more water. Eventually it started taking effect.

He looked at her as if to say, "Well, you don't expect me to use the toilet in front of you, do you?" But she didn't budge.

"Go ahead," she said. "I'm married. I've seen a man use the bathroom before. I'm not leaving. And keep drinking."

She soon heard applause. Obviously, the curtain had gone up. First the chairman and then the president of the Academy welcomed everyone, and then turned the proceedings over to the host, Robert Wagner. By now, Katharine Hepburn had made her way to the wings near the bathroom.

"Where's Inez?" she said to Susie Tracy. Inez had become a sort of security blanket for both of them at this point. Neither knew that she was three feet away in the bathroom with Frank Sinatra.

DH Robert Wagner made some heartfelt remarks about Spencer Tracy and then introduced producer/director, Stanley Kramer.

Stanley spoke eloquently and movingly. For Inez, who was making slow but steady progress with Sinatra, the longer the speeches the better. But through the door, she could hear Hepburn's voice, "Where is Inez?"

Stanley Kramer introduced Sidney Poitier. Self-effacing and funny, he too told stories that took time to unfold.

When Inez heard Poitier nearing the end of his scripted remarks, she knew Robert Wagner would soon be introducing Frank Sinatra. So she splashed cold water on his face, helped him put the studs back in his shirt, fix his tie and cummerbund, and led him out to the wings.

Hepburn saw him and said, "Hello Frank," and he greeted her warmly. She then turned to Inez. "Where were you? I've been looking for you."

"I've been taking care of some important last-minute details. Everything is fine."

On stage, Robert Wagner was saying, "Now, it's my pleasure to introduce Frank Sinatra."

Sinatra entered from stage left, walking with assurance, and was greeted with thunderous applause. He leaned on the lectern throughout his comments, which we realized were almost entirely ad-libbed. He was completely ignoring the script written by Comden and Green, but his stories were very funny and personal, and he delivered them in the easygoing manner for which he was famous. None of us in the audience had any idea that he'd been slurring his

Frank Sinatra on stage at the Majestic Theatre.
New York, 1986. Authors' collection.

words just forty minutes earlier. And we didn't question his leaning on the lectern. It just added to his casual demeanor.

Katharine Hepburn by now was standing center stage behind a black curtain. She was the only one who would not enter from the wings.

Frank Sinatra's scripted introduction of her was meant to be something like, "And now, ladies and gentleman, it gives me great pleasure to introduce the woman with the greatest cheekbones since Mount Rushmore: Miss Katharine Hepburn." Instead, he ad-libbed, "And now, the delicious Katharine Hepburn."

When Kate didn't hear her scripted cue, she turned to Inez Weinstein and said, "What happened to Mount Rushmore?"

Inez saw the curtain start to rise and said, "Never mind. The curtain is up. Just go!"

JK The theater erupted into a standing ovation of applause and shouts of "Bravo" as Katharine Hepburn walked forward and had her hand kissed gallantly by Frank Sinatra, who then walked off the stage. She approached the lectern, bowing slightly to acknowledge the cheers. She wore a long, black silk taffeta jacket by Rodier, from the 1940s, a black turtleneck, white silk scarf, and black pants, which were long enough to almost completely camouflage her black

Katharine Hepburn and Frank Sinatra during *A Tribute to Spencer Tracy*. New York, 1986. Authors' collection.

sneakers. (The previous year, she'd run her car into a telephone pole, causing her to almost lose her foot; the only shoes she could wear from then on were sneakers.) Her hair was mostly gray now, but still revealed a hint of the redhead she'd been in her youth. It was pulled up, in her usual way, with strands deliberately loosened and casual. No jewelry. She looked sensational and, out on that stage, in the center spotlight drinking in the audience's palpable rush of emotion towards her, she seemed at home.

She spoke for about twenty minutes. Everyone would have been happy if she'd gone on much longer, but with her impeccable sense of timing, she felt the moment had come for her to introduce Susie Tracy.

Susie was in the wings waiting for *her* scripted introduction. Hepburn was to say, "And now, I'm going to introduce you to Spencer Tracy's only daughter. I'll use a line that he used about me in *Pat and Mike*: *'Not much meat on her, but what's there is cherce."* Instead, she put her hand above her eyes as one does when looking into the distance, turned to her left towards the wings, and said to the audience, "Oh, excuse me; I think I see Spencer's daughter over there." And started walking across the stage. Susie said to Inez, "But that's not my cue!" By then, Kate had reached the wings, extended her arm for Susie's and led her onto the stage. Seeing the tape of that evening these many years later, one can still see the look of confusion on Susie's face as she walks with Hepburn to the lectern.

Backstage, Betty Comden, and Adolph Green were more than a little surprised. First, Frank Sinatra hadn't stuck to their script. And now Katharine Hepburn. Inez was just happy everyone had made it onto the stage.

Robert Wagner presented Susie with an enormous crystal sculpture to honor her father posthumously. She had it in her hands for a moment before Hepburn said, "It's too heavy. I'll hold it," and took it into her own hands. Now the look on Susie's face was one of consternation. If Kate dropped that crystal, it would have shattered into a thousand shards.

Susie spoke beautifully, from the heart. Her instincts about not wanting to be scripted were correct. Her remarks were well-thought-out, and felt very natural. Then she took the crystal from Hepburn and walked off stage with Robert Wagner.

Kate returned to the lectern and introduced the documentary by saying, "Thanks to the miracle of film and tape, Spencer's work will live on." She thanked us, MGM, WNET, PBS, Inez Weinstein, and the Academy for working so hard to make this evening possible.

The curtain rose again, and our program was projected on the big screen. When it ended, the audience cheered. It was "thrilling," as Hepburn had predicted.

All the participants came back onstage again with Katharine Hepburn in the center next to Susie Tracy. They were smiling as they took their bows.

Backstage, the biggest smile was on the face of Inez Weinstein.

DH Later that evening, Hepburn gave a small party at her townhouse on East 49th Street. There were drinks and hors d'oevres served by her housekeeper, Norah. Katharine Hepburn was radiant—and relieved. Robert Wagner and Jill St. John were there, as were Sidney Poitier, Stanley Kramer, Susie Tracy and her friend, Susan Moon. Frank Sinatra did not come. We and our guests, our associate producer, Cynthia Mitchell and her fiancé, executives from MGM, WNET, and the Academy of Dramatic Arts all were there to celebrate. And, of course, Inez Weinstein, who looked happy but tired. After we expressed our thanks and congratulated her on the success of the evening, she said quietly, "Let's go into the next room. I have something to tell you." And that's when we heard what had gone on behind the scenes at the Majestic Theatre.

Several of Hepburn's relatives and friends were also at the party and, when it was time to leave, we went up her to say, "Good night." She was talking with television veteran, Fred Friendly, and introduced us to him: "These are the two that did the film. Great, wasn't it?"

We shook hands with him and then said to her, "Thank you for a wonderful evening, and congratulations, Miss Hepburn."

She smiled and laughingly said to Fred Friendly, "You see, they still call me 'Miss Hepburn' because they're such good friends of mine." We knew it was her way of telling us the time had come for us to call her "Kate."

I gave her a kiss on the cheek and said, "Good night, Kate."

JK Dick Cavett called me the next morning. "What a splendid evening," he said. "And I'm so proud of you; I consider you my protégée."

I called Hepburn to tell her how sensational she was and how beautiful she looked. "It was a triumph."

"Yes," she said. "The audience was sweet. And Bobby Wagner, Stanley Kramer, and Susie were very good. But the stories that Frank Sinatra and Sidney Poitier told made it clear that Spencer and I had lived together."

"Nobody cared," I replied. "Everyone just was happy to be there and see you."

"Well, I do think we did Spencer proud," she said. "And the Academy was goddamn lucky to have your show. When I first met those people, they didn't have a clue how to put on an event."

"We were lucky too," I said. "It was amazing to see the program on a big screen. And by the way, the Academy taped the entire evening, but when I called them earlier to ask for a cassette of it, I was told they wouldn't give it to us—that it was just for their archives."

"Idiotic," said Kate. "Don't worry. I'm going to call them right now and tell them to send copies immediately. I need about five. How many do you want?"

"Two—one for David and one for me."

"Fine," she said.

Our cassettes arrived by messenger that same afternoon.

DH The following Monday was the PBS broadcast premiere of *The Spencer Tracy Legacy: A Tribute by Katharine Hepburn.* By the time Joan arrived at the office, there was a note waiting for her: *"Robert Wagner called at 9:45 am. Please call him back."* It meant that he'd tried to reach us at 6:45 am his time in California.

JK He answered the phone after two rings. I said, "Good morning. David and I received your message. Sorry we weren't here when you called."

"I just wanted to wish you good luck for tonight. I'm going to host the evening here at KCET (the LA public television station)."

I said, "You know, you're really something. First, you agree to participate in the program for no money. Then you come to New York to appear at the Majestic. Now you're going to introduce the show tonight on television. And I'll bet you'll be doing all the pledge breaks too."

"Yes, I am," he said. "Because I really loved Spence. I don't think you understand how important he was in my life. He treated me like a son, and I considered him my second father."

I then thanked him again and said I was sure he'd be responsible for raising a lot of money for public television.

"No," he said. "Not me. Your show will do that."

DH Joan had just hung up with Robert Wagner when Hepburn called, thanking us for the roses we'd sent to celebrate the premiere. A few days later, we also received a formal, hand-written note of appreciation from her. In it, she said, "*I should be the one sending you flowers. You did a wonderful job. Congratulations and love. Kate.*"

JK and DH She later told us that, after the show aired, she received over fifteen hundred letters, and more were arriving every day. "I reply to most of them," she said. "Especially if an eighty-year-old woman tells me I've somehow made a difference in her life. I guess I've become a saint. But I've learned to recognize the ones that just want my signature so they can turn around and sell it. I toss those letters in the garbage."

JK Then, in early June of that year, she invited us for tea in her garden. She was wearing a big surgical boot—not on the foot she'd almost lost, but on the *other* one.

"What happened to you?" I asked.

"I just wanted a matching pair," she said with a laugh.

"But you don't seem to be limping."

"I don't believe in limping. I just can't walk. Falling apart."

Norah served tea, ice cream and her scrumptious lace cookies. Hepburn picked up one of them and crumbled it over each of our bowls filled with ice cream. "That's the best way to eat them," she said.

Then she said, "I would have asked you to come earlier for lunch, but I just got out of the hospital an hour ago. The doctor didn't want to release me, but I insisted because it's June 10th, and I can't be in a hospital on the anniversary of Spencer's death."

Somehow, until that moment, we hadn't realized the significance of the date, and were deeply touched that she wanted to share that afternoon with us.

JK and DH In the years that followed, we would begin notes with, "*Dear Kate*," and send gifts with enclosed cards that said, "*For Kate*." But face to face, we still addressed her as "Miss Hepburn." It just felt right to continue giving her that extra token of respect.

David Heeley, Katharine Hepburn, and Joan Kramer.
New York, 1986. Photograph by Len Tavares.

ACADEMY OF TELEVISION ARTS & SCIENCES

cordially invites you

to attend

THE EMMY AWARDS PRESENTATIONS

1986

CREATIVE ARTS EMMY AWARDS

Saturday, September 6, 1986

Nominee Reception from 4:30 p.m. to 5:30 p.m.

Awards Presentation at 6:00 p.m.

Buffet Dinner and Dancing immediately following

the presentation at the Pasadena Center

THE 38TH ANNUAL EMMY AWARDS TELECAST

Sunday, September 21, 1986

5:00 p.m.

Nominee Reception from 3:00 p.m. to 4:00 p.m.

Doors close at 4:15 p.m.

Pasadena Civic Auditorium

Pasadena, California

GOVERNORS BALL

immediately following the Telecast

at the Pasadena Center

R. S. V. P.

BOTH EVENTS ARE BLACK TIE

Invitation to Emmy Awards.
1986. Authors' collection.

CHAPTER TEN

A Pink Hotel, A Yellow Box, and The Emmy Awards

DH The Academy of Television Arts and Sciences announcement brought some very good news. *The Spencer Tracy Legacy: A Tribute by Katharine Hepburn* had received three Emmy nominations: one for me as director; one for John L. Miller as writer; and one for the show itself, which meant that Joan and I, as well as Hepburn, were nominees, along with our two executive producers, George Page of WNET and George Paris of MGM. The *Nature* series, which I produced and George Page hosted, was also nominated—in a different category, fortunately, so the shows were not competing with each other.

JK I was, of course, thrilled, not just for myself and David, but for Katharine Hepburn and Susie Tracy, who had trusted us and never tried to exert any editorial control. This nod of approval from the Academy felt like icing on the cake, and it was very sweet indeed.

The Awards ceremony at the Pasadena Civic Auditorium was in early September, and George Page suggested we all stay at the famous pink Beverly Hills Hotel. Located just north of Sunset Boulevard, it was—and still is—"old Hollywood." Almost everyone who's anyone has stayed there; some even lived there for a time, including Spencer Tracy himself; so maybe it would bring us good luck. Hepburn, Errol Flynn, and many other movie stars had been regulars on the tennis courts, and the hotel's swimming pool has always been *the* place to be seen and noticed, especially when the loudspeaker pages a celebrity or wannabe, announcing that he or she has a call and should pick up one of the telephones strategically placed around the pool deck. It's rumored that those eager for recognition make certain they get paged by giving a nice tip to the front-desk clerk.

DH When Joan and I went to Los Angeles on business, we usually stayed at a hotel in West Hollywood; the price was reasonable and there were kitchens in all the rooms. When you're working on a project from dawn to dusk, it's a wonderful convenience to be able to make your own breakfast or late night snack instead of calling room service or going downstairs to the restaurant. So for us, staying at the luxurious Beverly Hills Hotel was a complete departure and a real treat.

JK I wish I could remember why, but I volunteered to make all the hotel reservations, even though we had secretaries who could have done it.

There would be six of us traveling from New York to LA and we needed a total of four hotel rooms: one for George Page and his partner, Dennis De Stefano; one for John Miller and his significant other, Carol Schneider; one for David; and one for me. However, we weren't all on the same flight, which meant that we'd be arriving at the hotel at different times. I'd had many phone conversations with the reservations agent and received confirmation numbers for each room. I felt a little like a den mother organizing a camp outing, but I actually enjoyed making sure all the arrangements were in place for what promised to be an exciting weekend.

It certainly lived up to the promise, but not quite in the way I had expected.

DH Joan and I were the last of our group to arrive on the Friday before the Emmy Awards. It was about 3:30 pm and there was a message from George Page waiting for us at the front desk: *"We're at the pool. Join us when you get in. Made a reservation for dinner at 6:30 in the hotel dining room."*

"Great," I thought. "We've time to get some sun, take a shower and maybe a nap and then dress for dinner."

And that's exactly the moment when things began to fall apart.

The receptionist said, "Mr. and Mrs. Heeley, your room is ready."

I said, "I'm afraid there must be a mistake. Miss Kramer and I have separate rooms reserved. Here are the two confirmation numbers."

She began searching her computer. Then she said, "Mr. Heeley, here's your key. A bellhop will help with your luggage."

JK I watched as David headed towards the elevator saying, "I'll see you at the pool."

The receptionist was examining her computer screen again.

"Miss Kramer, I'm sorry for the error, but the hotel is sold out. It's going to take a few minutes to find you a room."

"But I made these reservations two months ago, and I called yesterday just to be sure the confirmation numbers were correct. So what do you mean, you have to find a room for me?"

My anger and frustration were barely under control. I was the one who had done all the advance leg work, and yet I was the one standing at the front desk next to my suitcase, while everyone else was sitting on lounge chairs at the pool.

Finally, after what seemed an eternity, she said, "Here's your key. I hope the room will be satisfactory." I should have realized from that statement that something was a bit fishy, but I was just relieved to be led to the elevator.

The bellhop opened the door to the room and my heart sank. It was about the size of a closet. If I stretched my arms out to the side,

I would have been able to touch the walls. There was a twin-size bed on the left, a small dresser on the right, and a single chair near the window. The only walking space was a narrow path between the bed and the front of the dresser. The bathroom was tiny, with a shower stall, but no bathtub.

I said to the bellhop, "This won't do. Please wait while I call the front desk." When the receptionist answered, I said, "I can't stay in this room. It's unacceptable."

She could hardly have been surprised. She said, "Okay. Come back downstairs. I'll see what else I can find."

By then it was close to 4:30. I called David, who had just finished unpacking and was on his way to the pool.

"How's your room?" I asked him. "Is it small?"

He said, "No, it's quite large and very nice. How's yours?"

I wanted to kill him at that moment. "I don't have one yet. They tried to give me one the size of a broom closet. Now I'm back at the front desk while they look for something a little larger, but the hotel is sold out for the weekend."

"I'm sorry," he said. "I'm sure they'll find you a decent one. They have to. Come to the pool after you get settled."

By 5 o'clock, another key was handed to me. This time the room was large, bright, and beautifully decorated. But I heard a loud thumping sound and asked the bellhop where it was coming from. He went to the air conditioning unit under the window and began to fiddle with the controls. The steady thumping beat continued.

"I think something's wrong with this," he told me. "It doesn't seem to work, no matter what buttons I push."

I said, "I'm calling the front desk again. I can't stay here with that noise."

Once again, I was told to come back downstairs. And once again, the clerk tried to sound reassuring. "We always have cancellations, so eventually we'll get you a room."

She joined the list of people I wanted to murder. "Eventually?" I thought. "That could mean hours."

Finally, at about 5:30, I was led to a lovely room where everything was in working order. I had a splitting headache, was exhausted, hot, frustrated, stressed out, and furious. By the time I unpacked, I had to lie down. I called David and left a message that I'd be late for dinner and that everyone should start without me.

DH When Joan walked into the dining room at about 7, she didn't look at all happy.

She said, "Well, you'll all be glad to know I finally have a room, but I have a question for all the gentlemen at this table. What ever happened to chivalry? Did it ever occur to any of you to say, 'Joan, you can have my room? I'll be the one to wait for another one?'"

I tried to calm her: "It would have just caused more confusion to start switching rooms once they'd been assigned. And the hotel had an obligation to make good on your reservation."

She didn't buy it. "Right. But while you were getting a suntan, I was schlepping from one floor to another with the bellhop, with return trips to the front desk in between. My suitcase and I had a nice tour of the hotel." And with that off her chest she said, "Have you ordered yet? I'm starving."

After an excellent dinner, we all went to our respective rooms. It was only about 8:30 Pacific time, but we were sinking fast; our bodies thought they were still in the Eastern time zone and we were feeling the three-hour difference.

JK I'm always cold in hotel rooms with the air conditioning turned on, but it would've been too hot with it off. So I decided to look in the closet for another blanket. When I didn't see one, I called the housekeeping department and was told to check the closed, double-door cupboard above the closet. Even standing on a chair, it was too high for me to reach, and while I could see a pillow, I couldn't see a blanket. So I took a hanger, and used a sweeping motion to force the pillow to fall out and, along with it, a folded blanket.

As I picked up the blanket, a box tumbled to the floor. It had a bright yellow cover with bold red type: CHINESE SEX KIT. "What on Earth is this?" I wondered. "And what's it doing in this hotel?"

Of course, curiosity overcame my shock. I had to see what was inside. It contained a number of partitions, all of which were empty, except one, which housed a round plastic sphere, and inside the sphere were a number of silver beads.

DH When Joan and I met for breakfast, I noticed that she was carrying a plastic bag. After we'd ordered she said, "I have something to show you. It fell out of my closet last night when I pulled an extra blanket down." She was careful to keep it hidden by the tablecloth so that no one else could see as she showed me the box and one compartment with the little beads inside.

I couldn't help myself. "Did you already use everything else from it?" I asked her. "And how come your room came equipped with a Chinese Sex Kit and mine didn't? I'm going to call the front desk and complain."

JK "David, are you crazy? You can't do that. It's embarrassing. And there wasn't anything but the container of beads in the box when it fell out of the cupboard."

He said, "So that's your story, is it?"

At that point, I'd been working with David for over eight years and he'd realized early on that I was the perfect victim for his British humor. To this day, he tells everyone that I'm the best "straight man" he's ever met.

I said, "I wonder who had my room before I did? And where on earth does someone buy this kind of thing? By the way, what are the little beads for?"

"Use your imagination," he answered. "And I'm sure it's not hard to find a store that carries sex kits if you'd like to refill yours."

That evening, we were having dinner with two colleagues from New York. They picked us up in their rented car and as soon as David and I got into the back seat, they said, "We're going to a great

Chinese restaurant we've been to before."

I'd brought along the Chinese Sex Kit box in a plastic bag to show them.

"That's a coincidence," I said. "Look what I gave David as a present today."

"Joan, you're asking for trouble," he warned.

Undaunted, I took the box out of the bag. Without missing a beat, he said, "Joan had this Chinese Sex Kit, but by the time she gave it to me, it was empty."

For a flicker of a second, our friends looked back at me with new interest.

DH When we reached the restaurant, Joan put the bag containing the box on the floor under the back seat. We handed over the car to the valet parking attendant, went into the restaurant and had a great meal. But when we were driving back to our hotel, one of our colleagues discovered that a camera he'd left in the glove compartment was missing. Almost simultaneously Joan said, "And the bag is missing too."

The parking attendant, who was Chinese, must have been excited by the treasures he found in our car.

JK The following day, Sunday, was the Emmy ceremony. George Page called each of us that morning. "Let's meet at the pool in a half-hour to discuss who's going to say what if we win. There are a lot of us and we can't go up on the stage without working out our acceptance speeches in advance."

DH It didn't take long to agree what to say if we won, and then, to my surprise George said, "I've got to go take a shower and get dressed."

This was a big day for all of us. And I knew George well enough to realize he'd be nervous. But it was only noon and the limousines we'd ordered weren't picking us up until 4. (It's well-known that driving to and from the Emmys in your own car is a mistake. Those who have tried it find themselves in a parking lot far away, followed by a long walk to the venue. Years before, when we were first nominated, friends advised us to use a limo service.)

So I said, "George, we've got plenty of time. Why don't we have lunch now? The ceremony will go on for hours and it'll be a long time before we get to eat at the reception afterwards."

We all ordered sandwiches, and George gave the waiter seventy-five dollars before he even knew how much the tab would be. When the food arrived, he took a few bites, looked at his watch and said, "I *really* have to go to my room. There's a lot to do. I need to take a shower and then get two people into tuxes and bow ties. Dennis never can put the studs into his shirt or tie his tie. It's getting late."

It was catching. Joan was next. "He's right. I have to wash my hair and put on makeup. I'd better go too." I decided to try to be the calming voice. "It's only 12:45. Relax. It's a beautiful day. Let's enjoy the sun. You don't need three hours to get ready."

It almost worked. George lit another cigarette and Joan settled back in her chair. But five minutes later, he couldn't contain himself any longer. "I'm going to the room now, Dennis. Give me fifteen minutes to take a shower and then you can take yours."

At first Joan looked as though she was about to get up too, but she managed to hold out a full twenty minutes more, until Dennis left. "I'm getting nervous," she said, grabbing her towel. "I have to go now."

I knew they were antsy, but how could they possibly need three hours to get themselves together? John and Carol stayed until about 2:30, and I went to my room at 3. An hour was more than enough time for me.

After a shower, I began to dress: the tuxedo shirt with its studs, the pants, the cummerbund, and finally the bow tie. It was now 3:30, still a half-hour before the cars would arrive, so I started leafing through a travel magazine to pass the time. By 3:45 I decided I should go downstairs to the lobby to be there when George came down.

I went to the closet for my tuxedo jacket, and that's when I realized it wasn't there. I looked on the floor, in my suitcase, in the drawers. Now it was my turn to panic. Here I was, telling everyone to relax, that there was time to spare, and now I didn't have a jacket. I actually remember thinking, "What other jacket did I bring that might work?" The only two hanging there were light tan and denim blue.

I called the front desk, thinking, "This is The Beverly Hills Hotel. Someone here must have a tux jacket I can borrow."

"I'm sorry, sir," said the concierge. "We don't have tux jackets here. Why don't you rent one?"

I flipped through the phone book and found a tuxedo rental place not far from the hotel. "What size do you wear?" asked the person who answered the phone.

"What size do you have? I'll take anything at this point."

He finally convinced me that that wouldn't work, and I gave my size.

"Sorry sir. We don't have any jacket left in that size. It's Emmy weekend."

I called another rental store, which did have my size in stock.

"Can you deliver?" I asked. If I could get it in time, no one would know that I'd forgotten to pack my own.

"When do you need it?" asked the clerk.

"In the next two minutes."

"I'm sorry sir, but that won't be possible. You'll have to come here to pick it up."

I was done for.

I headed to the lobby, where George was pacing and smoking. The two limousines were already waiting outside. He took one look at me and realized that I wasn't wearing a jacket. Actually, it was the best thing that could have happened to him. He suddenly took control. "Get in the car. We're going to get you a jacket."

JK I was about to go down to the lobby when my phone rang. It was John Miller. "Joan, are you ready? The car is here and George and David have already left with Carol and Dennis."

I said, "What's going on? You and Carol and George and Dennis were supposed to be in that car. David and I were supposed to be in the other one and pick up Susie Tracy and her friend, Susan Moon."

"Well, David doesn't have a tux jacket, so they went to rent one."

We all met up on the steps outside the Pasadena Civic Auditorium. When I saw David, I said, "Nice tux. Don't you have something to tell me?"

He replied, "Not now, Joan."

David won the Emmy for directing, and John won for writing. George and I went home empty-handed.

John L. Miller, Joan Kramer, and David Heeley at a party after winning Emmys for *The Spencer Tracy Legacy: A Tribute by Katharine Hepburn.* Sherman Oaks, CA, 1986. Authors' collection.

Through the years, I've told the events of that weekend to several people. David usually tries to stop me by saying, "If you're lucky, Joan will tell you the story about my tux jacket." It's his way of saying, director-style, "Cut."

But it's too delicious not to repeat one more time.

***

JK and DH It sometimes feels as though Emmy weekends in Los Angeles result in strange happenings. Maybe not for everyone, but certainly for us.

Six years earlier, in 1980, we'd been nominated for the two Fred Astaire specials. Our executive producers for those programs were George Page and Jac Venza. We all stayed at the Beverly Hilton Hotel and the night before the ceremony, George and Jac invited us to have dinner with them at the famous restaurant, Chasen's.

They told us, "We thought it would be a treat for you kids."

DH Joan and I arrived in California on Friday, rented a car, and decided to spend Saturday afternoon at Disneyland. It was about a ninety-minute drive, so I'd worked out what time we'd have to leave in order to get back to our hotel, change clothes and be at Chasen's in time for the 6:30 reservation. We headed for the Disneyland parking lot at about 3:30, and found ourselves lost in a sea of cars. We couldn't remember where we'd parked ours, or even what color it was.

JK David tried hard to hide his concern. "We can't be the first to lose a car here. Maybe we'll have to wait until everyone else leaves. And we'll never make it to the restaurant on time." We found a pay-phone and left messages for George and Jac, explaining our predicament and promising to get to Chasen's as soon as we could. Then, by some miracle, David found the license plate matching the number on the key ring.

DH George and Jac were already seated in a booth sipping drinks when we arrived about fifteen minutes late. George was at one end and Jac opposite him. So Jac got up and Joan and I slid into the bench between them.

I'd known George for many years by then and recognized immediately that the vodka in front of him was not his first that evening.

And when we ordered drinks for ourselves, he asked for a refill. We decided what we wanted to eat, gave our menus to the waiter, and George passed out. He did so dramatically, falling forward, his head hitting his empty plate, which caused two of the crystal water glasses to crash to the floor in pieces.

Suddenly, all eyes in that restaurant were on us. And being a Saturday evening, it was packed.

JK Jac was clearly appalled. He told David, "Take him back to the hotel. I'll help you get him to the car." As both of them were trying to get George on his feet, I heard Jac say to him, "If you can't take responsibility for your end of the table, you'll have to leave."

I was now sitting there alone, with waiters mopping up and removing the shattered glass. It felt as though everyone was still staring in my direction.

When Jac returned, the room was calming down. He said, "By the time George got here, he was already a bit tipsy. How was Disneyland? I wish you'd told me you were going. I would have come along."

I thought, "Jac Venza at Disneyland? It's the last place I would imagine him wanting to go."

It seemed only a few minutes later that David came back.

DH Joan looked surprised. "How did you get here so quickly? And how is George?"

"I'm sure he's okay. I drove him to the hotel and saw him to the elevator. He told me he could make it from there."

Joan said, "I hope he's not slumped in the corner riding up and down. Why didn't you take him to his room?"

"I'd left the car in front and you can't park there. So I put him in the elevator and by then he looked fine. I think a change of air helped."

The next morning, I called George and he was completely sober, but annoyed. "Would you believe that Jac called me a few minutes ago to give me a lecture? He said, 'I hope you understand that the

Emmy Awards tonight are part of our business. If you show up drunk, you'll embarrass yourself, as well as me and the kids.'"

But in the end George had the last word. Or to be more precise, made sure *I* had it. He not only told Jac that he was very well aware how important this day was, but then gave a short "lecture" of his own. He said, "And Jac, if we win, David is the only person who should speak. We'll go up to the stage with him, but it's his night. If you say something, then I'll have to say something, and by then he won't have any time left. So don't open your mouth."

I was blown away. We all knew that Jac often made speeches about how difficult it was to raise money for public television. But I couldn't have been the one to tell him not to talk; he was one of my bosses; George was his equal.

JK and DH   When our limo arrived at Pasadena there were, as usual, television news crews covering the event. But this year there was little jockeying for position by the cameramen, because the Screen Actors Guild had called a strike a few days before, and almost all performers had decided not to cross the picket lines.

Fortunately the show did go on with last minute substitute hosts and presenters, and one of the Astaire programs did indeed win the Emmy.

DH   As we were heading for the stage, Jac whispered to me, "I've decided that you should be the one to accept."

I said, "Okay. Thank you."

The following morning Joan and I watched the *CBS Morning News* coverage of the event, which bemoaned the lack of glamour resulting from the strike.

"*It was a night of producers, writers, directors, but no stars,*" said the reporter.

On the phrase "*but no stars,*" the video cut to a shot of Jac, George and the two of us walking up the steps to the auditorium.

JK We had agreed that we wouldn't tell anyone about George passing out at Chasen's. But a few weeks later, at a party David gave for the premiere of the *Nature* series, we were astonished to hear George telling the story himself.

He ended it with, "And it's the only time I ever saw Joan completely undone."

George Page, Jac Venza, and David Heeley with Emmys for *Fred Astaire: Change Partners and Dance*.
Pasadena, CA, 1980. Authors' collection.

Sid Luft in his apartment.
Los Angeles, CA, 1984. Authors' collection.

CHAPTER ELEVEN

The Boxer and
A Singing Legend

Sid Luft was a mixed bag. To anyone who knew him, that must seem like the epitome of an understatement. A former boxer, he met Judy Garland at the nadir of her career. She had just been fired by MGM after what felt like a lifetime there[1], having started as a child performer in 1936, when she was only fourteen. Now approaching thirty, she didn't know which way to turn. Sid was exactly the person she needed at that time. His charm swept her off her feet (they married in 1952), and his self-confidence and drive helped push her in a new direction. He persuaded her to start performing in live concerts, at which she excelled, produced one of her most important films, *A Star Is Born,* at Warner Bros., and also negotiated a deal with CBS which led to a television special and eventually a series, *The Judy Garland Show.*

Long after their divorce, and Judy's death, and following many court battles, Sid succeeded in winning the rights to those TV shows. In the early 1980s, he made a deal with Bill Lamb, the new head of programming at WNET, for a profile of Garland to be

---

1   Her last film at MGM was *Summer Stock* in 1950.

done, focusing on her concert career. Sid would make available—fully cleared for broadcast—all the material he owned; WNET would provide the funds for the production. In exchange, Luft could distribute the show after its PBS broadcast window, co-owning the copyright with WNET. We were assigned to produce the program for the *Great Performances* series.

The prospect of creating a show about Judy Garland, with her singing some of the best songs ever written, was exciting, but we were wary of having to deal with Sid Luft. His reputation for being difficult, litigious, and crafty—perhaps even a scoundrel—was well-known. He was famous for claiming to own the rights to everything "Judy," and whenever he was challenged for using materials he didn't own, he'd launch a lawsuit. He believed that by the time each case was settled, enough time would have passed for the outcome to be irrelevant. In the meantime, he would continue using whatever he wanted. Many people in the business avoided him at all costs.

DH We were understandably nervous when we first met Sid in his Los Angeles apartment. But we were immediately disarmed by his charm. However, he was well aware of his own reputation, and near the end of the visit told us casually that he had been recording our entire conversation. Seeing the looks of consternation on our faces, he laughed, and said he was "just kidding." But we're still not sure.

He shared moving stories of his time with Judy, the ups and downs, the struggles to keep her drug free, and it was clear that he had loved her deeply and maybe still did. (When we arranged a private screening of the finished program, we could hear Sid sobbing when Judy sang "As Long As He Needs Me.")

At one point he played a video of the end of that first CBS *Ford Star Jubilee* special from 1955, where Judy, who had just finished her famous "We're a Couple of Swells" number, sat on the edge of the stage, still in her tramp outfit, and sang her signature song, "Over the Rainbow." It was a powerful and wrenching performance, much darker than the way she sang it in the 1939 film *The Wizard of Oz*. We knew immediately that we had found the climax of our program.

JK Sid and Judy had two children, Lorna and Joe, whom we filmed during one of our production trips to Los Angeles. Liza Minnelli, Judy's first child (with director Vincente Minnelli), also agreed to be interviewed. The date was set, and we ordered a limousine to pick her up from her New York apartment and bring her to WNET, where we and a crew were waiting. That morning, her publicist called me and asked if Liza could keep the limo for an hour or so after the shoot so that she could run a few errands. "Of course," I replied. Then, thirty minutes before she was due to arrive, the same publicist called again. "Liza won't be able to make it. There's a family emergency." It appeared that she had stood us up. However, much later, we learned what had happened that day. She had only recently returned home from a rehabilitation facility (unfortunately, by her own admission, she inherited Judy's "addiction gene"). And, although she had agreed to the interview, it was only as she was about to leave her apartment that she realized she was not emotionally ready to go on camera and talk about her mother. We had to respect that.

Lorna Luft with David Heeley and Joan Kramer.
Los Angeles, CA, 1984. Authors' collection.

JK and DH   As the planning for the program continued, and we were trying to decide who should host it, we realized the obvious choice was Lorna. She came across very well in the interview we'd shot, was level-headed, and had a clear connection to our subject.

We filmed her in the middle of an especially brutal New York winter (she was bundled up in furs for the few outdoor sequences—in Times Square and in front of Carnegie Hall), and the next day recorded her voice-over narration.

In the meantime, Sid had called to tell us that we could not use the version of Judy singing "Over the Rainbow" that he had shown us when we first met him. "It's my most prized possession," was his only explanation.

The program had to include her most famous song, and the only other version available to us was from *The Judy Garland Show* series, in a Christmas special that included all three children. Unfortunately, Joe, who was only seven at the time, kept interrupting. It was not one of Judy's better performances.

DH   Lorna's narration recording was going well, until she came to "Over the Rainbow." She stopped in astonishment.

"You can't use that," she said. "Joey never stops talking all through the song."

I explained that we had no choice because Sid wouldn't let us use the number from the 1955 special.

"What time is it?" she asked.

"Just before 2 o'clock," I told her.

"Good. Early enough for the next edition of *The New York Post*. The headline will be '*Daughter Kills Father*.' Where's the phone?"

Moments later she was talking to him in LA.

"Sidney," she said. "You have only one grandchild, who is my son. If you ever want to see him again, get that ******* tape sent here by FedEx."

"Lorna, calm down."

"Don't tell me to calm down! Call right now and arrange for that tape to be here by tomorrow morning."

Sure enough, there was a FedEx delivery the next day. And that performance of "Over the Rainbow" does indeed end the show, as we had originally planned.

JK and DH   But the broadcast was not the end of the story. Despite being required to provide material that was fully cleared for us to use, Sid somehow "forgot" to deal with the American Federation of Musicians, the Directors Guild of America, and many others. The lawyers at WNET spent many years dealing with all the claims that came in.

The program which aired had some elements which we had acquired from other sources, and which could not be cleared for home-video use. So we made a special version for Sid to distribute, which did not include those items. He ignored the tape we sent him, and used the broadcast version for all his releases. We don't know whether the rights holders tried to stop him, but suspect they did not deem it worth the considerable trouble.

Sid Luft passed away in September, 2005, at the age of eighty-nine. There was a private celebration of his life, which unfortunately, we couldn't attend. But we have to believe that it was more of a roast than a memorial—and he would have loved every minute of it.

David Heeley, Joan Kramer, Lorna Luft and Sid Luft before Emmy awards ceremony. Beverly Hilton Hotel, Beverly Hills, CA, 1986. Authors' collection.

Judy Garland.
1960s. Authors' collection.

CHAPTER TWELVE

Rainbow Over The White House

The show we produced about Judy Garland started to take shape in the spring of 1984. There are plenty of fascinating tales that swirl around this legendary performer, only some of which have been proven true. We wanted to be sure we'd separated fact from fiction, and one story in particular grabbed our attention. Verifying it involved a cast of characters that extended beyond showbiz to include some famous names in the world of politics.

At the time there was only one authorized biography of Garland: *Judy*, by Gerald Frank; and for it he interviewed every member of her family. Garland's eldest daughter, Liza Minnelli, tells a story about her mother at the time she was making her television series in 1963 and '64. As Liza explained, it was a grueling schedule and the production team was constantly changing. Judy would come to the studio to find new faces, different people to work with, and that, added to the stress of taping her shows before a live audience, left her exhausted and frustrated. At the end of the week, she would often come home and say to Liza, "What a week. I think I'll call Jack"—referring to John F. Kennedy, then the President of the United States—and she'd pick up the phone and place a call to the

White House. Each conversation ended the same way: Liza would hear her mother say, "Oh no, again? Do you really want me to do that again? All right…" And then Judy would sing the last eight bars of "Over the Rainbow" into the phone.

DH That story felt too good to be true. But if it *was* true, we certainly would want to use it in our program. We knew that Judy had campaigned for Kennedy and the families were friends. She had even rented a summer house in Hyannisport near the Kennedy compound. But did she really pick up the phone and call The White House just to chat and let off steam? And did the President always ask her to sing "Over the Rainbow" at the end of each call? The various parts of that story needed to be confirmed, despite the authorized nature of Frank's book.

This research was a task tailor-made for Joan, and she loved every minute of it.

JK I wrote a letter to Jacqueline Onassis on WNET letterhead and sent it to her apartment on Fifth Avenue. I told her we were producing a documentary about Judy Garland and, because there were so many myths and exaggerations surrounding her life, we wanted to fact-check a story we'd heard. I did not tell her where it came from or that Liza Minnelli was the original source. I simply asked her to confirm the basic details.

A few days later, I received a phone call from Nancy Tuckerman, formerly Mrs. Kennedy's social secretary in the White House, and now her assistant at Doubleday, where Jackie was an editor.

"Hello. This is Nancy Tuckerman for Mrs. Onassis. She asked me to call you in reply to the letter you sent her. She wants you to know that the story you asked her about is not true."

I was shocked and for a few seconds weighed whether or not I should take this a step further. Then I realized I had nothing to lose.

I said, "Mrs. Tuckerman, I think it's important for you to know where that story originated. It's in the only authorized biography of

Judy Garland and was told to the author by Judy's daughter, Liza Minnelli. If Mrs. Onassis is now saying that the story isn't true, then it means that Liza made it up. I must admit I'm rather flabbergasted that she would create a story that involved not just her mother, but also the President of the United States. Can you tell me, Mrs. Tuckerman, what *exactly* did Mrs. Onassis say? Did she deny every detail of that story, or perhaps just that those calls didn't take place 'often,' as I had mentioned in my letter?"

There was a silence and then she said, "I didn't actually speak to her about it. She received the letter at home, and sent it to me at the office with a note at the top: '*Call Joan Kramer. Story not true.*'" Then she added, "But if Liza Minnelli is the source, perhaps Mrs. Onassis just wasn't in the room when Judy called the President."

I replied in a voice that, in retrospect, must have sounded as though I was giving a lecture. "Mrs. Tuckerman, please correct me if I have my facts wrong. Mrs. Onassis started her career as a reporter/photographer and was married to a Senator who became the President of the United States. Then she was the wife of a world statesman and now she's an editor at a major publishing house. I'm certain she understands how important it is to fact-check a story. And she also clearly knows the difference between 'Story not true' and 'I don't know.' If she wasn't in the room during the President's conversations with Judy Garland, shouldn't her reply have been 'I don't know'?"

"Of course, she knows the difference. Therefore the story must really not be true."

I finished by asking if she'd speak to Mrs. Onassis about it again and call me back. I knew I'd never hear from her again.

DH I thought that was the end of it. But I should have known better.

JK The next day I called Senator Edward Kennedy's office in Washington, DC. I spoke to his press secretary, who said, "I'll ask the senator, but I doubt he would know." Of course, I never told him about my letter to, and response from, Jackie Onassis.

Senator Kennedy indeed didn't know. But he suggested that I call Evelyn Lincoln, who was President Kennedy's secretary, and even gave me her number.

"The story is absolutely true," she said.

"How can you be so sure?"

"Because whenever a call from a well-known personality came in, no matter what time of day or night it was, it was always put through to me first. And sometimes I was still on the line when I heard the President ask her to sing 'Over the Rainbow.'"

So now it was an even balance: one denial and one confirmation. I had to find a way to break the tie.

At that time, Caroline Kennedy was working for the Film and Television department of the Metropolitan Museum of Art. Most of the films with which she was involved eventually were acquired by WNET for broadcast on public television. And I was often assigned to "package" them, adding the WNET and PBS logos, etc. So she and I spent many hours together in edit rooms and she had an office near mine.

I didn't tell her anything about my letter to her mother, but I did say that I'd called her uncle's office and he'd suggested that I speak to Evelyn Lincoln, who'd confirmed the story.

Caroline said, "Evelyn Lincoln is a lovely person, but she's getting a bit old now, and sometimes her memory isn't what it used to be. So I don't think you should take her word for it."

"Did you ever hear about the calls from Judy to your father as you were growing up?"

"No. I did know Judy Garland and her husband, Sid Luft, because they and their family were our neighbors in Hyannisport during the summer. But I was much younger than her children, so they were closer to some of my cousins than they were to me.

"I have an idea though. Why don't you call Dave Powers at the Kennedy Library in Massachusetts and ask him? He was one of my father's closest aides at The White House, so he might be able to help. Tell him I told you to call."

Caroline was then Vice Chair of the Board of the John F. Kennedy Library Foundation. (Now she is Honorary President of the John F. Kennedy Library Foundation and a member of the John F. Kennedy Profile in Courage Award Committee.)

I went back into my office and dialed the number.

David Powers came on the line immediately and said, "Oh yes, I just heard from Caroline who told me to expect your call." I hadn't asked her to do that and she didn't tell me she was going to pave the way for me.

As soon as I started to tell the story, he interrupted me and said, "Oh, sure I remember. I was usually with the President in the Oval Office when Judy called and he never would let her off the phone without asking her to sing a few bars of 'Over the Rainbow.' In fact, he would hold the phone out so that I could hear her sing too."

That was good enough for me. Story confirmed.

Even today, so many years later, I'm disappointed at Mrs. Onassis' dismissive and erroneous reply. If I were from *The National Enquirer* I could understand her not caring about the question. But from public television?

And I'm also still grateful to Caroline Kennedy for her help. Thanks to her, I received two confirmations that day: one for the story about Judy Garland and President Kennedy; the other cementing my already-existing opinion that Caroline is kind and considerate and completely unaffected by her fame.

Judy Garland with John F. Kennedy. 1960. Authors' collection.

DH Our program does include that story, which is told over stills followed by news footage of Judy Garland singing for President and Mrs. Kennedy at a fundraiser. The sequence lasts fifteen seconds in an eighty-seven minute show. Confirming the facts took over two weeks.

Johnny Carson and James Stewart on the Universal backlot.
Universal City, CA, 1986. Authors' collection.

CHAPTER THIRTEEN

Jimmy and Johnny–Maybe

There was no doubt about it. At some point every major project hit a stumbling block that had the potential of causing it to collapse completely. After it happened with two or three shows, we came to expect a crisis on every one of them.

For *James Stewart: A Wonderful Life*, it was not long after we started pre-production. Stewart had agreed to participate in the program and we were several weeks into research and development, watching his movies, looking for news footage, and beginning the process of lining up interviews. In fact, we'd already sent a letter to President and Mrs. Reagan at the White House, since they and the Stewarts had been friends for over forty years.

DH It was about 7 pm on a Friday evening; I'd just arrived home when my phone rang. Our summer intern, Rachel Dretzin, was still in the office, and the moment I heard her voice, I knew she had bad news. Jimmy Stewart's long-time publicist, John Strauss, had called to tell us that Jimmy didn't want to do the show.

Usually, when a problem occurs on a Friday, I give myself the weekend to think it through. But this news spelled disaster and we had to find out quickly what was going on. I also knew that I was not the one who should call John. Joan had been his main contact and, in her usual way, had already developed a rapport with him.

JK   I was lucky; he answered his own phone. He apologized for the bombshell he'd just delivered, and then explained: "Stewart's agent, Herman Citron, is trying to negotiate a lucrative deal for Jim to write his autobiography. When he heard what you were doing, he told Jim to back out of it because he thinks the program will scoop the book. I'm really sorry."

I said, "John, I can't believe Citron is so short-sighted. Doesn't he realize that a television show can only cover a tiny fraction of what's in a book? You're a publicist; you know our show will be the perfect 'teaser.' It'll actually *boost* sales of the book."

"I tried to point that out to him, but it didn't work," he said.

"I assume he's aware that if Jimmy does pull out, we can still do this program without him? He's a public figure and we don't need his consent. Of course, it won't be as good a show, but we've been given the funding by PBS, so we're going ahead with it."

In truth, whether or not PBS would have continued to support the production without Stewart telling his own story was a big question. But it was the only stand I could take at the time.

I then pulled out my trump card. "And John, we've already written to President and Mrs. Reagan asking them for an interview. We told them that Jimmy has authorized the program and agreed to participate in it. I'm sure you can see how embarrassing it would be to tell them he's changed his mind."

That's the kind of information that hits a publicist right between the eyes. And it had the impact I was hoping for.

"I don't think anyone knew how far along you were," he said. "I'm going to call Jim and tell him what you've just told me. Hang on. I'll get back to you."

I did not hear back from him that evening or Saturday or Sunday. The entire weekend felt like we were "hanging on" by a thread.

On Monday morning my phone rang: "Jimmy's back on board. I spoke to him and Gloria (Mrs. Stewart), and just between us, I know that she went to bat for you. She told him that he'd already made a commitment to you and can't go back on his word. I think she also called Herman. I haven't heard from him, but I'd guess he's not happy. I am, though."

JK and DH It didn't take long for us to discover just how angry Herman Citron was. He also represented the Estate of Alfred Hitchcock, and had control over many of Hitchcock's films. Our next hurdle came when poor John Strauss called us to report that Citron would not give us permission to use excerpts from any of the films Stewart had made with Hitchcock, some of which were pivotal in Jimmy's career.

JK I asked if Stewart knew.

"No," said John. "I don't think Herman would be foolish enough to tell him. And I don't think it's a good idea to pit Jim against his agent again."

"But John, this show will have a glaring omission without any Hitchcock clips."

"I know that, and so does Herman. But I think we should just let this cool off for a few days."

And it was just a few days later, while still reeling from this news, that we received a call from Citron's office asking when we'd be in LA. He wanted to meet us.

JK and DH We felt as though we were walking into a lion's den, without any ammunition. He was on the phone when his secretary ushered us in. He shook our hands without smiling and indicated where he wanted us to sit. And we soon had another surprise: he was friendly and straightforward.

"I know I've given you trouble because I didn't want to hurt the sale of Jim's autobiography. But he's decided he wants to do your program, so I'm going to let you use the Hitchcock films. However, you can't have *Rear Window*; it's legally entangled and can't be shown at all." (The argument over who owned what in *Rear Window* became a landmark Supreme Court case known as *Stewart vs. Abend*.)

It was hard to believe we'd actually won this battle without any unpleasant confrontation. What we didn't know at the time was that it had taken a powerful force to make him change his mind: Gloria Stewart.

Once again, behind the scenes, she had come to the rescue. She never admitted it to us, but John Strauss told us it was she who'd called Citron and insisted he let us use the Hitchcock material. And although John never mentioned his own part in all this, we knew he was the one who'd alerted Gloria to the problem, knowing she wouldn't just sit by and let this profile of her husband be sabotaged by his own agent.

We hoped that was the end of our obstacle course for this program. It wasn't. But we had a breather.

DH Even now, it still amazes us that getting Johnny Carson to host the show was relatively simple.

Usually, Joan and I would make a list of stars, directors and other personalities who had a connection to our subject, and then debate that list endlessly. But from the moment we began to produce this program we'd been preoccupied with just keeping it afloat. So even though the choice of host was crucial, it was a discussion that kept getting pushed aside by more pressing issues. In fact, it wasn't until we were in Los Angeles driving to a meeting at MGM, that it struck us that the studio would undoubtedly be asking whom we had in mind as host and narrator. (MGM owned a large number of Stewart's movies and was providing clips and stills in exchange for ancillary distribution rights in the program.) To this day, I find it almost inconceivable that we waited until we were in a car, only twenty minutes away from an important meeting, before realizing we'd better come up with some names.

And that's when Johnny Carson popped into my head. Knowing how comfortable Jimmy Stewart was whenever he appeared as a guest on *The Tonight Show*, I felt the chemistry between him and Johnny could work just as well for us.

It was a no-brainer. Everyone loved the idea.

JK With a reconfirmed commitment from Stewart, I called John Strauss to ask how Jimmy would feel about Johnny as host, if—and it was a big IF—we could get him. John said he'd be thrilled.

It's important to remember that Carson was the king of late night television, an enormous star, who seldom accepted offers to do anything outside his own show except, occasionally, to host the Oscars. So we knew this was a long shot.

John suggested we contact David Tebet, an NBC talent executive, whom Johnny considered a trusted friend. In fact, Tebet had been instrumental in Carson becoming the host of *The Tonight Show* back in 1962. When I reached him, he immediately offered his help.

"Send me a letter and I'll give it to Johnny," he said.

A few days later, Tebet called with exciting news: "Don't tell him I told you this, but Johnny is going to do the show for you. He asked me to give you his home number and he's expecting your call. But let him tell you himself."

He answered his own phone, and I remember that first rush of excitement at hearing the voice of this talk show legend that I'd grown up watching as I tried to complete my homework. I thought his voice sounded slightly less baritone than it did on television, but it had the same clear quality. He said, "David Tebet gave me your letter. I'll be happy to do this if it's okay with Jim."

That was it. Instead of weeks of writing letters, making phone calls, and dealing with layers of representatives, we'd landed Johnny Carson in a matter of days. This was a cinch. Or so it seemed.

DH A few weeks later, on a clear California morning, Joan and I drove to Carson's home in Malibu at the tip of Point Dume. He'd already told us that he and Stewart were good friends. Both from the Midwest, they'd grown up with similar values, and Jimmy reminded Johnny of his own father, who'd been hard of hearing, as Jimmy was now.

After the usual handshakes, he showed us around his beautiful property with its sweeping view of the ocean. We could feel how proud he was not only of the house itself, but also of the new tennis courts, complete with guest accommodations, which he was having built just across the road. He was an avid tennis player, who could be seen in the stands at Wimbledon almost every year.

Joan Kramer and view from the back of Johnny Carson's home. Point Dume, CA, 1986. Authors' collection.

Following the tour, he took us downstairs to his den.

"I've been thinking," he said. "I'm the wrong person to host this show. You need Cary Grant."

This couldn't really be happening. Johnny was the perfect host and now he was backing out. Joan and I were both speechless. And he couldn't be serious about Cary Grant, who *never* appeared on television. But he was indeed serious.

"And I'm a friend of Cary's, so I'll ask him for you."

This was the sort of quandary few producers face. On the one hand, getting Johnny Carson was a major coup and we didn't want to lose him. On the other, Cary Grant would have been an unsurpassable "catch." But Grant was such a huge star he might overshadow Jimmy Stewart, the subject of the program.

We also wondered whether this was a test of sorts. If we leapt at the idea of Cary Grant, it might seem that we preferred him to Johnny. And even though he seemed down-to-earth and self-effacing, we knew that he, like most stars, had to have an ego and we didn't want to say anything that might bruise it.

He elaborated: "After all, you just did a show about Spencer Tracy with Katharine Hepburn as host. They not only knew each other, but they also made films together. I've never worked with Jimmy Stewart in the movies. Cary Grant has."

JK I finally found my voice. "Johnny, Hepburn hosting the program about Tracy was unique. What's special about your hosting this one is that you represent every member of the audience who has watched Jimmy Stewart on the screen for so many years. But you're one of the lucky ones who also happens to be his friend."

He nodded and clearly was pleased by that argument. Yet he said, "Why don't I just call Cary and see what he says?"

We reluctantly had to agree, but left his house feeling depressed. We'd just lost Johnny and had little-to-no hope he'd be able to talk Cary Grant into hosting the program. Worse, even if Grant wanted to do it, our concern that he'd take the spotlight away from Jimmy Stewart was growing deeper by the minute. It seemed that Johnny was determined to replace himself and would continue suggesting one big name after another until he found someone who was acceptable and available.

The next morning, the phone rang in my hotel room. It was Johnny.

"Cary is out of town with that one-man show he does about his career. So… I guess you're stuck with me."

It took me a moment to digest the impact of what I'd just heard. Was it possible that another enormous problem had suddenly vanished?

Then, with a sigh of relief, I said, "Johnny, you have no idea how thrilled I am to be 'stuck' with you."

JK and DH Only a few weeks later, on November 29th, 1986, the Sunday after Thanksgiving, there was a news flash on television: *"Cary Grant, Dead at 82."* Like the rest of the world, we were surprised and saddened. He had died in Davenport, Iowa, right before one of his appearances at a college there.

JK Johnny called me at home in New York. "Well, I guess you've heard the news."

I said, "Of course. I'm so sorry. I know you were friends."

There was a short pause, then, "Yes, he was a good friend of mine and I really cared about him. So don't get upset when I tell you what I thought of saying when you answered the phone."

"Okay, go ahead. I'm sitting down."

"I wanted to say: 'I asked Cary Grant to host your show and he dropped dead.'"

James Stewart, Joan Kramer, and Johnny Carson between takes on the Universal backlot. Universal City, CA, 1986. Authors' collection.

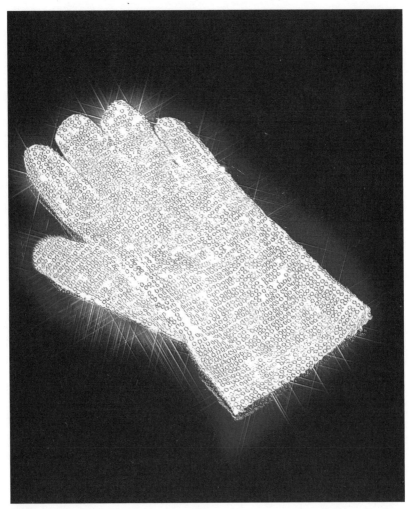

Authors' collection.

CHAPTER FOURTEEN

Dirty Laundry and
A Rock Concert

The cast of characters in this story includes an unlikely group: Katharine Hepburn, Jane Fonda, and Michael Jackson. And it was Hepburn, herself, who told us the story during lunch at her house in New York.

She had agreed to participate in our profile of James Stewart, but she had a favor to ask.

"I've also promised to do an interview for a piece about Michael Jackson, so can your film crew shoot it on the same day? I'll already be in makeup for you, so it would make sense to do the other one right afterwards."

Since she already knew us and our crew, that made sense. But what caught our attention was her mentioning Michael Jackson.

JK "Do you know him?" I asked.

"Why? Does that surprise you? As a matter of fact, that book on the table over there belongs to him. He left it here when he came to visit."

"Okay. Now I'm filled with curiosity."

"Oh yes, we're good friends," she said. "I met him when I was up at Squam Lake in New Hampshire making *On Golden Pond*, and he came to visit Jane Fonda. They were already friends and she invited him to the location. She introduced him to me, and he was very soft-spoken and sweet.

"Then, Jane said to me, 'I have to go back to Los Angeles for the weekend, so could you look after Michael for me?'

"I said, 'What the hell am I supposed to do with this kid? I hardly know him.'

"'Oh, you'll find things to do,' she said. 'He's crazy about you.'

"She'd found him a room in the attic of an old house. When I went there on Saturday morning, the room looked like a hurricane had hit it. I said, 'Michael, clean up this place—right now.' And he said, 'Yes, Miss Hepburn,' in a voice I could hardly hear, and he began picking up all those clothes and piling them on a chair. I said to him, 'Don't you ever do your laundry?' And he said, 'Someone usually does that for me.'

"I said, 'Come with me. We're going to a laundromat just down the street.'"

DH It's a scene that should have been captured on film: Katharine Hepburn and Michael Jackson walking into a public laundromat, with Kate showing Michael how to feed quarters into the washing machines.

She said, "People were a bit taken aback to see us, but then went about their own business and left us alone."

While they sat and watched his clothes tumbling around, she said, "Michael, take off those goddamn sunglasses. I can't see your eyes." And he promptly obliged.

"So that was the beginning of our friendship. Now, whenever he's in New York, he comes to visit. The last time, he said, 'I'd like to buy some books. Can you recommend any that you think I should read?' I asked Kathy (her niece, Katharine Houghton, who played Hepburn's and Spencer Tracy's daughter in *Guess Who's Coming to Dinner*) to take him shopping at Barnes and Noble and they came back with three shopping bags filled with books I'd suggested. He proudly showed them all to me. And I can guarantee that he's never cracked the spine of any one of them."

JK She also invited him to dinner and asked what he'd like to eat.

"Just vegetables," he said.

She told us, "So, Norah made this beautiful vegetarian dinner, with almost every vegetable you can think of. When he arrived, I asked him, 'What's your favorite vegetable, Michael?' He replied, 'Cauliflower.'

"'Really? How fascinating,' I said, as I realized it was the only one not on the menu. But I decided to let him discover that for himself.

"And then, he invited me to one of his concerts at Madison Square Garden."

Actress that she was, she paused for shock value.

I said, "And did you go? I don't quite picture you at a Michael Jackson concert."

"Yep," she said. "He insisted I come. I took Phyllis and Schuyler (her great-niece, Schuyler Grant)."

Another great scene for a movie: two octogenarians and a seventeen-year-old walking down the aisle at Madison Square Garden to seats in the second row. Apparently, word spread like wildfire that Hepburn was in the audience, with everyone wanting to catch a glimpse of her.

Soon after 8 pm, the concert started. But as with most rock concerts, the main attraction isn't the first one to appear. So as the clock ticked away, Kate became increasingly angry.

"Let's go," she said. "He's late and I don't want to wait any longer." Schuyler explained that he wasn't late—that this was just the opening act for him.

"Well, then why didn't he tell me that so we could have arrived later?"

Schuyler prevailed on her to wait it out, since Michael knew they were in the audience.

And then, finally, out he came. Hepburn was horrified—by his erotic pelvic moves and the volume level of the entire performance. The young man with the quiet voice and shy personality had turned into a sex object on the stage in front of her.

She said, "Let's get out of here. I don't ever want to see him again. He's vulgar."

Again, it was up to Schuyler to convince her not only to stay, but then to go backstage, where he was expecting her after the concert.

Another frenzied melee erupted when she walked through the stage door. And in a voice everyone there could hear, she said, "Michael, what was that? Asinine. And lewd."

"I'm sorry, Miss Hepburn," he said, speaking again in his soft, childlike voice. "But that's what I do when I perform on stage."

"Well, take my advice. And don't ever do it again."

DH A week after she told us that story, our crew set up in her living room for our James Stewart interview. As usual, we were a very small group: Joan and I, a production assistant, lighting director, cameraman and sound engineer. By the time we'd finished, the producers of the documentary about Michael Jackson had already arrived. Obviously everyone on their staff wanted to meet Katharine Hepburn and found an excuse to show up: two producers, writers, a director, an assistant director, a production assistant, and several others whose titles weren't obvious.

When Kate saw this crowd she said to us, "Stick around. When I get rid of that bunch, we'll have lunch."

Joan and I went into an adjacent room and watched the interview on a monitor. It didn't take long to realize that the questions were making Hepburn increasingly uncomfortable.

"What's your favorite Michael Jackson song?"

"I don't know the name of any goddamn one of them."

"What do you see in Michael Jackson's future?"

"I see Michael Jackson."

I felt my stomach muscles tense as this continued through several more questions. I thought she was going to throw them all out at any moment.

After about fifteen agonizing minutes, it was over. When they were on the way down the stairs, she said to us, "Thank God they're leaving. Now let's eat."

As usual, lunch was a cup of Norah's homemade soup, and a sandwich. And, of course, for dessert, Sedutto's mocha chip ice cream and lace cookies.

JK and DH   We never saw the finished documentary about Michael Jackson. And we doubt that Hepburn did either.

And, as far as we know, she never went to another one of his concerts, which undoubtedly was best for both of them because he clearly, and astutely, never took her advice about his performance.

Photograph by Len Tavares.

David Heeley meets President Ronald Reagan and Nancy Reagan.
The White House Library, 1986. Authors' collection.

President Ronald Reagan and Nancy Reagan greet Joan Kramer.
The White House Library, 1986. Authors' collection.

CHAPTER FIFTEEN

A Visit to the White House

DH Among the many photographs that hang on the wall of my loft in Manhattan, there's one in particular that almost always provokes comments. It's a picture of me shaking hands with Ronald Reagan. Those who don't know my political leanings usually tap dance around, trying to determine how I felt about him and his presidency. I eventually let them know that I met Ronald and Nancy Reagan on business, and it had nothing to do with politics.

JK and DH They were high on our list of potential interviewees for the profile we were producing about James Stewart. It was well known that they shared a long friendship with the Stewarts, one which dated back so many years that none of them could recall when it first began. Gloria Stewart did remember that she knew "Ronnie" before she ever met Jimmy, and that she and Nancy were friends long before the Reagans married. The Stewarts were also staunch Republicans, and Jimmy frequently campaigned for Ronald Reagan when he ran for Governor of California, and later for President.

We were aware that arranging an interview in the White House with the President and First Lady would not be easy. They undoubtedly received hundreds of letters every day and read very few of them personally. However, since the one from us involved a good friend of theirs, we thought there was a fair chance it would eventually be brought to their attention.

The response came in about ten days. It was on White House stationery from Frederick J. Ryan, Jr., Director of Presidential Appointments and Scheduling. He said he was writing on behalf of the President, who would not be able to *"participate in a program on the life and career of the late James Stewart"* because of his full schedule.

THE WHITE HOUSE

WASHINGTON

September 5, 1986

Dear Mr. Heeley and Ms. Kramer:

On behalf of the President I thank you for your recent letter in which you request that he participate in a program on the life and career of the late James Stewart for Public Television.

Although he would like to be able to do this, his projected fall and early winter schedule is so heavy that it will not be possible.

With best wishes.

Sincerely,

Fred Ryan

FREDERICK J. RYAN, JR.
Director, Presidential
Appointments and Scheduling

Reply to our request for an interview with President and Mrs. Reagan. 1986. Authors' collection.

At that time, in 1986, Jimmy Stewart was still very much alive. Unwittingly, Mr. Ryan had done us a favor. Had he not referred to the *"late"* James Stewart, we probably would have believed the excuse. But his blunder not only indicated that our request had never made it past his desk, but it also gave us valuable ammunition for a second attempt.

Our initial reaction was to have some fun at his expense by informing him that Mr. Stewart was going to be rather surprised to hear that two of his oldest friends think he's dead. But our associate producer, Cindy Mitchell, suggested a more sensible approach. By a fortunate coincidence her fiancé, John, lived next door to Sheila Tate, who had only recently left her White House position as Nancy Reagan's press secretary. Cindy thought Sheila might be able to give us an insider's advice, and offered to contact her for us.

JK I soon had a message on my desk: "*Call Sheila Tate at 10 am Tuesday morning.*"

She came on the line immediately.

"I heard about the letter you received from Fred Ryan. Poor Fred. He's overworked and obviously didn't do his homework. I can assure you that the Reagans would have agreed to an interview about Jimmy Stewart if they knew they'd been asked.

"Now if you still want them, let me handle it. But don't try embarrassing Fred. The staff will protect him and you still won't get the interview. I'll call Elaine Crispen, who's now in my old job as Mrs. Reagan's press secretary, and ask her to get involved. But when you talk to her, just start from scratch with your request and don't mention Fred Ryan's letter. I'll have already told her the whole story and she doesn't need to hear it again."

I remember saying, "But Sheila, is that the way to approach the President—by going through Mrs. Reagan's office? Our letter was addressed to both of them."

"Trust me. This is the way to do it."

I was surprised. Like most people at that time, I was not aware of the extent of Nancy Reagan's power within the White House. The stories about her far-reaching influence on her husband's decisions had not yet been made public by some members of his staff who later claimed that she was responsible for them being fired.

Sheila Tate called back within twenty-four hours.

"I've spoken with Elaine and filled her in on the background. Here's her direct line. She's expecting your call."

Elaine Crispen was businesslike but friendly.

"I hear you're doing a profile about the late James Stewart," she said with a laugh.

"Mrs. Crispen, you said that. I didn't."

"I know. Fred made a mistake, but let's see if we can fix it. I'll talk to Mrs. Reagan and I should have an answer for you by tomorrow."

She called the next morning with good news. And then added, "You'll be hearing from Fred Ryan to schedule the time."

It was hard not to laugh when he called, and there wasn't even a hint of recognition that he'd dealt with this before.

"Hello, this is Fred Ryan, Director of Appointments and Scheduling for the President and Mrs. Reagan. How is Monday afternoon, November 10th at 4 pm for your interview? If that works for you, I need you to send me a list of the topics you want them to discuss. Now let me connect you to Elizabeth Board, who is Director of The White House Television Office."

Elizabeth also asked for the same list "so that I can get the speech writers going on this." That took me aback somewhat.

I said, "Elizabeth, what speech writers? Everyone else who's on the program is answering questions in an informal, conversational way. If the President and Mrs. Reagan read a speech from a teleprompter about their old friend, Jimmy Stewart, it'll feel very odd. They know him so well. Can't they just talk off the cuff?"

"They almost never do anything without being scripted," she said, "and they're very good at making it *not* look or sound like a speech. But I do see your point. Let me talk to Elaine and I'll call you back."

Finally, it was agreed that our questions would be given directly to the Reagans so they would have time to collect their thoughts. But there would be no speeches written for them and no teleprompter.

DH We were asked for our birth dates and social security numbers and, apparently we each now have an FBI file, as does anyone who interviews the President.

Arriving at the White House gate a few weeks later, we were given name tags and clearance passes, and taken upstairs to Elaine Crispen's office on the second floor. There was another small staircase nearby, which she told us led up to the private living quarters. We expected her office to be large and luxurious. It wasn't. It was tiny, but well furnished and comfortable, with photos of the Reagan family on the walls and shelves. She gave us the list of questions we'd sent, which now had the President's and Mrs. Reagan's check marks next to the ones they were prepared to answer. Among the very few not marked was: *"When did you first meet Jimmy Stewart?"* The reason became clear later.

Mr. Frederick J. Ryan, Jr.
Page 3

10. Apparently, the President has given Mr. Stewart a western belt, which Mr. Stewart wore to the ranch last year when he and Mrs. Stewart attended Mrs. Reagan's party. (There is a shot of Mr. Stewart and the President looking at the belt). Would the President and/or Mrs. Reagan tell us the significance of the gift...why a western belt... when did the President give it to Mr. Stewart...on what occasion, etc?

#7 - if possible

11. Mr. and Mrs. Stewart were invited to stay at the White House on at least one occasion that we are aware of. On the wall in the Stewarts' home there is a photo in color of Mr. Stewart standing next to a rabbit made of shrubbery which is over seven feet tall, and which apparently, was taken in the White House. The photo is signed: "For Jimmy, you never told us he was green!" It is signed "Nancy" and "Ron". Obviously, a reference to the film and play HARVEY, in which Mr. Stewart starred, what were the circumstances of the green rabbit being in the White House at that time. Did the President and Mrs. Reagan obtain it just for the visit of the Stewarts? We'd like to hear the complete story.

Know personally - how many compare w/image & what is that image that is so special to the Am. people.

12. Can the President and/or Mrs. Reagan tell us how the screen image of Mr. Stewart compares to the real man, the man they know as actor and friend?

#4

13. What do the President and Mrs. Reagan feel that Jimmy Stewart represents to the American public? Why do so many people relate so strongly and with such great warmth to him?

14. Can the President and Mrs. Reagan place Mr. Stewart in the annals of American cinema?

#5

15. How will James Stewart, actor and man, be remembered?

Again, the above thoughts are merely meant as suggestions, and we are well aware that we've listed more than we expect the President and Mrs. Reagan to have time to address. But as I explained to you on the telephone, we know that the President and Mrs. Reagan have

Interview questions with the Reagans' comments.
1986. Authors' collection.

The crew was setting up in the White House Library on the main floor when Elizabeth Board told us, "You'll have twenty minutes. That should be plenty." Obviously she had scheduled more for the President and First Lady to do on camera that afternoon. Twenty minutes didn't seem like "plenty" to us, but we were in no position to argue.

JK Just before 4 pm, Ronald and Nancy Reagan walked into the library holding hands and smiling. She was wearing a red dress (red had become known as her signature color) with simple, but elegant gold jewelry. He was dressed in a dark suit and tie, looking very dapper. His hair appeared to be naturally black; it didn't look dyed. (Everyone in our office had asked us to take a close look because most people thought it was impossible for him not to have a gray hair at his age.)

A White House photographer was standing by, and his camera flashed as each of us shook hands with the President and then with Mrs. Reagan. This is most likely standard procedure since almost everyone who meets the President of the United States wants a record of the occasion.

DH Joan remarked to me later that she didn't see any sign of Secret Service agents.

I told her, "Just because you can't see them doesn't mean they're not around. Don't try doing anything to the President or I'm sure they'll jump out of the woodwork."

Shooting the interview with one camera meant that for most of it, the Reagans were in a two-shot. Only rarely did I zoom into one of them, since I wanted to capture the reactions of each as the other was talking. Joan sat next to the camera asking the questions.

JK Even though the President hadn't checked the question about first meeting Jimmy Stewart, I decided to ask it anyway. He explained that under the old Hollywood studio system, actors met at publicity events and parties and, therefore, it was almost impossible to recall where or when he actually first met Jimmy.

However, Mrs. Reagan said, "*I* can tell you when I first met him." As a young teenager, she and her family were summer guests at the country home of actor, Walter Huston, whom she referred to as "Uncle Walter." One day, director Joshua Logan came to try to persuade Huston to star in the play, *Knickerbocker Holiday*. And Logan brought along his friend, Jimmy Stewart, who played the ukulele and sang "Judy." Nancy admitted that she was immediately smitten. "By the time he left, I had a terrible crush on him." Then, looking directly into the camera, she said: "Gloria, you understand, of course."

The President laughed and, when she had finished the story, he turned to her and said, "You wouldn't like to tell them how you tried to convince 'Uncle Walter' not to do *Knickerbocker Holiday*, would you?"

She smiled and gently reminded him, "This is for a program about Jimmy, dear."

That was the first hint that, with only the slightest encouragement, he was ready to launch off the subject. We, of course, were acutely aware that the clock was ticking on our allotment of twenty minutes. Otherwise, we would have been happy to hear whatever stories he wanted to tell.

DH We had found news footage of Stewart campaigning with Reagan when he was running for Governor of California. At the podium, Mr. Reagan told the audience that Stewart's military rank was "Major General," which he apparently repeated at every stop along the way. Joan asked him to tell us that story.

He said that the master of ceremonies would usually introduce Jimmy by talking only about his movie career. Then Stewart would introduce him, and he would remind the audience that Jimmy was also a war hero.

"I'd say, 'He's actually *Major General* Jimmy Stewart.' Then, on one occasion, the emcee *did* include his military career and introduced him as 'Brigadier General, James Stewart.' When it was my turn to speak, I said, 'My apologies to the emcee, but it's *Major General* Jimmy Stewart.'

"Well, later that evening, Jimmy caught up with me and said, 'R-r-r-Ron, that fella up there t-t-t-tonight was right. It is *Brigadier General*. I just never corrected you because it sounded so good.'" The President did a terrific imitation of Stewart's famous hesitations and obviously relished the chance to perform. The actor in him was still very close to the surface.

He also still wanted to believe that Stewart had been promoted. As an afterthought, he said, "And now, I think Jimmy *is* a Major General in the Reserves." He wasn't. And he was no longer in the Reserves either. In 1968, when he reached the mandatory retirement age of sixty, Brigadier General James Stewart retired from the Air Force Reserves, having served in the military for a total of twenty-seven years. Fortunately, Joan thought it would be impolitic to point out to the Commander-in-Chief that he was not only wrong again about Stewart's rank, but also didn't seem to know that he had retired from the Reserves over eighteen years ago.

JK I knew it was definitely time to move on to the next question. I said, "Mr. President, we've read about your reaction to Mr. Stewart's appearance at your first pre-inaugural gala in January, 1981."

He nodded and said, "Nancy and I were sitting in the box seats with family and friends. Jimmy came out on stage wearing his full dress military uniform and, at the end of his comments, he saluted me. Then I, of course, stood up and returned the salute. And yes, it's true. That was the moment when it came home to me that I actually had this job."

The interview was going well so far. But then I had a question that had been suggested by Gloria Stewart. A few weeks earlier, I had asked her if she knew of any unusual stories about the friendship between her husband and the Reagans. She said, "Ask about the engraved western belt Ronnie gave Jimmy."

Now, even though I'd done many interviews over the years, I broke a cardinal rule: never ask a question unless you have at least some idea of what the answer will be. I should have asked Gloria to tell me the story. Unfortunately, I didn't.

So I dove in. "Mr. President, I understand that you gave Mr. Stewart an engraved western belt. What was the occasion?"

He began: "There were two women who had promised their mother that they'd take care of their mentally-challenged brother. He was a grown man, but he was like a little boy. He had a teddy bear and loved sitting with it in a rocking chair."

Even at that point, I was getting nervous about his story. But I had no choice. I had to let him go on.

He explained that while he was Governor of California, the agency that provided financial support to the disabled had notified the two sisters that the subsidy checks for their brother were about to be discontinued. The sisters had written letters to various departments within the state government, begging for help, but were getting no results, and time was running out.

"Finally, they wrote directly to me," he said. "And I'd always told my staff that if a letter came in describing a problem that couldn't be solved through the usual channels, I wanted to know about it. So I read their letter and immediately assigned one of my aides to see what could be done."

DH By then it felt as though the story had already gone on for an eternity. Mrs. Reagan, aware that she was on camera, sat quietly staring into space, every now and then looking at her husband, perhaps trying to give him a signal to tie up the loose ends.

Since I was behind Joan, I couldn't see her face, but I could sense her tension. I knew she was as concerned as I was that the President was using up what was left of our time, talking about something that seemed to have nothing to do with the question she had asked.

JK I remember sitting there with a frozen smile, trying to maintain eye contact and enthusiasm, since I couldn't bring myself to say, "Excuse me, Mr. President, but what does all this have to do with Jimmy Stewart?"

And so he continued. It turned out that the problem had been caused by a bureaucratic snafu and, when he sent word to the sisters that it had finally been corrected, he also sent one of his own rocking chairs as a gift for their brother—hand-delivered by a highway patrolman.

In some perverse way, I was now fascinated by how he planned to end this tale.

He said the family was so grateful for his intervention—and the rocking chair—that they sent him a beautiful engraved western belt. "The engraving work was some of the best I'd ever seen."

After writing to thank them for it, he received another, just as beautiful as the first. "Well, it got to the point where I couldn't use any more belts myself, so I asked if I could *buy* one for a friend. And that's the one I gave to Jimmy Stewart."

I finally felt my stomach muscles relax and breathed a sigh of relief that he'd actually connected the dots. But I already knew that this story would never make it into our show. Indeed, it remained on the cutting room floor, and I still kick myself for not asking Gloria for the details when she suggested it.

DH The interview went on for longer than twenty minutes, much to Elizabeth Board's dismay. But there was nothing I could do about it. The President just kept talking, telling us that because of his current position, his favorite Stewart movie was *Mr. Smith Goes to Washington*.

When it was finally over, I asked each of them to do cut-aways for editing purposes: close-ups of them looking at each other, nodding, and then turning back to look at Joan. The President seemed a bit hard of hearing at one point, so Nancy said, "Look at me, dear." He laughed and said, "All right."

Even after the camera was turned off, they continued to talk about Jimmy and their days in Hollywood together. They were certainly friendly and charming. It was as if they had nothing else on their minds that Monday afternoon.

JK As David and I were on our way out, I stopped in the ladies room and noticed that the paper towels were embossed in gold with the presidential seal. So I took a dozen of them, put them in my purse and gave them as souvenirs to our staff in New York. I did wonder if I'd be searched and accused of stealing, but, as with Frank Sinatra's paper towels, I assumed that if they're available for people to use and throw away, I was probably safe in taking them.

Two weeks later, our official White House mementos arrived—an envelope containing the photos taken of each of us with the Reagans.

JK and DH It was only a few days after we returned to New York that the Iran-Contra scandal broke with full force. The papers were filled with the story, accusing Reagan of a cover-up. And we realized how lucky our timing was. Had our interview been scheduled any later, it would never have happened. By then the President had more important matters to deal with. It occurred to us that, based on our experience with Fred Ryan's mistake about the *"late James Stewart,"* it's just possible that Ronald Reagan never knew how the Iran-Contra situation spiraled into a debacle. His aides could have been "handling it" without him knowing what they were doing, just as Mr. Ryan had initially "handled" our request for an interview. Maybe that's too simplistic an analogy. We'll never know.

When the Reagans left the White House in January, 1989, we read that Fred Ryan was among only two top presidential aides who would remain on their staff and move back with them to California. He eventually became Chairman of the Board of Trustees of The Ronald Reagan Presidential Library and Foundation. And in 2014 he was named publisher of *The Washington Post*.

In the Stewarts' garden: David and Joan with Jimmy and Gloria Stewart.
Beverly Hills, CA, 1986. Authors' collection.

CHAPTER SIXTEEN

"Don't Mess With Him"

It was September, 1986, when we first met Jimmy and Gloria Stewart in person. They lived in a comfortable home on Roxbury Drive in Beverly Hills. It was modest by Hollywood standards, although they had bought the land next door so that they could have a larger garden. Many famous celebrities, including Lucille Ball, Peter Falk, Rosemary Clooney, and Ira Gershwin, had lived on that street, and so it was striking that almost none of the houses were surrounded by walls or gates. Most had security signs posted on the lawn, but other than that, they were completely exposed to anyone passing by.

When we arrived in mid-afternoon, Gloria was waiting for us in the living room, which was furnished with chairs and sofas upholstered in brightly-colored prints. She was a strikingly handsome woman, and greeted us with a big smile.

"Jimmy will be down in just a moment," she said.

We told her how grateful we were for all her help, which she acknowledged only by smiling enigmatically. She told us she'd found some home movies, stills, and other memorabilia in the basement and would give them to us before we left that day.

DH We hadn't been talking for more than a few minutes when I heard someone coming down the stairs. Moments later James Stewart entered the room.

My first reaction was one of shock. He was tall, but that was hardly evident. The frail old man with wispy gray hair was somewhat bent over, looking tired and lacking in energy. He smiled and shook hands, but all I could think was that we had made a big mistake. We'd fought so hard to get to this point, and now I had grave doubts that this person could carry a ninety-minute special. A jumble of thoughts cascaded through my head as we discussed our ideas for the production. I was trying to come up with a "Plan B," but inspiration eluded me, since the concept for the program—and the one PBS had funded—was based entirely on Stewart telling his own story.

On the way back to the hotel I shared my worries with Joan. She was as concerned as I was, but she couldn't think of an alternative either.

The next time we saw him was only slightly more reassuring. He was dressed casually again, and was still pale, but this time he was wearing his toupée, which made him look younger. As before, he didn't have much energy, but was enthusiastic about the project. We left with a glimmer of hope and managed to convince ourselves that we should proceed as planned.

JK Our first day of filming was in the Stewarts' home that November. The makeup artist and hairdresser were already upstairs with them when we and the crew arrived. We'd decided that I'd interview Gloria first in the living room, then David would interview Jimmy in the library.

Gloria looked beautiful on camera, wearing a pale pink silk blouse, black slacks with a belt, a gold necklace and earrings. She wasn't at all self-conscious. Over the years she'd been interviewed many times, so the process was familiar to her. She spoke eloquently about their marriage, their children, and the impact her husband's

Gloria Stewart about to be interviewed by Joan Kramer.
Beverly Hills, CA, 1986. Authors' collection.

performances have had on audiences, including her. She told us
that even before she knew him, he was her favorite actor because he
could make her laugh and then cry within a single scene. She'd also
admired the innate honesty that came through in his performances.

They'd met at the home of Mr. and Mrs. Gary Cooper, who
had arranged for her to be Stewart's blind date that evening.

"Of course, it wasn't a blind date for me," she said. "But Jimmy
had no idea whom he was meeting. I remember that Ann Sothern
and Ronnie Reagan gave me a lift. There were six of us at dinner,
and we went to a nightclub where Nat King Cole was performing."

On their first few dates, he took her to play golf and then drove
her home. She recalled, "I think we golfed for two weeks before I
finally said, 'You know, I eat too!'"

After an eight-month courtship, they married in August, 1949.
He was forty-one; she was thirty-one. She already had two young
sons by her previous marriage, so Jimmy became a father and a
husband at the same time. Then, in 1951, the Stewarts had twin
daughters, Kelly and Judy.

I knew I had to ask her about her eldest son, Ron, a Marine in the Vietnam War, who was killed just days before his twenty-fifth birthday. Both she and Jimmy had supported the war, and she spoke straightforwardly about Ron's death, but in a way that spoke volumes about her loss and the irony of its timing. Later, John Strauss told me that after her son's death, Gloria no longer went to church with her husband. And when reporters asked Jimmy how he felt about his stepson's death, he replied, "It's a terrible loss. I think about him every day, and am proud of him. He died doing his duty for his country."

DH After Joan had finished her interview with Gloria, we took a short break while the crew re-set the lights and camera in the library for Jimmy. It was a room filled with books, family photos, and memorabilia from his career and the Stewarts' many trips to Africa. Moments later I heard him coming down the stairs.

When he entered the room I was in as much shock as the first time we met him. But now it was for the opposite reason. The frail old man had completely vanished. In his place was James Stewart, the movie star. He stood straight and tall and there was now a vigor to his step. A light, subtle makeup had removed the pallor from his face and, as always for public appearances, he was wearing his toupée. Dressed in slacks, with a white shirt, a black sweater vest, a muted black and red tie and one of his favorite checkered sport jackets, he looked ten years younger than he had two months before.

We shook hands and he maneuvered his way expertly around the lighting and sound equipment to get to the chair. Knowing that he was going in front of a camera had rejuvenated him. The interview lasted almost two hours, breaking only briefly to change tapes, and he clearly enjoyed telling stories about his career and the people with whom he'd worked.

Stewart was a real pro. He knew how to lace his stories with humor and self-deprecation. He said that he'd never forgotten the advice given to him by actor Ted Healy when they were working together in the 1936 film, *Speed*: "Never treat your audience as customers. Always treat them as partners."

"I've never stopped believing that's true," he told us.

We'd read that there was one topic he never talked about publicly: he felt that his experiences serving in WWII were too personal and that those memories should remain private. Yet, a profile of him would not be complete without covering that period of his life. I knew I had to ask him about it and I eased in by saying, "I know you enlisted in the service several months before America entered the war."

He shook his head and replied: "No, that's not correct. I was drafted."

I thought he'd made a mistake. When we paused to re-load the camera, I asked him if it were true that he'd been drafted because all our research said he'd voluntarily enlisted.

He said, "I know that's what the publicity department at the studio put out. They thought it was in keeping with my image. Well, it's wrong. I was drafted." He'd just debunked over forty years of a myth that had become so ingrained in the public's perception of him that even President Reagan said in his interview that Stewart had enlisted.

And several weeks later, when Johnny Carson received his narration script and came to the line: "*James Stewart was drafted*," he called and said, "I think this is wrong. He enlisted, didn't he?" We told him we'd always thought so, but Jimmy told us he'd been drafted. Johnny said, "Why don't you call and ask him one more time?"

Joan did, and he repeated, "I—was—drafted. It's the only lottery I ever won."

I then stepped into what I knew was dangerous territory: "Mr. Stewart, can you describe for me a typical day when you were the lead pilot in a bombing mission?"

He looked directly at me without smiling and said, "No."

That was it. No explanation. Just one word: "No."

David Heeley interviewing Jimmy Stewart.
Beverly Hills, CA, 1986. Authors' collection.

JK The firmness with which he refused to answer that question was not surprising. In doing research, I talked to many people who knew him. One was producer/director Hal Kanter, who'd worked with him on the 1971 television series, *The Jimmy Stewart Show*. Everyone with whom I'd spoken before told me what I'd expected to hear: he was a very good actor, thoroughly professional, well-educated, and a perfect gentleman. Nobody had a negative word to say about him. I wasn't looking for negatives, but I did want a full picture of this man whose image was "aw shucks" and "just one of the folks." Were the image and the real person one and the same?

I asked Hal Kanter, "What was it like to work with him on a daily basis? Was he always as easygoing as he appears?"

"Yes, he's wonderful to work with, and yes, most of the time he's quiet and gentle," he said. "But don't fuck with him. He knows exactly what he's doing, has strong opinions, and can dig in his heels when he wants to. Remember, he's remained a staunch Republican in a town where most of his friends are Democrats. He's been a star in Hollywood, where divorce is rampant, but he's been married to the same woman for almost forty years, with never a breath of scandal. And most importantly, never forget that he served in World War II and was the lead pilot in over two dozen bombing missions. Something got him through that war; something made him choose to stay in the Air Force Reserves for years, finally retiring as a Brigadier General; something made him support the Vietnam War even though one of his stepsons was killed in it; something makes him stand by what he believes in no matter what. There's a toughness, a stick-to-your-guns kind of courage and strength underneath that genuine niceness. People sometimes think because he's that nice, he's easy to manipulate. Believe me, the best advice I can give you is don't mess with him. Don't ever try pulling the wool over his eyes and you'll get along fine."

DH At about 3:30, John Strauss whispered to me, "I think you should wrap it up soon. Jim's running out of steam." I didn't see any sign of it, but I trusted John's instincts.

The day had gone better than we'd dared to expect and we went back to our hotel happy and relieved. Jimmy Stewart was more than able to hold his own, and "Plan A" was now securely on track.

***

JK Once Johnny Carson confirmed that we were "stuck" with him, we knew he wouldn't back out. What we didn't know was that he was such a movie buff—and especially a Jimmy Stewart movie buff. We asked if he wanted any research materials or tapes of any films. He said, "I don't need anything. I was a fan of his from the time I was a teenager in Nebraska, and I've seen all his pictures."

DH We scheduled the shoot with Jimmy and Johnny together on the Universal backlot where Stewart had made many films, including

Harvey and several westerns. Another advantage of shooting there was that both he and Carson were good friends of the studio's Chairman, Lew R. Wasserman, who at one time had also been Jimmy's agent. It was undoubtedly as a result of their friendship that Universal had not only agreed to let us use the lot, but didn't charge us a dime in rental fees.

JK Then I got one of those calls from John Strauss.

"Joan, we have a problem. Jim doesn't want to shoot at Universal."

"Why? He thought it was a good idea a few weeks ago. What happened? It's all been arranged."

"I don't know. He just called and told me he doesn't want to shoot there. He wouldn't give me a reason."

By then John had become a trusted ally. So after delivering the "official" message from Stewart, he felt comfortable enough to share his personal opinion. "Jim can be stubborn once he makes up his mind about something. And my guess is that he thinks going to Universal will be an inconvenience for Johnny Carson."

"But I know that Johnny's more than happy to shoot there. He's always been crazy about movies, and about Stewart's in particular, so going to a studio backlot where Jimmy made some of his films will be a real kick for him. He certainly doesn't see it as an inconvenience. In fact, he told us to be sure to schedule it for a Monday because that's his day off from *The Tonight Show*."

John said, "Let me talk to Jim again. I'll get back to you."

A few hours later, he called. "Well, I was right. Jim says if you're sure it's okay with Johnny, then it's okay with him."

At 8 am on Monday, December 15th, 1986, two limousines drove onto the Universal backlot: one carrying Jimmy Stewart from his home in Beverly Hills, the other with Johnny Carson from Point Dume. We'd asked them both to bring additional wardrobe, and Jimmy also had his favorite cowboy hat, which he'd worn in almost every one of his westerns.

Not long after they arrived, Johnny came up to me and said,

"If Jim tells me one more time how nice it is of me to be doing this, I'm going to strangle him. Doesn't he know who he is?"

"No. He thinks *you* are the only star here today."

A few minutes later, Jimmy said to me, "Isn't it wonderful of John to be doing this?"

I smiled and said, "Yes, it sure is."

And a few minutes after that, I overheard Stewart thanking him again, which in turn led to Johnny telling me, "He's still at it, even though I've told him so many times how much fun this is for me. Maybe he doesn't believe me."

Johnny Carson, Jimmy Stewart, and David Heeley between takes. Universal City, CA, 1986. Authors' collection.

DH The weather was near perfect. After a chilly start, the sun burned off most of the clouds and it became comfortably crisp with just a slight overcast.

It was to be full day of shooting on one of the shortest days of the year. We knew that we'd lose the sun at about 4:30 and, since all our shots were exteriors, there was no time to waste. The Universal backlot spreads over many acres, so we were lucky that the locations we needed weren't too far apart. However, by documentary standards, our crew was enormous, with two cameras, a dolly, a crane, tracks to lay, a generator and a truck full of lighting equipment. Thus every move required a good deal of time and effort to break down, pack the trucks, and reassemble everything at the new site.

Although the crew was fast and efficient, our two stars always had time to kill between shots. Having made movies for so many years, Jimmy was used to sitting and waiting. But Johnny worked in a television studio with a permanent set, and so for him the waiting must have seemed interminable. He was used to taping what was essentially a live, unedited program for broadcast later the same night. Here he was putting himself in an unfamiliar situation, venturing outside his usual comfort zone. He wasn't used to multiple takes or being on location and, at the beginning of the day, I could sense that he wasn't completely at ease despite his calm demeanor. But he was a real pro, and I was impressed by how quickly he adapted once we were under way and the cameras were rolling.

Between set-ups, he sat in one of the director's chairs and often talked with us quietly about the upcoming scene. For example, he said, "I think we should take it in small pieces so Jim can concentrate on one story at a time. If we try to cover too much at once I think we may run into trouble." He was concerned about Stewart's stamina and wanted their conversation to feel as relaxed as possible.

Much of it was ad-libbed and unscripted, although based on topics and a general structure we had all decided upon earlier. However, there were a few scripted pieces we needed Johnny to do alone to camera. And since he was used to working from cue-cards, and preferred them to a teleprompter, we hired the same cue-card man who worked with him on *The Tonight Show*.

Jimmy sat nearby watching him and was very supportive.

"That's great, John," he'd say.

Johnny was clearly pleased and I could see that he'd settled into the routine and was indeed having a good time. Once or twice he blew his lines and said, "Bullshit. How did you like that one, Jim?" And there were other times when he wasn't pleased with his own performance. "I didn't like that. Let's do it again. Sorry. My fault." Then, when he did it to his satisfaction, as well as mine, I'd hear, "When are the Emmys? This is definitely Emmy material, isn't it?"

For one shot, I asked Stewart and Carson to walk down the western street while talking about the film, *The Cheyenne Social Club*. The camera was tracking alongside them on a dolly, and I'd drawn a line on the ground near the end of the camera's tracks to indicate where I needed them to stop walking. In the first take, Jimmy was only halfway through describing the plot of the movie when they reached the finish line. But, without the slightest hint in his voice or change in his facial expression, he continued, "So my friend and I go up from Texas to Cheyenne and then—uh—now we've come to the end of the road." His ad-lib was so natural that it caught Johnny off guard and, for a second or two, he just continued looking at Stewart, waiting for him to go on with his story. Then, realizing what had happened, he suddenly broke up.

"When Jim hits his mark," he said laughing, "that's it. It's over. Over and out."

Of course, the solution was to have them pause during the walk. Jimmy timed the next take perfectly, and that's the one we used in the show.

During another set-up, coming through the swinging doors of a saloon, Jimmy was carrying his old cowboy hat.

Johnny said, "That hat belongs in the Smithsonian."

Stewart replied, "I tried to give it to them, but they turned it down."

JK and DH The catered lunch was served outdoors at tables with red-checked tablecloths. Very simple food—chicken, potato salad, fresh vegetables, and brownies for dessert. Jimmy and Johnny stood in line at the buffet table along with us and the crew, and then sat across from each other on folding chairs. Both of them were rather

Jimmy shows Johnny the cowboy hat that he wore in over twenty westerns. Universal City, CA, 1986. Authors' collection.

quiet. They did talk about flying their own planes when they were younger, but the conversation was low-key. It seemed as though neither one wanted to encroach on the other's free time.

Most of the afternoon was spent on the "Colonial Street" section of the Universal lot, where *Desperate Housewives* would be shot some twenty years later. This is where the façade of the *Harvey* house still stands.

DH *Harvey* was one of Stewart's most popular films about an enormous rabbit who's invisible to everyone but Jimmy's character, Elwood P. Dowd. They were best friends, spoke to each other and went everywhere together, much to the embarrassment of the rest of the family.

We filmed a brief sequence in which Jimmy and Johnny come out of the front door of the house.

Johnny says, "You did promise you'd introduce me to Harvey."

Jimmy turns and says, "Harvey, come out here," looking up, since the rabbit is apparently taller than he is. "I want you to meet a very good friend of mine, Mr. Johnny Carson."

After greeting the invisible rabbit, Johnny ad-libbed, "Big mother, isn't he?" Unfortunately, by the old rules of what was

Jimmy Stewart and Joan Kramer in front of the *Harvey* House. Universal City, CA, 1986. Authors' collection.

considered proper language on television, that take was left on the cutting room floor.

Johnny asked how Jimmy's association with Harvey started. Stewart began to explain, but lost his train of thought and tried to cover with his usual "um"s and "uh"s as he made several attempts to get back on track: "It's a strange thing, uh, I've wanted to do, uh, when I first, uh." He eventually gave up and said, "Uh, I've just run out of talk." Without missing a beat, Johnny looked at me and said, "Do you want to cue Harvey?"

I had read that the author of the original story, Mary Chase, had considered making Harvey an imaginary canary, not a rabbit, and I thought it might be interesting to have Jimmy talk about that. The minute I suggested it he said, "No. That would be very bad. Talking about a canary would be too confusing and it would ruin the image of Harvey. Everyone knows that this particular friend of mine is a rabbit."

He said it nicely, but there was a determination in his voice that made me realize immediately that the decision was final. Just as he'd flatly refused to answer the question about the bombing missions he'd led during the war, here was another instance where we saw him stand his ground over something he didn't want to discuss.

JK He was obviously a complex character, which is probably part of the reason he was able to be so believable in such a wide variety of roles. And he aged well on the screen, playing parts that were appropriate for him as he matured. I remember the film scholar, Jeanine Basinger, telling me on the phone, "I think there are four main directors who shaped Stewart's career, and each of them used his image in a different way. In Frank Capra's pictures, Jimmy was the small-town, all-American who faces problems and stands up for what he believes. Then he did all those westerns with director, Anthony Mann, who took the Stewart image and made him a quintessential cowboy, always on the right side of the law. Alfred Hitchcock took the 'every man' in Stewart and put him in impossible, suspenseful situations. And John Ford made him a cowboy again, but this time he was not always the good guy."

DH In one of the last shots of the day, Johnny asked Jimmy how he'd like to be remembered. Stewart said he hoped it would be as "a guy who believed in hard work and decent values, love of country, love of family, love of community, and love of God."

Johnny said, "Well, I think you embody all of those things. And thank you for your wonderful life from all of us." And they shook hands.

I said, "Cut. That was terrific. But I need another take because an airplane flew over while you were talking."

Johnny said to me quietly, "Oh. How can you ask him to do it again? It came out so pretty the way he said it. And I don't think you're ever going to get the same feeling a second time. Can't you live with the sound of the plane?"

Stewart had obviously overheard some of this conversation and said to me, "Just put music over it so it'll drown out the plane."

I thought for a few seconds and then agreed not to insist on a second take. I knew that Jimmy could have repeated his performance, but realized that it was Johnny who didn't want to do it again. He'd been genuinely moved by Stewart's answer and would have felt awkward trying to re-create his own emotional response.

Thinking back on that day, I remember a conversation with Carson in his dressing trailer when he told me that over the years, he'd received offers to star in feature films. He said, "I always turn them down. I know what I do best, and if I tried acting in movies, the critics would just be waiting to attack me. And they'd be right." Years before, he had appeared in a few not very memorable pictures and even in some episodes of television series, but mostly in cameo roles in which he played himself. I thought it was interesting that this star, who obviously had an ego, knew how to keep it in check. He had a clear understanding of his weaknesses as well as his strengths, and was sensible enough not to venture into areas where he knew he was likely to fail.

We finished the last shot just as the sun was going down. But Joan and I had a tradition to keep. We always had a "graduation picture" taken at the end of a major shoot, so we asked the crew and our staff to gather around Jimmy and Johnny in front of the *Harvey* house. We sent a copy of the photo to Stewart, Carson, and every member of the crew.

Nice memories.

The end of the day.
Universal City, CA, 1986. Authors' collection.

Johnny Carson on the Lorimar (former MGM) lot. Note the cue-cards on the left.
Culver City, CA, 1987. Authors' collection.

CHAPTER SEVENTEEN

"I Can't Work Without The Bells"

A month or so after shooting at Universal, we were back in LA to film Johnny doing some scripted links and recording the narration.

We'd planned to leave New York on a Friday, meet him at his home on Saturday to go over the final script, do the narration on Sunday morning, and shoot with him on Monday, his usual day off from *The Tonight Show*. However, that Friday morning we could hardly see out of our windows. During the night, New York had been hit by a powerful Nor'easter, which resulted in cancelled flights at all three airports.

JK I called Johnny.

"You're snowed in, aren't you?" he said. "That's why I moved to California." I told him that now we'd be leaving New York early on Saturday and would get to Los Angeles in time to come to his house in the afternoon and go over the script together. He said he was comfortable with the way it was written, so it wasn't necessary to meet; he'd see us on Sunday at the recording studio. He also reminded me to bring along the photos from the shoot at Universal;

he was eager to see how they'd turned out.

As luck would have it, a stomach bug hit me late in the afternoon on Friday and kept me up most of the night. The next morning, I tried to convince myself that I was well enough to travel, but soon realized I couldn't spend five hours on an airplane. David left as planned, but I went back to bed and made a reservation to leave early the next day. With the three hour time difference, I'd arrive at LAX early enough to get to the narration session.

My alarm went off before sunrise on Sunday morning, and I was on the first flight out of New York. We landed on time and I took a taxi straight to the recording facility, where the receptionist directed me to Studio B. But when I opened the door, the room was strangely quiet and empty. Finally I found a sound engineer in the control room.

"Isn't this where Johnny Carson is supposed to be recording narration for a show about Jimmy Stewart?" I asked.

"It's over," he said. "They all left about twenty minutes ago. Johnny's on his way home and I assume you're the Joan that David went to pick up at the airport."

This was before cell phones, so I had no means of contacting him. My only choice was to take another taxi to the hotel and wait there.

DH I couldn't find Joan at LAX, which made me wonder if she was still too sick to travel. So I drove back to the hotel and discovered that she had already checked in.

Her first question was: "How did you get through the narration so quickly? There were over a hundred different pieces to record."

"He was so fast I couldn't believe it," I said. "When I told him we had eight hours booked, he said, 'You've got to be joking!' He did the entire script in just over ninety minutes. He's so used to live television, he just knows how to get it right the first time. There were very few sections I could ask him to do again. It was over so quickly it almost makes me nervous; I hope we didn't miss anything."

David and Johnny.
Culver City, CA, 1987. Authors' collection.

JK and DH We'd arranged for the next day's shoot to be at MGM in Culver City, where Jimmy Stewart had spent most of his early career as a contract player. The lot had been bought by Lorimar, but most of it was exactly the same as when MGM owned it. The studio assigned Johnny one of the old star dressing rooms, and we asked him to be there at 8 am.

We knew that he had once had a reputation for being temperamental and difficult. In his younger days he liked to drink and, by his own admission, liquor brought out his worst side. However, when we'd met him at his home and then on the day with Jimmy

Stewart at Universal, he was always pleasant, at times funny, at others shy and quiet, but never difficult.

This shoot at Lorimar would be different. He'd be alone with us—no Stewart this time—and it occurred to us that we might find a very different Johnny Carson, one not so easy to work with.

JK I always believed that our associate producer/production manager, Cindy Mitchell, should some day be a florist. She loves flowers and knows exactly what to order so that they fit the personality of the recipient. She'd found a highly recommended Beverly Hills florist and ordered an arrangement for Johnny to be delivered to the studio at 7:30 am.

"Make it big, beautiful, masculine, and one color."

The tall, all-white arrangement was exquisite; we put it in his dressing room.

When Carson arrived on the lot a half-hour later, we all shook hands and Cindy took him to his dressing room. A few minutes later his makeup artist came out looking for me.

"Johnny would like to see you," he said.

I thought, "Uh-oh. Something's wrong. Maybe he's changed his mind about the script. Here it comes—the other side of Johnny Carson." I would have preferred not to go alone, but David was busy setting up with the crew, so I knew I had deal with this myself.

The door was open and he was sitting in a chair studying his lines.

"Good morning, Johnny. Is everything okay? Do you need anything?"

"Oh," he said, "I just wanted to thank you for the flowers. They're beautiful. Would you mind if I took them home to Alex?" (Alexis Maas was then his fiancée, soon to be his wife.)

"The flowers are yours. Of course you should take them home. I'm so happy you like them."

Then, knowing the crew wasn't quite ready, I took out of my tote bag the envelope containing pictures from the shoot at Universal, gave him some to keep and asked if he'd autograph the others.

He said, "Sure, but what kind of pen do you have?" I only had a black ballpoint.

"That'll damage the photos," he said. "We need a felt tip. Leave them with me and I'll send them back to you in New York." I looked at him without saying anything, but he read my mind. "You don't believe you'll ever see them again, do you?"

I said, "If I don't give our staff signed pictures of you, I'll get lynched."

He smiled. "I promise. In fact, I'll send them by FedEx." I had no choice but to leave the envelope with him—reluctantly.

DH He was as professional and easy to work with as he'd been before. Of course, there were a few snags.

Usually, when you film on a studio lot, it's necessary to hire Teamsters to drive talent and equipment on and off the property. Most are union shops, and productions working there must play by the union rules. However, we were a small crew making a public television documentary, so the Lorimar studio manager had told us that we didn't need to use Teamsters. We drove ourselves onto the lot; our crew drove themselves; and Johnny arrived in a limousine we'd provided.

JK I'd just returned from the dressing room when I felt someone tapping me on the shoulder. I turned around to find a large, burly man with a deep frown on his face.

"I'm the Teamsters' rep here," he said. "I just saw Johnny Carson get out of a car. Is he working with you? Why wasn't he driven onto the lot by a Teamster?"

Cindy had noticed what was happening and had already gone to find the studio manager. And I knew that if you're going to choose a union to get in trouble with, you don't choose the Teamsters. So I smiled my sweetest smile, put out my hand to shake his, and decided I had to try to keep talking until Cindy came back.

"It's nice to meet you," I said. "We're doing a documentary for

PBS about Jimmy Stewart, and Johnny Carson agreed to host it; of course he's only being paid scale. You see that man over there? He's our director, and he has a wonderful expression: 'My knees hurt from working in public television.' You know how we're always begging for money. By the way, how about a donut? And we have coffee to go with it." The frown softened. He followed me to the craft services table and helped himself. Then, with barely a "goodbye," he left to go and deal with some other production. By the time Cindy and the studio manager arrived on the scene, the Teamsters' rep was nowhere in sight.

DH One of the other problems was people traffic. We were shooting outside a soundstage where the television series, *Dallas,* was filming. People were constantly walking in and out of the stage door and, every time we were about to begin a take, someone would appear in the background of our shot.

At one point, Linda Gray, who played Sue Ellen Ewing on the series, came out and was surprised to see Johnny.

"What are you doing here?" she asked.

"Well, PBS doesn't pay much. But two hundred bucks here, two hundred there. Every little bit helps."

Johnny with Linda Gray outside the *Dallas* soundstage. Culver City, CA, 1987. Authors' collection.

In the meantime, Cindy found the *Dallas* production manager and asked a favor. She explained that we only needed about twenty minutes to get our shot, and wondered if the *Dallas* cast and crew could take an early lunch break so that we could do what we had to and get out of their hair. To be perfectly honest, they were the ones in *our* hair, but we could hardly complain after we'd decided to shoot right in front of their stage. Besides, they were a big, expensive production and a steady client on the Lorimar lot; we were very small potatoes in comparison. But within a few minutes, they all disappeared. We got our shot and moved on. Somehow production managers understand each other.

Soon we found ourselves with another issue. During several of our scenes, we were hearing church bells ringing in the distance. We'd wait for them to stop, but as soon as the camera was rolling, they'd start to ring again. At last, during a brief period of silence, we were able to shoot a take without interruption. However, Johnny blew his lines.

"Sorry. Let's do that again," he said. "I can't work without the bells."

JK At the end of the day, we took the floral arrangement from his dressing room and put it on the floor of the limousine. It was so tall that the flowers reached the roof of the inside of the car. He made it a point to show me that he had the envelope of photos I'd given him. We all said our "goodbye"s and "thank you"s, and he drove off to his home at Point Dume. The trip would take about forty-five minutes.

Back at our hotel, Cindy called the florist.

"I want to tell you what a wonderful job you did. Whenever I order flowers by phone, I never know what's going to show up. But your arrangement was perfect. In fact, Mr. Carson liked it so much he took it home to his fiancée."

"Miss Mitchell, thank you so much for calling," he said. "But Mr. Carson beat you to it. He just called us from his car."

I waited another half-hour and called Johnny at home.

"Is everything all right?" he asked when he heard my voice. "Did you get everything you need? If not, I can come back."

"Everything is fine. I'm calling for another reason. You just taught me a life lesson."

"What did I teach you?"

"Do you always call florists?" I asked him.

"How do you know I called the florist?"

"Because we just did to thank him, and he said you'd beaten us to it."

He said, "I've been calling florists for years. I know a lot of people call only when the flowers are lousy. I've always believed that they deserve to hear when the flowers are wonderful."

We flew back to New York the following day, Tuesday. I was still at home on Wednesday morning when FedEx delivered a manila envelope, addressed by hand with a black felt tip pen. Inside were the photos, each autographed by Johnny as promised. I still have the envelope. And the picture inscribed to me is framed and hanging on my wall.

David and I had been worried about dealing with the "real" Johnny Carson. We needn't have been. Throughout our association with him, he was a class act. On screen and off.

Joan, Johnny, and David after the final shot at Lorimar.
Culver City, CA, 1987. Authors' collection.

Johnny and Jimmy.
Universal City, CA, 1986. Authors' collection.

CHAPTER EIGHTEEN

"Stay in Touch"

A few weeks before the PBS broadcast of *James Stewart: A Wonderful Life*, we flew to California to hold a special screening of the program for Jimmy, Gloria, Johnny and his fiancée, Alex Maas, who brought along her father. We also invited John Strauss, David Tebet, and Herman Citron.

We rented a screening room and ordered a catered breakfast of fruit, muffins, coffee, etc. When everyone had arrived, we noticed that Johnny chose to sit in the back, away from the others, drinking cup after cup of coffee. Apart from us, he was the most nervous person in the room. Somehow it wasn't unexpected; he was accustomed to getting immediate reactions from his live studio audiences, but here he'd had to wait six weeks after we shot his on-camera sequences and recorded his narration to see how it all turned out. Mainly, we think, he was concerned about whether he had served Jimmy Stewart well.

He had his answer the moment the show ended. Of course, the people in the room were predisposed to like the program, but they seemed genuinely happy with it. Jimmy and Gloria thanked and congratulated Johnny, and Gloria confessed that she had been moved to tears several times. Jimmy told us how pleased he was and that we'd saved him from ever having to write his autobiography.

"You've done it for me," he said. We were most gratified by that remark since the issue of his writing a book had almost sunk the project before it had begun. Herman Citron was standing close enough to have heard that comment, but we weren't paying attention to him at the moment.

Hearing their positive reactions was a great relief. It's nerve-wracking to show a finished program to those involved in it, and risky if it's before the first broadcast. People could have all sorts of last-minute regrets: "Maybe I should have worn a different color." "My hair doesn't look quite right." "Did I give my best reading of that line?" "Since the show hasn't aired yet, can we re-shoot that scene?"

Screening for a group lessens the risk, and there's a built-in atmosphere of celebration. For us, it's a moment of truth. During the months of production, we've had to walk a fine line, developing and nurturing relationships with the participants, while trying not to let those relationships affect our editorial decisions.

Johnny stayed until the others had left and told us how proud he was to be part of the show. However, he asked us to check a line in his narration because he thought he'd given the wrong date for one of Stewart's films. We did check it and called him later to assure him that the date was correct.

JK   The premiere of the program was scheduled for Friday, March 13th, 1987. Our publicist had distributed press materials to newspaper and magazine reviewers across the country, and had sent excerpts from the program to various television shows including, of course, *The Tonight Show*. I decided to call one of the producers there to confirm that he'd received the package. He said, "Oh, yes. We have it, but we never publicize shows that will appear on other networks."

So I called Johnny, and we had a very nice chat.

On Tuesday, March 10th, James Stewart was a guest on *The Tonight Show*. When Johnny introduced him, he said that hosting the profile was the best time he'd had in all his years in television. They talked about Jimmy's films, showed clips from the program, and Johnny made a point of repeating the title and its airdate. In all, he and Stewart did what amounted to a forty-minute promo. It was very rewarding for us, and I called Johnny the next morning to thank him. He said, "If I can, I'll mention it again over the next few nights. My sister has already seen it and thought it was terrific. But of course, she's my sister, so she had to say that!" (The PBS station in the city where his sister lived had decided to air the program several days before its nationwide broadcast.)

The show received excellent reviews and became the highest-rated program in the *Great Performances* series to date. Jimmy wrote to us several times, expressing his appreciation and telling us that he was still receiving letters from people all over the country.

A few months later, the program was nominated for an Emmy Award. When a subject's name is part of the title of a documentary special, that person is an automatic nominee along with the producers. So we all received nomination certificates from the Academy of Television Arts and Sciences and, if the show had won—which it didn't—Stewart, David, and I would each have received an Emmy statue. We'd wanted to enter Johnny separately for a nomination as host, but he asked us not to. He said, "I don't think it's appropriate. It's Jimmy's show."

DH When we were in LA to attend the Emmy ceremony, Jimmy and Gloria invited us to their home for a "good-luck drink" the evening before.

Stewart said, "You managed to cover a lot of ground when we shot at Universal. How did you do all those different set-ups in just one day?"

I replied, "We had a great crew. And the talent wasn't bad either."

Gloria and I began talking about nature preservation, since she was deeply devoted to that cause and knew that I was the executive producer of the *Nature* series. The conversation included a discussion of reptiles, and I said I hoped to commission a program about snakes because so many people have a fear of them. Gloria said, "I think they are fascinating creatures and, as a matter of fact, I would have liked to have had a python as a pet."

Jimmy looked at her without any expression on his face, and then said to us, "Now, you know I've been married a good long time." And with perfect timing, he slowly turned to her again. "What do you *mean* you would have liked to have had a python in this house? You never told me that."

"I never told you because I knew you wouldn't want one," she said. "But I think it would've been great."

"I'm still learning things about her I didn't know," he said to us. Then he turned back to Gloria. "I wonder what else you haven't told me."

"Probably quite a lot," she replied.

He said, "We've had several unusual pets over the years, although never a snake. One of them came home with us after a trip to Africa with our twins."

The girls were about twelve at the time and they'd fallen in love with a small bushbaby. They pleaded to keep it as a pet.

Jimmy explained, "Well, you know there are rules about bringing live animals into the United States, and the girls didn't want to wait until the bushbaby went through a quarantine process. So I snuck it onto the plane under my shirt and jacket. Since we were sitting in first class, I thought once we were in our seats, no one would notice. Well, during the flight, I fell asleep and when I woke up I realized the bushbaby wasn't under my shirt. The lights in the cabin were off, so I got down on my hands and knees and crawled around, feeling under other people's feet, trying not to wake anyone up, but desperate to find that animal. I finally did, stuffed it back under my shirt and we made it through Customs without any problems. It lived with us in this house for many years until it died."

Gloria listened quietly as he told the story. She then said, "Are you finished now?"

"Yes, why?"

"I want you to know that not one word, not a single word of that story is true," she said to us. "Except that we did have a bushbaby. But it was sent home from Africa according to all the rules, was quarantined and tested, and then we picked it up and brought it home. Jimmy did not sneak that animal onto the plane."

"I certainly did. Don't you remember me crawling around on all fours looking for it? Or maybe you were asleep."

We're still not sure who was telling the truth. We do know that Stewart was quite capable of creating tall tales. And it may also have been part of his and Gloria's normal banter for him to tell a fable so that she could challenge it.

John Strauss and Jimmy Stewart.
Universal City, CA, 1986. Authors' collection.

JK John Strauss called me about a week later.

"Joan, you won't believe what a day I've had with Jim. It would have made a great movie."

I was immediately intrigued. "What happened?" I asked.

He explained that he'd arranged for Stewart to be interviewed at 10:30 that morning by a woman who was writing an authorized biography of Cary Grant. John always came early and sat in on such interviews. However, he had car trouble, which delayed him. When he arrived at about 10:45 am, he noticed a young, blond, well-dressed man standing at the front door.

"Who are you?" John asked.

The man had a distinct Australian accent. "I'm here to see Jimmy Stewart."

John said, "He's doing an interview. You can't see him now."

At that moment, Jimmy opened the door. "Hello, John. Come on in." Then he looked at the young man and said, "I told you to come back at noon."

As the man was heading towards the sidewalk, John thought, "I never saw that guy before, but obviously Jim must know him." Then he and Stewart walked to the den where the author was waiting to continue her interview. She left about an hour later and, just as John was about to leave too, Gloria came in from the garden.

She said, "Would you mind sticking around a little longer?" Before he could ask, "Why?" the doorbell rang and she went to answer it. She brought the blond young man into the den and then went back outside. Jimmy said, "I'm sorry I couldn't talk to you before, but I had to do another interview first. Now, how can I help you, son? Sit down."

John thought, "What does he mean *another* interview? If this guy is here to interview Stewart, I certainly didn't set it up."

The man explained that he was from Melbourne, Australia, and it had been his life-long dream to come to Hollywood to meet his idol. He'd worked until he had enough money to afford the trip. Jimmy smiled. The story continued. "So six months ago, I came here and was lucky. I finally got to meet my idol—Muhammad Ali."

Jimmy looked quizzically at John, who said, "You're telling us that your idol was Muhammad Ali?"

"Oh yes. I've always admired him. When I got to LA, I asked a taxi driver if he knew where Ali lived. He didn't, but happened to know the address of his manager. When I explained that I'd come all the way from Australia to meet Ali, the manager took me to his house. Ali was wonderful. We hit it off right away and he invited me to stay in his guest house. So I was here for three months. When I got back to Australia, I met a reporter and told him about my experience. He wrote a whole article about it and I've brought it along to show you, Mr. Stewart."

He handed a large newspaper clipping to Jimmy, who put on his glasses and dutifully began reading it. When he'd finished, he looked up and said, "This is very interesting. So what do you want to talk to me about?"

The man said, "Well, after a while I wanted to come back to California to meet my other idol. So I saved money and here I am."

Again, Jimmy smiled. But John thought, "If we're lucky, this guy is going to ask for an autographed picture. But I wouldn't be surprised to hear him ask if he can stay upstairs in the guest room."

He was wrong on both counts. The man said, "You see, my other idol is Sylvester Stallone. And since you've lived in Hollywood for so long, Mr. Stewart, I thought you could introduce me to him."

Jimmy looked completely bewildered and replied, "I'm really sorry, son, but I've never met Sylvester Stallone. John, do you know him?"

By then, John was on his feet. He told the young man to follow him into the foyer and then said, "I don't know Sylvester Stallone, but here's the number of his publicist. Try calling him and maybe he can help you. Now it's time for you to leave."

But the man said, "Before I go, I must thank Mr. Stewart for seeing me."

John assured him it wasn't necessary. "I'll tell him how grateful you are," he said, as he closed the door.

Back in the den, Jimmy was still sitting in his chair. He said in his typical way, "He seemed like a nice fella. But, John, what do you think that was all about?"

Just then, Gloria walked into the room and asked, "Has he left yet?"

John said, "Yes. He's gone. Now will both of you please explain to me how that guy got into this house in the first place?"

Gloria spoke first. "I let him in. I knew an author was coming to interview Jimmy. When the bell rang about 10 o'clock, the house-keeper was upstairs, so I opened the door and naturally thought that man was the author. So I took him into the den. You see, I didn't know the author was a woman."

Jimmy continued, "John, I know you told me it was a woman, but I guess I forgot to mention that to Gloria. So when I came downstairs and saw that fella sitting here, I thought maybe the plans had changed. I asked him, 'Are you here to talk about Cary Grant?' And when he said, 'No,' I figured I must have forgotten about another interview I was supposed to do. I probably should have asked him what we were going to talk about, but I didn't want to insult him by admitting I didn't remember. So I just told him to come back at noon."

Gloria added, "And since I overheard Jimmy tell him to come back, I let him in again."

John tried hard to remain calm: "I know none of us is getting any younger, but in all the forty years that we've been working together, when have I ever forgotten to call you to re-confirm interviews? When I spoke to you yesterday, I didn't mention a second interview because there wasn't another one.

"Do you realize how lucky you are? That guy could have been an ax-murderer. Here you have security signs all around the house, and he just walked up to the door, rang the bell, and you let him in without ever asking who he was or why he was here. And not just once, but twice! I can't believe the nerve of that guy. I wonder how many other homes in Beverly Hills he tried to talk his way into before he came to yours. Now it wouldn't surprise me a bit if he winds up living in Sylvester Stallone's guest house for a couple of months."

After John left and was driving to his office, he began to see the humor in what had just happened. He thought, "Why was I so surprised? That's Jimmy, the only movie star I ever heard of who comes out of the house and waves to the fans on the tour buses."

By this time, I had tears rolling down my face from laughing. The situation was so ridiculous that it bordered on farce. But John was right. It could have been dangerous.

JK and DH Our relationship with John Strauss evolved from strictly business to a close friendship that also included his wife, Renee. Through the years, we spoke often by phone and whenever we were in Los Angeles, they invited us to their home for an afternoon by the pool, followed by a home-cooked meal. Renee always gave us roses and freshly picked limes from their garden to take back to our hotel.

During one of those visits, John showed us a scrapbook, which included an original drawing of Harvey by Jimmy Stewart. It was a close-up of the rabbit's head, with both ears up, one slightly bent. And he was wearing a big, striped bow tie. There were only a handful of these original sketches in existence because Jimmy only did them for a few charity auctions or for close friends. I said, "John, do you think he'd draw one for each of us?"

He said, "Let me work on it. It may take some time."

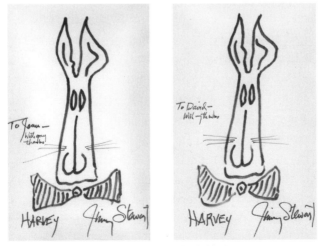

Harvey sketches for Joan Kramer and David Heeley.
1993. Authors' collection.

Several months later, I received an envelope. In it were two original Harvey sketches and each had two signatures at the bottom: Jimmy Stewart's and Harvey's. One was inscribed, *"To Joan, with my thanks,"* and the other, similarly inscribed to David.

Sadly, John died in 2001, but we and Renee are still close friends.

***

The Stewart profile had received an enormous amount of publicity and many national and international honors. When all the reviews had been gathered into a book, we sent Jimmy and Johnny copies. Johnny called when he received his and, needless to say, was very happy with the overwhelming positive response, not just to the show, but also to him as its host.

At the end of the conversation, he said, "Please stay in touch, and when you come out to LA, let's get together."

Not long after that, we indeed were going to be in LA and took him up on his suggestion. He invited us to a taping of *The Tonight Show* and arranged for a stage manager to take us to his dressing room. We talked for about ten or fifteen minutes and then walked with him to his car. Once again he said, "Let's stay in touch," and drove off with a wave. That turned out to be the last time that we saw him in person.

JK However, we did speak on the phone over the years, and he was always eager to chat. We know that "warm" is not a word that was often used to describe him, but he was certainly warm towards us.

In 1991, when we were producing a profile of Henry Fonda, I called Carson. Since Stewart and Fonda were such close friends, and since Johnny was a friend of Jimmy's, I thought perhaps he might have known Fonda too. He said he'd met him a few times and had him on his show, but didn't really know him. When our program was completed, we sent him an advance copy, asking that he not show it to anyone else. We received a hand-written note saying he's sure his *Tonight Show* audience will enjoy seeing clips from it before it airs. Then he added: "*Just kidding.*"

Occasionally, we asked him to host another profile. We hoped to produce one about Jack Benny and, because we knew how much Johnny admired him, we felt he was the perfect choice as host.

He called and said, "If Jack were still alive, I would have loved to do it. But I'm not comfortable being on camera without someone to talk to. That's why the one with Jimmy worked for me; we were able to have a conversation."

A few years later, we considered doing a show about Bob Hope, and another about George Burns and asked Johnny again. In each instance, he explained, "I don't feel about Bob Hope or George Burns the way I feel about Jimmy Stewart. But if you ever find a subject that I really care about as much as I do about Jim, I'd be happy to work with you again." Unfortunately, we never did.

He once told us, "I don't feel any need to leap in front of a camera just to be on television, because if I don't believe in a project from the beginning, it would show. I'd come off as insincere and, more than likely, I'd make a complete fool of myself." He paused for a moment and then continued, "I hope this won't sound unkind, but I'm not like Lucille Ball, who was brilliant when she was young and doing *I Love Lucy*. But as she got older, she kept trying to re-create the same character with the same kind of broad humor, and it didn't work. It wasn't funny any more. I don't ever want to fall into that kind of trap. Just because something worked years ago doesn't mean it will work again now. Timing is everything."

JK and DH When Johnny Carson announced his retirement in 1992, many of his favorite guests were invited to appear on *The Tonight Show* during his last few weeks as its host. We heard that Jimmy Stewart was among them, but that he turned down the offer. We believe we know why.

Not long before, we'd been told confidentially that Gloria was terminally ill with lung cancer. Jimmy had already become increasingly reclusive, likely as a result of her illness, and also because he believed he could no longer accept acting roles due to his hearing loss. He did wear a hearing aid, but still had a hard time understanding what people said to him unless they spoke very loudly. When it was suggested that he still could work and read his lines from cue-cards, he adamantly refused. If he couldn't react to other actors' dialogue in the usual way, he preferred not to work at all. He did make a few exceptions, including the interview he did for us in 1991 about his friend, Henry Fonda. But by 1992, he obviously felt he couldn't make any more personal appearances, not even with Johnny.

Gloria had been a heavy smoker all her life. Although she was ten years younger than Jimmy and looked in robust health when we last saw her in 1988, the cigarettes took their toll and she died of lung cancer in February, 1994, about three weeks before her seventy-sixth birthday. Jimmy was so distraught and depressed that he seldom left his bedroom, often even eating his meals there, and only rarely agreeing to let anyone come to visit him. Even his long-time friend and former agent, Lew R. Wasserman, told us he'd been calling regularly, but the housekeeper always said that Jimmy wasn't able to come to the phone and didn't want to see anyone.

With the exception of Stewart's children, John Strauss was the only person he *would* see. John felt it was important to keep up the routine they'd always had, in which he'd go to the house about once a month and tell Jimmy about the requests he'd received for personal appearances, and to give him his fan mail. John recalled that once, when he forgot to bring along the mail, Jim asked, "Don't you have any letters for me?" That's when he realized how much it meant for Stewart to know that people still took the time to write to him. And every so often, John could get him to sign some photos for fans who'd requested them.

On July 2nd, 1997, James Stewart died at the age of eighty-eight. It was a little over three years after Gloria's death, and he had lived a solitary and unhappy life since then. After so many years together, he just couldn't function without her by his side.

JK When we heard the news of his death, I knew I had to call Johnny. His housekeeper answered, and he came on the phone within a few seconds. I told him how sad David and I were, and at the same time, how lucky we felt to have had the chance to work with Stewart.

He said, "I feel exactly the same. He was one of a kind."

Then he said, "Over the past couple of years, I'd been calling him every few weeks, but he never would talk to me. His housekeeper always said, 'He's sleeping,' or 'He thanks you for calling, but can't come to the phone right now.'

"But two nights ago, *Destry Rides Again* was on television, and I watched it even though I'd seen it many times before. I always thought Jimmy and Marlene Dietrich were terrific in it. When it was over, I decided, 'What the hell, I'm going to try calling him.' As always, the housekeeper answered and asked me to hold on. I was astonished when the next voice I heard was Jimmy's. He said, 'J-J-John, how are you?'" (Johnny did a perfect imitation of Stewart.)

"I told him I'd just watched *Destry* on the tube and how wonderful I thought he was in it. He said, 'Yeah, that was a good one, wasn't it?'

"Since he seemed willing to talk, I said, 'Jim, I was thinking recently how much fun it was for me to do that profile of you. The day we shot at Universal was amazing. And people still talk to me about that program.'

"Jimmy said, 'I remember it too, John, and I'm still grateful to you for giving up your time to do it. We did have a good time, didn't we?'

"'We sure did, Jim. Hey, how about my coming over to see you one of these days, just for a few minutes?'

"'Sure, I'd really like that. Why don't we talk next week and we'll set a date?'

"'Great. I'll call you again at the beginning of the week.'

"After I'd asked how his children were, he thanked me for calling and we hung up. The conversation must've lasted for about ten minutes. I expected him to sound weak, and he did sound a little tired. But I was encouraged that he'd talked to me and agreed to see me. Although, I'm not sure he wasn't just being polite about my coming to visit. But he sounded like Jimmy, and I was so glad I'd decided to make that call.

"That was Monday night. Then this morning I heard the news that he'd died. It makes me wonder if he had a premonition that he wouldn't live much longer and that's why he came on the phone. Sort of a last goodbye. I don't know. Maybe I had the same premonition too. It's just such a coincidence that I hadn't been able to talk to him for years and then just happened to call two nights ago. I still can't believe we had that conversation and now, thirty-six hours later, he's gone."

Johnny and I spoke frequently over the next few years. The last time was just a few months before his own death. He told me that he was planning to sail to the East Coast on his boat and would call so we could meet for dinner. We don't know whether or not he actually made that trip, but we never heard from him again.

JK and DH When he died in January, 2005, both of us took it very hard. Jimmy Stewart's death hadn't been all that unexpected. But Johnny's came as a complete shock.

In the days that followed, as we read the newspaper obituaries and watched the television programs paying tribute to him, we realized what a unique experience it was for us to have worked with him. We knew it was special at the time, but sometimes when you're so busy, you don't think about just *how* special it is until much later. We genuinely liked him, and knew that the feeling was mutual. And we're very pleased that he really did want to "stay in touch."

He had said that Jimmy Stewart was "one of a kind." He was right. And so was Johnny Carson.

Authors' collection.

Bette Davis.
Photograph by Fabian Estivals/Sygma/Corbis.

CHAPTER NINETEEN

Tea and Daggers

DH It was in the late 1980s, probably around 1987, that Michael Black called. He'd been Fred Astaire's agent when Joan and I produced two programs about Astaire seven years earlier and, although we'd spoken occasionally with Michael since then, it was unusual for him to be calling us.

"I've recently acquired a new client," he said. "Not long ago I found a note slipped under my door. It said, 'I hear you're an agent. I need an agent. Will you represent me?' and it was signed 'Bette Davis.' It turns out she lives in my building."

He went on to explain that Davis had a collection of home movies and that she and her assistant/companion, Kathryn Sermak, were putting together a film using some of that footage. But he felt they needed some advice, and thought we might be able to help.

"What kind of help do you think they need? Do they want us to produce their film, or show doctor it, or what?"

"No, no. None of that," he said. "They just need some guidance and I thought that you and Joan were the people they should talk to. I'll give you some background. Kathryn Sermak had been Bette Davis's personal assistant, but after Bette was so hurt by her daughter's book *(My Mother's Keeper)*, she now thinks of Kathryn as her surrogate daughter and she trusts her completely. They've started making this film and I'd really appreciate it if you'd let Kathryn call you."

I couldn't find a good reason to say "No." But something told me this wasn't going to be easy. Reluctantly, I agreed.

She called the next day. It was a friendly voice and she thanked me for taking time to talk to her. She told me she had done an interview with "Miss D." and they were using that, together with Davis's home movies, to produce a profile of her. They had edited about fifteen minutes so far.

Not sure where the conversation was going, and wanting to encourage her to tell me more, I asked a simple question to start the ball rolling.

"Are you shooting film or tape?"

There was a silence, long enough to make me realize she didn't know.

"When you're with your editor, are you watching television monitors or splicing pieces of film?" I asked.

She said, "Oh, we're looking at it on television."

That gave me the answer (in the late 1980s it was rare to edit film using tape editing techniques, which were still relatively clumsy). I didn't push the issue any further.

"How can I help?"

"We have a lot more to do, but Michael suggested I talk to you before we go on. Miss D. and I are coming to New York next week, because she has a dental appointment. She's devoted to her dentist in New York and won't use anyone else. So while we're there, can you and your colleague, Joan, come for tea? How about 4 o'clock on Tuesday?" I agreed to the appointment and asked her to send a videocassette of what they'd already edited.

It arrived the next morning, and as soon as we had watched the first few seconds, both Joan and I realized we'd been handed a "hot potato." Our opinion was not going to be what they wanted to hear.

Kathryn, herself, was the on-camera interviewer. She looked beautiful, but clearly had no experience in this area and did not know how to phrase questions in a way that elicited stories; many of them already gave away the answers, leaving Davis with nothing much to say. There was also the problem caused by the stroke Bette Davis had suffered a few years earlier. She was obviously trying to hide the effect it had on her facial muscles by wearing a hat with a white net veil. Therefore, while we were hearing her speak, we couldn't really see her, which was disconcerting. On top of that, the structure of the veil interfered with the lines that make up the television picture, and the result was dizzying. And they had chosen to use very little home movie footage, which struck us as strange since both Michael and Kathryn had emphasized that this film would mark the first time that Davis was allowing any of it to be seen.

I called Michael immediately. "The film has a lot of problems and there's no easy fix. I can't imagine what we're going to say to them. Can you get us out of this?" He used his most persuasive tone, "They just need to hear from someone with experience. Please meet them and try to offer some suggestions."

JK We arrived at their suite in the Hotel Navarro on Central Park South at precisely 4 pm. Bette Davis opened the door herself. I knew she was short, but didn't expect her to be so thin. She was dressed in what looked like a Chanel suit. It was somewhat sad to see her in person now, because she'd suffered from a number of serious illnesses, which had taken their toll on her appearance.

David and I introduced ourselves and she invited us in. "I've ordered tea," she said, in what was still a strong, commanding voice.

Then she looked at me and said, "You look familiar. Where have I seen you before?"

I explained that I used to work for *The Dick Cavett Show,* and was involved in booking her for the interview in which Dick asked, "When did you lose your virginity?" She laughed and said that she'd never forget that appearance and that people still mention it to her.

The doorbell rang and a waiter arrived with a cart that had small sandwiches, cookies and a tea service.

As she was pouring tea for us, a door opened at the far end of the room and Kathryn Sermak entered. But she didn't just come into the room, she made an entrance worthy of a scene in a drama. I still remember what she wore: a black velvet gown with a diamond—or rhinestone—brooch at the bottom of the deep v-neck. The dress was almost floor length, with a very full skirt, one side of which she held out so that it flowed as she glided across the room towards the chair next to us. She was wearing high heels, which were also black velvet, with a sparkling brooch at the front of each. Her jewelry included a cascading diamond necklace that reached down into her cleavage, and matching chandelier earrings that were long enough to almost touch her shoulders. In the other hand, she held a cigarette in a long black onyx cigarette holder—one that would not have been out of place in a Bette Davis movie.

I later described the scene as reminiscent of the way Loretta Young, wearing a flowing gown, would make her entrance each week at the opening of her 1960s television series.

Kathryn sat down, took a puff of her cigarette, and said, "Hello, I'm Kathryn Sermak."

I just stared at her, not quite able to digest what I was seeing.

DH Bette Davis smiled at her and then turned to us, "I saw the piece you did on Spencer Tracy with Katie Hepburn and thought it was very good. But our film is different. And before you give us your reactions, let me say that I think Kathryn has done a remarkable job. Don't you agree?"

Suddenly all eyes were on me, including Joan's. My heart sank. I had to say something, but didn't quite have the nerve to burst Bette Davis's bubble of enthusiasm. So I used the old trick of avoiding the question by asking some.

"What are your plans for the film? How long do you want it to be and how do you think it should be distributed?"

It was Kathryn who replied. "We think it should be at least two hours. And we know you work for public television, so we thought the two of you could help us raise the money to finish it and get it onto PBS."

This was not at all what I had expected. My diversionary tactic had only caused us to fall deeper into a hole.

I tried to get out of it by explaining that WNET, like most public television stations, had a fundraising department and that we were not allowed to step on its toes. I'm not sure I sounded very convincing.

But then Joan came to the rescue. In fact, she plunged in head first.

JK David can vouch for the fact that it's not often I find myself speechless. But I was still somewhat stunned by Kathryn Sermak. I felt guilty leaving him "holding the bag," but I rationalized, "He's the only man in the room; they know he's a director; and he speaks with a British accent." But when I heard that they wanted us to become their fundraisers, I found my voice.

"Miss Davis, you mentioned the show we did with Katharine Hepburn about Spencer Tracy. I think you should know it took over three years to raise the money for that program, even though Hepburn was the host. The point here is that I don't think you, Kathryn, should be on camera asking questions. No one knows you. You could still ask the questions, but *off* camera and phrased in such a way that Miss Davis's answers make sense without the audience hearing the questions. It's a style commonly used in documentaries and it works well. It also saves program time.

Bette Davis interrupted, "But then it will look as though I'm talking to no one. And besides, I think Kathryn is very good. I know it won't take three years to raise the money for this show." The implication was as clear as her ego. She thought a profile of her was more saleable than Hepburn's about Spencer Tracy. She also believed that her own fame and clout would make everyone accept

Kathryn Sermak as the host.

Although my suggestion had gone over like a lead balloon, by then, I really didn't care; I knew we were in a no-win situation.

Suddenly I thought of another idea. I said, "How about a 'scrapbook' framework? It would allow the two of you to sit next to each other and talk about Miss Davis's life and career as you turn the pages and look at pictures. The camera would zoom in to some of the images, and as they filled the screen, they'd come alive as film clips and stills."

"I don't like that at all," said Davis. "It's contrived."

DH She put down her cup of tea, went to the door of the suite, opened it and said, "Thank you for coming."

It wasn't subtle. Bette Davis was throwing us out.

All I could think of was her performance in *The Private Lives of Elizabeth and Essex*, except that she didn't slap our faces as she did Errol Flynn's. Our audience with her had lasted all of twenty-five minutes, which felt like two hours.

As soon as we were back in our office, I called Michael Black. "What's going on here? They clearly didn't want to hear the truth about their film, and we felt we were witnessing a real-life version of *All About Eve*. Kathryn seemingly wants to be a star and Bette Davis obviously is trying to help her become one."

He said, "I'm sorry you had such a rough time, but I knew that they wouldn't listen to me. I'm just the agent."

JK and DH As far as we know, their film never was completed. But several years after Davis's death, TNT aired a documentary called *All About Bette*. As we watched it, we recognized some of the footage of her in that unforgettable hat and veil; the same we'd seen in the fifteen-minute cassette that Kathryn had sent us.

Bette Davis died in 1989. Her son and Kathryn Sermak were named co-executors of her estate.

Authors' collection.

David Heeley with Lauren Bacall on Warner Bros. lot.
Burbank, CA, 1987. Photograph by Mitzi Trumbo.

CHAPTER TWENTY

Bacall and Bogie

here had been programs made about Humphrey Bogart, but never one hosted by his widow, Lauren Bacall. They had married shortly after their first film together, *To Have and Have Not,* and became one of Hollywood's most famous couples, until his untimely death at the age of fifty-seven. We discussed the idea of a profile with Roger Mayer, head of Turner Entertainment Co.[1], which controlled the rights to many Warner Bros. films, including Bogart's most famous. Roger was enthusiastic and said he'd be willing to enter into a co-production deal with WNET, giving us free access to the clips and stills in exchange for Turner having the rights to distribute the program in other media outside the PBS broadcast window. PBS was on board too, agreeing to finance the show as a *Great Performances* special for a fundraising Pledge Week. Now all we needed was Bacall.

We wrote her a letter and, soon after, her agent, Hal Ross at

---

1   For many years, Roger had been an executive at MGM, before Ted Turner asked him to run TEC. In 2004, he was the recipient of the Jean Hersholt Humanitarian Academy Award.

William Morris in Los Angeles, called to say that she was interested. We asked him to set up an appointment for us to meet with her. When he didn't call back, we called again. He told us he was trying to sell the idea to other broadcasters and was waiting to hear from one of the major commercial networks.

We were appalled. Even in the cutthroat entertainment business, it did not seem very honorable to be shopping around our project to others. But we had an ace up our sleeve: Roger Mayer, one of the most above-board executives in Hollywood. Although Roger was a friend of Hal Ross, and might have been able to make more money from a commercial network deal, he stood by his verbal agreement with us, and told Ross that if anyone else tried to produce a program with Bacall about Bogart, they would not have access to any Warner Bros. film clips[2].

That was the end of that problem. But there would be others.

JK We eventually met Lauren Bacall in her agent's office in Beverly Hills (she lived in New York, but was in LA at the time), and took her to lunch at a restaurant nearby. We reminded her that we'd met before, when she did an interview for the show we'd produced about Katharine Hepburn in 1981. Bacall and Hepburn were close friends and she told us she'd seen our program about Spencer Tracy, which Katharine Hepburn hosted. She expressed surprise that Kate had done that show, since she'd never before agreed to talk about her relationship with Tracy. She was even more surprised when we told her that Hepburn had actually suggested the program herself.

It's just a guess, but in retrospect, we believe that Bacall's decision to work with us was based at least in part on Katharine Hepburn having trusted us to produce a program that was just as personal to her as this one about Bogart was to Bacall.

---

2   Warners made *The Maltese Falcon*, *Casablanca*, *To Have and Have Not*, and many more important Bogart movies.

DH She was forthcoming and pleasant and we came away liking her. But her reputation for being difficult was well known, so we were wary.

The next obstacle was her fee. It took a long time to come to terms with her agent's demands, but finally a deal was made. Getting a fully-executed contract was another matter. We had to push ahead with production in order to meet the PBS airdate. But we were always aware that we were on thin ice until the contract was signed.

The next time we met was in her apartment in the Dakota, on New York's Central Park West. She asked us to find a way for her eldest son, Steve Bogart, to work on the program. So we hired him as a consultant. Steve looked remarkably like his father, but didn't seem terribly interested in the project. He did loan us some photos, and was always available to talk. Having lived with the Bogart name—and indeed, legend—all his life, he admitted that only recently had he reached the point where he wanted to know more. (Years later, he would write a book about his father and then produce and host a television program based on it.)

Bacall told us that she had a collection of home movies in a storage facility and agreed to have it sent to us on the condition that we make copies for her, Steve, and her daughter, Leslie. It was valuable and unique footage, since she had accompanied Bogart to Africa for the making of *The African Queen,* and shot home movies there of Bogie, Hepburn, director John Huston, and a lot of crocodiles. The problem with it was that she was not a great cameraperson. Like many other novices, she used a film camera as though she were shooting stills. As soon as a subject was properly framed, she moved on to something else, so that almost none of shots lasted more than a couple of seconds. Fortunately, she occasionally gave her camera to someone else, possibly a crew member, so some of the footage was usable.

The Burbank Studios gave us permission to shoot Bacall on the Warner Bros. lot, where she and Bogart had worked for many years. She found it an emotional experience to be back at the place where her career started and where she met Bogie.

But now we found ourselves dealing with a difficult, demanding Lauren Bacall. And remember, we still didn't have a signed contract.

Although she had seen and approved the script beforehand, she wanted to change large chunks of it. So valuable time was spent in conferences in her dressing trailer, re-writing each piece right before shooting it. Then the new copy had to be put onto prompter, taking up even more time.

Lauren Bacall in Warner's Prop Department with the Maltese Falcon. Burbank, CA, 1987. Photograph by Mitzi Trumbo.

JK While the crew was setting up new shots, Bacall and I walked around the lot. In the hallways of the buildings are many original posters of Bogart's movies. She asked if she could have them. The studio manager explained that they were not allowed to remove them from the walls. The same thing happened in the prop department. She wanted one of the replicas of the Maltese Falcon, a request which also was denied. Then we went to wardrobe, where she asked if they had one of Bogart's famous raincoats. They didn't, but she said she'd like one if they ever found it.

She worked easily with the crew, but the air was filled with tension, and shooting went very slowly because of all the re-writing.

Back in New York, we had scheduled her for one more day on-camera and a day for narration. Then, out of the blue, I received a call from Hal Ross: "You're going to have to shoot and narrate Betty Bacall in London because she's been invited to attend a big event there and won't be in New York when you need her."

I reminded him that we'd worked out the schedule with her approval, and didn't have the time or money to travel to England.

"Well, you'll have to," he said. "She's leaving next week."

We knew we were in a bind. Even if we could afford to go to London and hire facilities there, the trip would make mincemeat of our already tight schedule. After discussing the situation with Jac Venza, our executive producer, we decided we had no choice other than to stand tough. I called Ross back and said, "Miss Bacall made a commitment to do this program on a schedule that was convenient for her. So now there are two choices. She can keep her commitment to us as planned, or she can go to London and we'll hire another person to narrate the program." It was a clear ultimatum.

There was a silence. Then he said, "I'll get back to you."

Half-an-hour later, my phone rang. "She's canceling her trip, but she's furious."

DH We knew that our next encounter with Lauren Bacall was going to be difficult.

She arrived for the shoot clearly angry. Her makeup artist, who had gone to her apartment to do her makeup, told us she'd been fuming all morning and was unpleasant and uncooperative. On set, she did what she had to do, but refused to talk to me or Joan. Most communication was via the lighting director.

In tribute to her professional skills, the footage looks fine. No one watching the program would guess that there was a frigid atmosphere throughout the day. At one point, between set-ups, her attention was diverted to our contracts administrator, Lynne Autman, who limped into the room with a broken leg in a cast. Bacall noticed the cast and began a friendly and sympathetic conversation with her. Lynne was a master at chatting with talent and getting contracts signed. She pulled it off again. Bacall signed without missing a beat.

The next day was the narration session. I went into the recording booth with her. Joan was outside in the control room, but could hear everything being said in the booth.

Bacall was still furious. She said, "How dare you do what you did? I was given nothing short of an ultimatum. Kamikaze tactics. You used kamikaze tactics to threaten me."

I tried to reason with her. "Miss Bacall, we had agreed to this schedule and we don't have the time or money to go to London."

"No, I never agreed to these dates. How dare you threaten me?"

I had had enough. I got up and started walking towards the door.

"Where do you think you're going?" she asked.

"I resent the way you're talking to me," I said. "I'm leaving."

JK I saw David walk out of the recording booth and followed him as he headed for the elevator. I said, "What are you doing? She'll leave."

He said, "She won't. Just leave her alone. She's accusing me of lying."

It takes a lot to make David angry, and this was the first—and last—time I saw him walk out on anyone.

As we got off the elevator, we bumped into Jac Venza, who knew we were working with Bacall that day.

"Have you finished already?" he asked.

"No, she's being very difficult. I just left her in the narration booth," David told him.

"What? Why?"

"It's a long story, Jac. I'll tell you later. Right now I have to look for a piece of paper."

Fortunately Jac trusted David enough not to ask any more questions, but he must have been concerned. David found the letter in which Bacall had agreed to the schedule, and a few minutes later was back downstairs.

DH Bacall had remained in the booth, reading the script. When I went in, she said, "Sometimes when I'm nervous and under stress, I don't always handle things very well. I'm sorry. Let's get on with it."

She was now co-operative, professional, and even funny from time to time. The session went extremely well and I never needed to refer to the letter.

JK and DH That stand-off was an even bigger turning point than we could have hoped for. We broke for lunch and the three of us ate together on paper plates with plastic forks. By then we were chatting amiably and once again we saw the Lauren Bacall we'd first met months before in California. She talked movingly about her life after Bogart's death, her children and grandchildren, and how she was struggling to stop smoking. And while we knew some of the stories from our research, hearing them directly from her made us realize that her reputation as "difficult" was the armor she used to protect herself from being disappointed, hurt, or taken advantage of by others. She was only thirty-two when Bogart died, leaving her a widow with their eight-year-old son, and four-year-old daughter. Then she was engaged to Frank Sinatra, only to be publicly humiliated by him when he ended their relationship abruptly. Several years later, she married Jason Robards, Jr., and had a son, Sam. But Robards was a heavy drinker then, and it took a toll on their marriage. By the time they were divorced, she was almost forty-five years old, and alone again—this time with *three* children. She even talked about her need to keep working. She said, "Everyone thinks I'm a rich widow and divorcée who is secure financially. It's not true. I've been on my own for a long time and I need to pay the rent like everyone else."

JK Bacall was in Europe when the show premiered nationally on PBS. But she had heard that it had received great reviews. She sent us a postcard, and signed it "*B. Bacall.*" That was the closest she came to using "Betty" with us—the name by which she's called by all her friends. And even though she hadn't seen the finished program, she agreed to help publicize it. She was interviewed by *The New York Times* for a Sunday feature article about David and me, and she appeared on *Good Morning America* by satellite from London.

When she was back in NY, we learned that *Bacall On Bogart* had been nominated for an Emmy. As host, she was also a nominee. We didn't win, but she told us she'd never before been nominated and was thrilled that it happened for this program.

She suggested we get together for lunch to celebrate. We took her to the Russian Tea Room, where she insisted on being given Table Number 1 at the front. That was the so-called "status" table, where the restaurant always seated well-known personalities.

We arrived just a few minutes after she did. As we entered, she was near the cloakroom not far from the door. When she saw us, she opened both arms wide, embracing David and me.

"You see, we made it," she said. "And no one killed anyone."

David said, "We came close."

JK and DH It was at that lunch that she asked us, "Who are you going to do next?" And before we could answer, she said, "I think you should do a profile of Bobby Kennedy. He was a friend of mine, and I think audiences would be fascinated by the man behind the politician. I remember being invited to his home in McLean, Virginia, not long after one of his children was born. I don't remember which one because he and Ethel had eleven altogether, but I asked to see the new baby and he took me upstairs to the nursery. The sun was pouring in through the curtains, the baby was beautiful, and it felt idyllic. I said quietly, 'What a life.' He looked at me somberly and said, 'Yes, but what a world.' I'll never forget that afternoon, how deeply he felt about his children's—and everyone else's—future, and how much he hoped to help make a difference in people's lives.

"I think you should seriously think about doing a profile of him and I'll help you in any way I can."

We did write a proposal, and sent it to the series, *American Experience*. But it never went any further.

Over the years, we had remained friendly with Lauren Bacall. For our 1993 program, *Katharine Hepburn: All About Me,* she again let us use her home movie footage shot in Africa. The old wounds were not deep and they had healed easily. And the more we got to know her, the more we liked her. It's just a shame we had to go through so much to get there.

Bacall on Bogart cast and crew.
Burbank, CA, 1987. Photograph by Mitzi Trumbo.

Joanne Woodward with Group Theatre members Eunice Stoddard and Ruth Nelson.
Cinematographer Rick Malkames at left and David Heeley on right.
Brookfield Center, CT, 1987. Photograph by Don Perdue.

CHAPTER TWENTY ONE

Joanne and The Group

I t is sometimes a shock to look back and realize the depth of ignorance we had before starting a project. The most striking example involves a program that took the longest to produce, was the most difficult and contentious, yet in the end was one of the most satisfying.

JK It began in February, 1982, with a phone call from Joanne Woodward.

"Did you see today's obituary for Lee Strasberg?" she asked me. "We're losing our theatrical heritage. I'm realizing there aren't many members of The Group Theatre left, and we have to capture their memories before it's too late. Let's make a documentary about it for PBS."

David and I both had some limited knowledge of theater history. I knew that Lee Strasberg was most celebrated for his teaching at The Actors Studio, where several generations of actors, among them Marilyn Monroe, Al Pacino, and Paul Newman, learned his technique called "The Method." Strasberg's method was revered by many, and scorned by others. Although controversial, he was without doubt one of the most influential forces in American theater. But I didn't know anything about his background.

"What's The Group Theatre?" I asked.

Joanne was horrified. "Are you telling me you don't know anything about The Group? It was the seminal force in the history of the American theater, and all of us who work in movies, television and on the stage are its descendants, because the original members of The Group went on to become some of the most important acting teachers and directors in this country. I studied from Sandy Meisner; Paul [Newman] studied from Lee Strasberg; Marlon Brando studied from Stella Adler; and Gadge [Elia Kazan] is still directing today. I'm sending you a book by messenger. It's *The Fervent Years* by Harold Clurman, and it tells the whole story of The Group Theatre. Harold was one of its three founding directors along with Strasberg and Cheryl Crawford, and now Cheryl is the only one of them still alive. Read it right away and give me a call."

The book arrived. I read it. David read it. We both had the same reaction. Clurman sounded like an egomaniac, and the members of The Group Theatre a bunch of 1930s radicals. I called Joanne.

"Who did Harold Clurman think he was? He was convincing working actors to give up their jobs in the middle of the Great Depression. That's irresponsible. And The Group sounds like some sort of commune—everyone living together, and hoping to create some newfangled form of theater. Clurman was just a play reader for the Theater Guild—a nobody, really. He comes across as a bit crazy and so do those who went along with him."

Joanne listened quietly to my outburst and then said, "Joan, you and I share a love of the ballet. By your way of thinking, George Balanchine would never have gotten the support of Lincoln Kirstein, and there would never have been a New York City Ballet. They wanted to revolutionize ballet in America just as the members of The Group wanted to revolutionize the American theater. They did it by putting on plays that reflected the times in which they were living, and by developing a new approach to acting. They were brave and dedicated pioneers and we really have to do this program. Talk to Jac."

DH Unlike us, Jac Venza knew plenty about The Group Theatre. "It's an interesting idea," he said. "But what is there to show? We can't just have talking heads. The Group only lasted ten years and I don't think any of their performances were ever filmed. There have been revivals of some of their plays, but not with the original casts. I don't see the elements for a program here."

That sounded like a definite "No" to me, but not to Joanne.

"When can I come over to talk to Jac?" she asked.

She presented her case to him with passion. "I'll become Barbara Walters," she said. "I'll interview everyone, and then we'll persuade famous Group descendants to re-create scenes from Group Theatre productions. I'll get Paul, Al Pacino, Dustin Hoffman, Ellen Bustyn. And we have to move fast before it's too late. We've already lost Lee Strasberg and Harold Clurman—and the rest of the original members still alive are in their eighties. When can we start?"

She's not an Oscar-winning actress for nothing, and by the time we all left Jac's office, she had a commitment to do the show. It was the beginning of a five-year saga. The project became her obsession and, for a time, our albatross. It almost cost us a friendship.

JK The National Endowment for the Arts gave us a $15,000 Research and Development grant. As soon as the money came in, we began to film interviews.

The first were in November, 1983, with Ruth Nelson, Sanford Meisner, Sylvia Sidney, Morris Carnovsky, Phoebe Brand, Cheryl Crawford, Sidney Kingsley, Margaret Barker and Gerrit Tony Kraber. They were still passionate about their days with The Group and were often moved to tears remembering the successes and the conflicts they lived through. Joanne found it easy to talk with them. But it was interesting to see that she sat bolt upright when she interviewed her own teacher, Sanford Meisner. There was still the strong boundary of respect between her, the student, and him, the teacher she revered, and at one time feared.

Joanne Woodward and Sanford Meisner.
New York, 1983. Photograph by Don Perdue.

Joanne Woodward and Sylvia Sidney.
Westport, CT, 1983. Photograph by Don Perdue.

Sylvia Sidney had an entirely different view. She was already a famous movie star when Harold Clurman invited her to star in The Group's 1939 production of *The Gentle People*. The year before, she'd married Luther Adler, and in so doing, she also became a sister-in-law of Stella Adler, both original members of The Group. When I first contacted Sylvia by phone she said, "It was like a cult. They were all crazy—completely brainwashed. It felt like Jim Jones in Guyana[1]." Unfortunately, she wouldn't repeat that on camera. But she did say that The Group fell apart because "everyone began sleeping with everyone else."

During a break in filming, Joanne whispered to me, "Can we use that?" Yes, we could, and did.

DH Another actress who was critical was Luise Rainer, an MGM star of the 1930s. She was romantically involved with Group actor/playwright, Clifford Odets, and although they didn't marry until 1937, she was an eyewitness during the company's formative years and we wanted to hear what she had to say about it. She was living in Switzerland when we wrote her a letter asking for an interview. In her hand-written reply, she said that she never quite understood what the members of The Group were so excited about, because she grew up working in European theater ensembles, such as Max Reinhardt's, where reflecting the world through the theater was the norm. So she didn't feel The Group Theatre was all that impressive. Nor did she feel that her comments would be appropriate for our program. We wrote back immediately and said we indeed would welcome her views because it was our aim to present a portrait of The Group that was not just a puff piece. Unfortunately, that was the last we heard from her; repeated letters never received any replies.

JK The money was dribbling in slowly, but we grabbed every chance to do more filming whenever there was an opportunity. On a trip to

---

1   In 1978, Jones had convinced his followers to take poison and commit suicide.

California for a program we were making about Judy Garland, we managed to squeeze in interviews with Group members Martin Ritt, Robert (Bobby) Lewis, Michael Gordon and Virginia Farmer.

In New York, at the end of a day of shooting with Katharine Hepburn for the show we were producing about Spencer Tracy, while the camera was still rolling, I asked her about a story we'd thought was apocryphal. However, she confirmed that it was true.

In late 1930, she was still an unknown, having never made a movie, when she was invited by a friend, Eunice Stoddard, to attend one of Harold Clurman's early meetings, where he laid out his plans for The Group Theatre.

Hepburn told us, "I listened about what a wonderful thing it was going to be, and that everyone was going to play little parts, and they were going to do wonderful plays. I thought, 'They're all going to be rather invisible.' After the meeting, when Clurman asked me if I'd be interesting in joining, I said, 'I'm going.' He said, 'You're what?' And I said, 'I'm leaving. I don't want to be a member of a group. I want to be a great—big—star.' And I left."

DH As Joan pushed her to give us her opinions on The Group's actors, "The Method," etc., I saw that Kate was becoming increasingly irritated, even though she continued to give polite, but not very meaty answers. I couldn't believe that Joan wasn't seeing the warning signs or was choosing to ignore them. I was getting more and more uncomfortable while she persisted in asking more questions. Until Hepburn finally said, "I have nothing more to tell you. You've now gone too far."

I wondered if she was going to throw us out of her house.

JK We knew that we had to do everything possible to get an interview with Elia Kazan, a renowned stage and film director, who'd started out as an actor when he joined The Group in 1932. He also became its most controversial member. During the Communist witch-hunts of the 1950s, Kazan "named names" when called as a friendly witness before the House Committee on Un-American Activities. Among those he named were several of his former colleagues in The Group Theatre, ruining their careers—and their lives. In the years since then, he never capitulated, never apologized, and many Group members refused to speak with him or even be in the same room.

Elia Kazan and Joanne Woodward.
Westport, CT, 1984. Photograph by Don Perdue.

Joanne Woodward, Morris Carnovsky, and David Heeley, about to shoot a scene from *Awake and Sing.*
New York, 1986. Photograph by Don Perdue.

267

When I approached him, he adamantly turned us down: "I'm writing a book and don't want to give it away in a television program." I told Joanne we had hit a brick wall and asked if she would call him. It would be harder for him to say "No" to her. Finally he relented, although his lawyer created a special release that stipulated how many minutes of his interview could be used in the finished show.

DH Joanne came up with a number of good ideas. We shot a Master Class with Bobby Lewis guiding her, Anne Jackson, Ken Howard, Austin Pendleton, and Glynnis O'Connor through some acting exercises. And we filmed Morris Carnovsky re-creating scenes from *Awake and Sing*, one of The Group's most famous plays. Carnovsky had been cast as the grandfather in the original 1935 production when he was in his thirties, and had to wear makeup to appear much older. Now in his eighties, he looked the part without any help.

We found the site in Brookfield Center, CT, where The Group members spent their first summer together in 1931, and we filmed Ruth Nelson and Eunice Stoddard there while they reminisced.

JK and DH Early on, we had contacted Helen Krich Chinoy, the leading expert on The Group Theatre. She was a theater scholar, recently retired as head of Drama at Smith College and had published a collection of interviews with some members of The Group, who all knew and respected her. Thank God for Helen. She became our invaluable consultant, collaborator and sounding board. She understood instinctively that while a television program about The Group had to be accurate and on sound scholarly ground, it also needed to be entertaining.

As time went on, and the hours of footage continued to mount, we had the growing sense that there was no end in sight. It felt as though we were shooting elements almost randomly, catching who and what we could. It was *not* the way to make a documentary, and we knew it. We often said to each other half-jokingly, "How can we get rid of this?" But Joanne was our friend and we could not let her down.

Nor could we give up on the commitments to Jac, PBS, or Helen.

JK Then there was Paul Newman. On more than one occasion, he asked me, "When is this program getting out of my house and my hair? Joanne has just told me she doesn't want to go on a summer vacation because she wants to work on The Group."

I remember saying, "Paul, please take her on vacation. We don't know when or how we'll finish it. We have hours of footage and no more money."

JK and DH One summer, the Newmans' old friend, Stewart Stern, came to stay with them in Connecticut. He was a brilliant writer (*Rebel Without A Cause; Rachel, Rachel; The Ugly American*), but at that time was struggling with writer's block. Joanne thought that he, having been a member of The Actors' Lab, an offshoot of The Group, could make significant contributions to the program. So she enlisted his advice, hoping that it would also help him get back to writing.

What resulted were problems we hadn't anticipated. We became splintered factions. Stewart and Joanne began coming up with ideas that were mostly impractical—and expensive. In fairness, some of their suggestions, such as dramatizations, are often used in documentaries. But it's a style we didn't like then, and still don't. So we found ourselves in the uncomfortable and embarrassing position of being "the bad guys."

At one point we heard that they'd written a letter to Arthur Miller, asking him to serve as the writer of the program. Fortunately, they hadn't yet mailed it and we asked them not to. While Arthur Miller was a brilliant playwright, he'd never written a documentary.

JK Tension was mounting. I could hear it in Joanne's voice on the phone. She felt deeply about the importance of recording for posterity an important part of the history of the American theater. But her dedication to the project, to Stewart, to what she hoped the finished program would represent, was starting to feel like an obsession. Or maybe, we just were not equally as enthusiastic. There's no doubt we were also feeling some guilt.

DH We all were struggling with the same basic problem. The show needed more than interviews and stills. It needed a modern "hook," something on which to hang the story. And that "something" had to be affordable on a public television budget.

Joanne came to the rescue. In 1987, she convinced Nikos Psacharopoulos, then head of the Williamstown Theatre Festival, to let her direct a production of *Golden Boy* to celebrate the fiftieth anniversary of The Group's original production, so that we could shoot footage of the rehearsals and the performance. She cast Dylan McDermott and Margaret Klenck in the leading roles. And Nikos also agreed to a Sunday afternoon "Special Event" celebrating The Group Theatre, which we could also film. It was presented on the main stage of the Williamstown Theatre Festival before a live, standing-room-only audience. All surviving original members were invited to come and speak, as well as a distinguished group of descendants, including Paul Newman, James Naughton, Kate Burton, Maria Tucci, Ellen Burstyn,

Maria Tucci, Paul Newman, and James Naughton at the *Tribute to The Group* Theatre. Williamstown, MA, 1987. Photograph by Don Perdue.

Barbara Baxley, Shelley Winters, with Joanne as host. It was written by Steve Lawson, who had been a writer on the television series, *St. Elsewhere,* and was a longtime artistic associate of Nikos. There were film clips, music, and scripted reminiscences. It was a superbly successful event in its own right, and just what we needed. And we asked Steve to become the writer of our program.

JK and DH We had accumulated more than twenty-eight hours of film footage for what would be a ninety-minute program. But Joanne still wanted to shoot more. We had to keep our professional hats securely on our heads, which put the friendship with her on very thin ice. We explained that we already had too much material, and that we couldn't shoot any more.

"But if I find the money, why do you care?" she said. "The worst that will happen is that we'll donate the film to an archive."

It was Jac who finally put his foot down. He told her that WNET was not in the archive business, that he'd scheduled an airdate for the show, and it was now time to start editing.

As our editor we hired Alan Berliner, whom we had met when we worked at ABC's *20/20.* At that time he was an assistant film editor, and we were impressed by both his organizational abilities and his sensibilities[2]. He was a very wise choice.

DH By this time, we and Joanne were barely speaking. Nevertheless, I told her that I believed the interviews we'd shot were so strong that they should be the basis of our program. So we suggested that she and Stewart borrow our production assistant, Rachel Dretzin, to go through the massive volumes of transcripts and try to create a skeleton of The Group's story. It was a tough job, requiring patience and probably many gallons of coffee. Alan took their selected interview choices and did a rough assembly on film.

---

2   Alan Berliner went on to become an award-winning filmmaker in his own right.

It was Stewart Stern who eventually realized the magnitude of the project. He said to Joanne, "We're not documentary producers. David and Joan are. I think we've gone as far as we can go ourselves."

JK and DH They had in fact done us a huge favor. The preliminary weeding out allowed us to come in with a fresh view and see what additions and changes were needed. There was still a vast amount of work to be done, but now it was manageable. Slowly, we began to put the story together. The interviews became the spine, and elements from the Williamstown *Tribute to The Group* helped flesh it out, together with other film clips, newsreel footage, stills and graphics. And we lucked out when we discovered that a vault in California contained screen tests of many of The Group's actors performing scenes from Group Theatre plays.

Joanne had come up with a splendid idea for the program's closing credits. She suggested we contact the many famous actors and directors who had been taught by original members of The Group, and ask them to record an audio tape saying, "My name is… and I studied from…," and also to send us an eight-by-ten photo. They included Meryl Streep, Warren Beatty, Maureen Stapleton, Marlon Brando, Julie Harris, Walter Matthau, Faye Dunaway, Sydney Pollack, Peter Bogdanovich, among others. Their voices and pictures became the backbone of the credit sequence, re-enforcing the continuing legacy of The Group Theatre.

When we had completed a rough-cut, we invited Joanne to come and see it. She watched in silence; we knew she was less than pleased, still upset that Jac had told her there would be no more filming, except for her scripted on-camera links.

The Neighborhood Playhouse, her acting alma mater, agreed to let us shoot the links there. She was professional, delivering her pieces well and with warmth. But between shots, she was cool, as she was in the narration session that followed. But we all did what we had to do.

JK In the meantime, we had hired the famed jazz pianist, Dick Hyman, to compose original music for the program. He did it in the form of an elegant classical chamber piece.

Jac Venza gave the fine-cut his seal of approval, and the airdate was approaching. Publicity cassettes went to the press and the advance "buzz" was enormously positive. Joanne began getting phone calls congratulating her on the show.

What happened next was typical of her generosity. She came to the realization that the program had turned out well, and decided to throw a party to celebrate its completion. It was in her apartment in New York, and everyone who had participated was invited. But there was one problem.

"What am I going to do about Gadge [Elia Kazan]?" she said to me. "If I ask him, no one else will come."

There was a pause. "I know how to handle this," she said. "I'll call and tell him the truth…that I can't invite him to be in the same room with Ruth Nelson, Morris Carnovsky, Phoebe Brand, and the others. He's not dumb. He'll understand why. But I'll suggest he have dinner with Paul and me some time next week." That's exactly what she did and the party was splendid.

JK and DH *Broadway's Dreamers: The Legacy of The Group Theatre* premiered on June 29th, 1989, to excellent reviews, and was honored with many awards. We had insisted that Joanne share our producers' credit, so when the program won an Emmy for Outstanding Informational Special, all three of us received statues.

JK David and I went to the Academy ceremony in Los Angeles, and I remember calling her in Connecticut after we'd won, even though it was very late on the East Coast. Paul picked up the phone.

"I'm sorry if I'm waking you up." I told him. "But The Group Theatre program just won an Emmy."

"Whoopee!" he shouted.

"I'd like to give Joanne the good news. Can you please wake her up?"

He said, "I think I just did."

JK and DH In the years since, whenever Joanne was acting or directing, we'd get a call from someone on the set asking for a cassette because, "Miss Woodward wants to show it to the cast and crew." And Paul gave a grant through his Newman's Own Foundation for all the interviews in their entirety to be donated to the Lincoln Center Library's Theater Archives, where future students of theatrical history can watch them as part of their research. Unfortunately, by then, Joanne's fears over losing more of The Group's original members had become a reality, as we learned that many of the ones we'd interviewed had died.

However, the postscript to this story is a happy one. After the five, often-agonizing, years it took to produce—half the life of The Group Theatre itself—Joanne is as proud of the program as she is of any she's ever done. And it's one of our proudest achievements too.

David and Joan with their Emmys.
Pasadena, CA, 1990. Authors' collection.

Audrey Hepburn with *The Fred Astaire Songbook*.
Geneva, Switzerland, 1990. Authors' collection.

CHAPTER TWENTY TWO

Audrey in Switzerland

Rarely did we ever produce more than one profile about the same subject. An exception was Fred Astaire, about whom we actually did three. The first two in 1980, when we had the opportunity to meet Astaire, celebrated his dancing[1], and received almost unanimously positive reviews. However, John J. O'Connor, the television critic for *The New York Times*, while praising the shows, mentioned *"more effort might have been made to highlight Astaire, the singer."* We never forgot that comment, and in 1991 decided to produce *The Fred Astaire Songbook*.

As usual, it had a wobbly beginning.

By then Astaire was no longer alive, so the first step was to get the co-operation of his widow, Robyn Smith Astaire. She had developed a reputation for trying to stop the use of any excerpts from her husband's films or even photos of him without her permission[2],

---

1   See "Fred Was First."

2   The most notorious case involved the televising of *The Kennedy Center Honors*, which in 1992 was paying tribute to Ginger Rogers. Film excerpts were always provided to the program on a "most favored nations" basis; rights-holders waived charges, but only if all other rights-holders followed suit. Robyn Astaire refused to co-operate with the no-fee policy, so no Astaire/Rogers dance numbers could be shown.

which came with a large price tag attached. And she trusted very few people. Among the few she did trust was Roger L. Mayer, the head of Turner Entertainment Co. (TEC), which held the majority of Astaire's films. Roger had made a deal with Robyn that allowed him to license excerpts, and in return, she received a percentage of the fee. The deal also included his agreement to tell her in advance of any such usage.

We already had asked TEC to be a co-producer of the program, along with WNET (Turner provided whatever elements they owned in return for future distribution rights following the PBS broadcast window), so Roger was one of our executive producers. He suggested we come to LA to have dinner with him and Robyn. The date was set, and she suggested the restaurant in the Bel Air Hotel. We arrived on time, as did Roger. But no Robyn. After waiting fifteen minutes, he decided to call her. No answer. Another twenty minutes later, he called her again, only to reach her answering machine. After another half-hour, he said, "I don't think she's going to show up, so let's order."

The next morning, he reached her.

"What happened to you last night? I even called you the day before to re-confirm."

"I'm so sorry," she said. "I thought it was meant to be tonight. Let's all have dinner this evening at L'Hermitage; my treat."

Once again we and Roger met at 6:30 pm, and were led to a corner table. The maitre d' told us that Robyn always wanted to sit facing the wall, apparently in an effort not to be recognized.

At 6:45 Roger said, "I wouldn't be surprised if she stood us up again."

Five minutes later, the head waiter came with a message: "Mrs. Astaire called from her car. She's on her way and asked that you order appetizers and drinks." She finally arrived shortly after 7. She was pretty, wearing a pair of slacks, a blouse and a jacket. We all shook hands, and then she began talking to Roger. It was as though we were not there.

At one point, she asked him, "Are you wed?"

Always composed, he replied, "Yes, Robyn, I've been 'wed' for many years." Then, still focusing only on him, she asked, "Why do film companies like yours think they deserve to keep making money from my husband's films?"

He was beginning to show a bit of impatience, but responded calmly, "Robyn, studios don't make movies to just keep them hidden on shelves. And, by the way, that brings us to the project we're planning, so why don't we let Joan and David tell you about it."

DH We reminded her of the 1980 programs, and had brought along a copy of the letter of congratulations we received from Astaire after they had been broadcast. And we mentioned the John O'Connor comment.

"So now we're making good on it and doing a show about your husband's singing. And we'd greatly appreciate your co-operation. Do you have any materials that we might use, such as sheet music or any of the original scores for the songs he wrote?"

She smiled and said, "I know how much Fred liked your earlier programs and because he loved to sing and write music, I'll be happy to help with this show in any way I can."

"Good," said Roger. "And while they're in Los Angeles, why don't you let them have a look at what you have in the house?"

"Of course. Can you come tomorrow afternoon? How about 2 pm?"

JK This was going smoother than we had expected. Until the next morning. I hadn't left my hotel room, and the phone hadn't rung, but at around 10 am I saw the light on it blinking. Robyn had left a message with the front desk: "Can't confirm this afternoon until about noon."

12 o'clock came and went. When we hadn't heard from her by 12:30, I called. The answering machine picked up. Another half-hour went by. I called again and left another message.

DH I was going stir-crazy waiting in my room for news, so I told Joan I was going out for a walk. When I came back, she still hadn't heard from Robyn.

Finally, at 1:45, fifteen minutes before we were supposed to have arrived at her house, Joan received another message through the front desk: "Can't see you today. I'm out flying my plane cross-country."

JK I called Roger. "We've been stood up again. Since when has Robyn become a pilot?"

"I think she told me a while back that she was taking flying lessons," he said. "She wants to fly for FedEx or DHL or one of those delivery services. But why she made an appointment with you, and why a housekeeper didn't answer when you called, and why she left messages at the front desk instead of talking to you directly, are all mysteries."

About a week later, after we'd returned to New York, Robyn eventually did call me. And she delivered a bombshell: she wanted to host the program.

DH Our next surprise was when our executive producers, Roger and Jac Venza, told us they didn't think it was such a bad idea, since many people knew that Astaire had married a former jockey and might find it fascinating to see her.

I was skeptical. She was not an actress or performer, and had no on-camera experience. (I had had to deal with inexperienced hosts in the past, never with very satisfactory results.) And she hadn't given us any reason to trust that she'd keep to our schedule and budget. Jac listened to all my reservations.

"Give it a try," he said.

Our lawyer sent her a contract, which she signed and returned. She then asked us to send tapes of our shows, so she could study some of our other hosts.

JK And then another bombshell: a call from her attorney to say that she didn't want to host the program and, worse, she was withdrawing her permission for us to produce it.

Knowing that she was litigious, what followed was a round of phone calls between attorneys at WNET in New York, PBS in Washington, Turner Entertainment Co. in LA, and Turner Broadcasting in Atlanta. There were conference calls, faxes, and more calls. The production schedule was tight, so David and I had to cross our fingers and proceed on the assumption that it would all be worked out. We were scheduled to leave for another trip to LA the day after Labor Day to start shooting interviews.

The Friday afternoon before the long weekend, we finally heard from WNET's general counsel: "Everyone has agreed. You should go ahead as planned. Just find someone else to host the show." The decision was based on the fact that we had a fully-executed contract with Robyn Astaire, that a check for her first payment had been sent, and that she was now in breach of that contract. "So if she tries to sue us, she doesn't have a legal leg to stand on. And we've informed her attorneys that we're going ahead without her."

DH Actually it was a great relief, based on my original concerns. And we never heard another word from Robyn or her lawyers.

Of course, we now were facing the challenge of finding another host. We made a list of people who had worked with Fred Astaire and our top choice was Audrey Hepburn. However, she lived in Switzerland and we'd had no success getting her to appear in our original Astaire shows ten years earlier. But this time we got lucky. I happened to mention her name to a colleague, John Heminway, who worked in the next office to mine at WNET, when he said, "I know one of her best friends. If you'd like, I can make a call and see if I can put the two of you together."

JK His friend was Jacqueline Blanc, who lived in Lausanne, not too far from Audrey Hepburn. And within a few days, I found myself talking with Robert Wolders, Audrey's long-time companion. He asked some general questions, and seemed interested in our plans for the program. The following week, in the middle of our third conversation, suddenly he said, "Hold on, Audrey would like to speak with you."

Like so many other people, I was a great admirer of Audrey Hepburn's beauty, her movies, her voice, and the fact that she put aside a lucrative career as an actress to become a Goodwill Ambassador for UNICEF, traveling to some of the most difficult places on earth where she tried to comfort sick and dying children—using her fame to raise awareness of their plight. She was someone I had always hoped to meet. So when I heard that voice on the phone for the first time, I was thrilled. She was easy to talk to, straightforward, and wanted to be part of the show.

There was only one catch: our timetable was in conflict with hers; she couldn't come to the United States when we needed to film her. So it was agreed that we'd go to Switzerland.

DH I had some mixed feelings about her hosting our program. In theory, she fit the bill perfectly, but I'd seen her in the role of host recently and, while she looked beautiful and elegant, to me she came across as somewhat cool and distant. I certainly didn't want that feel for our show.

The solution came out of a conversation that Joan had with one of her close friends, Leonard Gershe. He wrote the screenplay for *Funny Face*, the only film that Audrey made with Astaire.

Joan told him of my concern. He said, "The problem is that every time she agrees to appear on television, producers ask her to wear a formal gown. They're trying to make her look even more elegant than she already is. And it's a big mistake because she then feels she has to play the part of 'super-elegant' and it doesn't work. She doesn't need any help being elegant. My advice, for what it's worth, is to get her to wear a pair of slacks and a shirt or a sweater, and let her sit on a chair or in the corner of a sofa with her feet curled up under her. That's the Audrey I know. She loves to dress casually, and while the elegance is still there, she's completely down-to-earth."

JK We flew to Switzerland and stayed at the Hotel de la Paix, overlooking Lake Geneva. It was early November, and cold, but beautiful. Our first order of business was to survey the suite at the Intercontinental Hotel, which our UNICEF contact, Christa Roth, had suggested we use as a location for filming.

It was my first time in Geneva, so after the survey, we walked over a bridge and into the old town, where we had a snack at a small café. By then we were tired and chilled, so we returned to our hotel. I stopping briefly to buy—of course—some Swiss chocolates and a small cuckoo clock.

The next morning, Audrey and Robert Wolders arrived at the Intercontinental in their own car and I met them in front of the hotel. She was wearing a red coat and slacks and no jewelry. She was as beautiful as I had expected her to be, and I felt comfortable with her immediately. I led her and Rob up to the suite where David and the crew were setting up.

DH She had brought several shirts and sweaters from which to choose. One was a simple blue and white striped blouse. Another was a pale pink sweater, which I thought suited her perfectly.

She said, "I was surprised and so happy that you want me to dress casually."

I thought, "Thank you, Leonard Gershe."

And I had decided to take the rest of his advice too. I asked her to sit in the corner of the sofa. And she instinctively curled her legs under her. She looked as though she could have been relaxing in her own home.

Our art department had made a prop for the shoot: a fake book with the title, *The Fred Astaire Songbook*. Audrey held it in her lap and occasionally turned a page, as though reading it. After the program aired, we received many requests from viewers wanting to know where they could buy a copy.

JK During our phone conversations, I had asked Robert Wolders what to order for Audrey's lunch.

He said, "She likes pasta, tomato juice, bananas and chocolate. Believe it or not, she loves to eat." It certainly didn't show, because she was even thinner in person than she appeared in photos and on film.

Later in the afternoon, I asked her to sign about twenty copies of a lobby card for *Funny Face*. She willingly agreed, and inscribed each one personally. Then, to allow the ink to dry, she spread them out on the bed—and every other available surface in the bedroom. She pointed out that the lobby card shows her wearing a blue scarf when it was actually yellow in the film itself.

Rob had gone out to a business meeting. When he returned, there were autographed lobby cards everywhere and no place to sit!

DH The shoot was very smooth. We had sent Audrey the script ahead of time, so there were no problems—until the last page. It had her saying, "If perfection is what we strive for, then certainly he succeeded." And ended with, "… I was the object of that perfection." She had crossed out the entire last paragraph, because she objected to that final phrase, feeling that it sounded as though she was putting herself in Astaire's league. I knew that the end of the program would be lame without it, but understood her concern. After a brief discussion we both agreed to a subtle but significant change in the final sentence. Now she says, "And for one brief moment, in our world of film fantasy, I was allowed to be a part of that perfection." She delivered the line with understated emotion that provided a perfect coda.

After the on-camera sequences, we set up for the voice-over recording. And that's when we discovered her sense of humor. Realizing I was originally from Britain, she suggested that she do the narration with a Cockney accent, the way she spoke in *My Fair Lady*. And the first time I asked her to do another take, she said, "Willie Wyler; he thinks he's Willie Wyler"—a reference to the director of her first film, *Roman Holiday.* Wyler was legendary for always wanting numerous takes.

JK During one of our breaks, we had a conversation about her fan mail. She told me that most of it comes from women, requesting advice about fashion, makeup, etc. "And over the years, I've also received letters from people who were furious when I cut my hair in a film, such as in *The Nun's Story.* And I also had a lot of people angry at me when it was announced that I'd play Eliza Doolittle in the film version of *My Fair Lady.* They accused me of stealing the part from Julie Andrews, who played the role on the stage. I was upset by those accusations, but the fact was that Julie Andrews hadn't yet made a name for herself in the movies, and the producers weren't going to give her the part even if I turned it down. It was a plum role, the script was terrific and so I accepted the offer. If I hadn't, they'd have given someone else the part."

I then asked her about her work for UNICEF. "When you travel to third-world countries, do you take your own food and water?"

She said, "UNICEF makes sure we have drinking water, but often there was not enough water for a bath."

I thought, "Here's the meticulous, beautiful Audrey Hepburn. It's hard to think of her not being able to bathe whenever she wants."

DH When we had finished, she and Rob asked us to spend the following day at her home in Tolochenaz, just outside Lausanne. Joan and I hated to turn down the invitation, but we had to catch a plane to return to New York, since our production schedule was very tight and we had a firm airdate.

JK Even before we'd met her, Audrey had agreed to be the host of a series called *Gardens of the World.* It was scheduled to be broadcast around the same time as the premiere of our *Fred Astaire Songbook*[3].

---

3   Eventually the *Gardens of the World* series was postponed, and did not air until 1993.

So we spoke to the producers of the *Gardens* series, and our publicist and theirs agreed to cross-promote both shows. That meant that whenever she appeared on a program to talk about either one of them, she would try to mention the other. But we could hardly expect her to publicize ours without having seen it. So, once again, we broke our rule of not letting participants see a program before it airs, and sent a cassette to her in Switzerland.

A few days later, David and I received a telegram:

"Dearest Joan and David,

Just saw your Fred Astaire Songbook and I cannot tell you how pleased and impressed I am. Congratulations to you all.

Gratefully with love,

Audrey."

JK and DH We saw her and Rob again the following year in New York when she was being honored by Cartier, and she made sure that we were invited. She seemed as happy to see us again as we were to see her. After that, we continued to stay in touch by phone.

JK A side-story here: during Iraq's invasion of Kuwait, news broadcasts were filled with statements by the Iraqi spokesman, Tariq Aziz, and we noticed that in some of them he was taped in the room at the Geneva Intercontinental Hotel that we had used for our shoot with Audrey. I called her to ask if she'd recognized it too. She said, "I'm so upset by the news, and how dare he sit in the exact same place that I sat...on *our* sofa?"

JK and DH In the fall of 1992, reports began to appear that she was ill. At first, everyone thought she had come down with a gastrointestinal infection after a UNICEF trip to Somalia. But as the months and weeks went by, the reports became more ominous.

On January 20th, 1993, David and I were in our office, watching Bill Clinton's Presidential Inauguration, when we heard a news bulletin that Audrey Hepburn had died. We felt as though we'd been punched in the stomach. And to this day, we can kick ourselves for not delaying our trip back from Switzerland so that we could have spent some time with her at her home.

But we're lucky to have known her and to have had the opportunity to work with her. And we're still friends with Rob Wolders.

David Heeley, Audrey Hepburn, and Joan Kramer.
Geneva, Switzerland, 1990. Authors' collection.

Joan Kramer and Henry Fonda.
Bel Air, CA, 1980. Authors' collection.

CHAPTER TWENTY THREE

Henry and Jane and Ted and Peter

"Darling, why are you crying?" Ted Turner asked his fiancée, Jane Fonda. We were on the back patio of her house in Santa Monica, having lunch and discussing the final details of the next day's shoot. It was for a program about her father, Henry Fonda, which we were producing for Ted's network, TNT.

JK and DH If you believe in Fate, you might say that our producing this program was pre-ordained. But Fate seldom chooses the easy route.

We met Henry Fonda in 1980, not long after he'd finished what would be his last film, *On Golden Pond*, marking the first and only time he worked with Katharine Hepburn. We were making a profile of her for PBS and he'd agreed to be interviewed for it.

His wife, Shirlee, didn't want a film crew in their Bel Air home, so we set up outside near the pool. The background was a panoramic view of Los Angeles, which would have been breathtaking if it had not been for a residue of smog that smudged the famous city skyline.

DH Fonda came out before we were quite ready. After shaking hands with him, I decided to read the list of about ten questions that Joan and I had prepared, thinking it would give him time to collect his thoughts. I began:

"Mr. Fonda, when did you first meet Katharine Hepburn?" He was standing next to me with his head slightly bowed.

"I really don't have anything to say about that," he said quietly.

I didn't expect that, but I pressed on.

"Can you tell me if there is any difference in the way you each approached your roles in *On Golden Pond*?"

"No. I don't have any thoughts about that."

"What's the first Hepburn film you saw?"

"I have no idea."

JK I was about two feet away as this scene played out and even though it was a cool, brisk morning, I started to feel really hot. We were about to do an interview with a big star who had nothing to talk about.

DH He listened patiently to all the questions, and sparked to none of them. I thought, "Why did he agree to this? He just worked with Hepburn and can't think of anything to say? What are we doing here?"

By then, the crew was ready and I asked him to sit in front of the camera while I sat alongside it, facing him and holding my list of useless questions.

I realized that we might be wasting film, but since I had no other choice, I said, "Mr. Fonda, I'm going to ask you the same questions. Don't worry if you can't answer some of them, but let's give it a try." He nodded.

Henry Fonda and David Heeley prior to interview.
Bel Air, CA, 1980. Authors' collection.

"Can you tell me when you first met Katharine Hepburn?"

There was a brief pause, which seemed like an eternity. Then suddenly the quiet, diffident man was transformed; in front of our camera was Henry Fonda, the actor.

"Strangely, we had never met during the last forty-five years that we've both been here. I'd known Spencer, but I never had met Katharine. And she walked straight up to me and she said, 'Well, it's about time!'"

His voice was strong, and he was full of energy. It was as though he'd suddenly had a shot of adrenaline.

He had tears in his eyes when he recalled their first day of filming. Right before the cameras rolled she gave him Tracy's favorite hat.

"And I collapsed. This beautiful, crushable brown felt hat. I wore it in the first scene of the picture, and when we'd finished that scene, I gave it back to her, since I thought she meant for me to just use it as wardrobe. But she said, 'No it's yours. I want you to have it.' And I have it."

JK When the interview was over, I asked if we could see the hat. He went into the house and a few minutes later came out carrying

Spencer Tracy's hat.
Bel Air, CA, 1980. Authors' collection.

it. We propped it on the edge of a bench and shot footage and still photographs of it.

JK and DH Soon after *Starring Katharine Hepburn* was broadcast in March, 1981, we received another of those phone calls from PBS: "So who are you going to do next?" At the top of our list was Henry Fonda. We wrote him a letter asking for his co-operation and he agreed. But we didn't know that he was seriously ill. He had been nominated for an Academy Award for his performance in *On Golden Pond*, but was too weak to attend the ceremony. That evening, he won his only Oscar as Best Actor, and his daughter, Jane, accepted it on his behalf.

DH On August 12th, 1982, I received another call from PBS, but this time it was to deliver bad news: they had decided to turn down our proposal. That afternoon came even more bad news: Henry Fonda had passed away. We felt as though he'd died twice on the same day.

JK When a reasonable amount of time had passed, we wrote a letter to Jane, saying that since her father had agreed to a documentary (perhaps for another network), we'd still like to do one, and asked if she'd be the host. We received a reply signed by both her and Shirlee Fonda, Henry's widow. In it, they explained that while they very much wanted a program done about him, it was important for the family to produce it themselves. They never did.

Some eight years later, in 1990, we were on location in Atlanta co-producing the television movie, *The Perfect Tribute,* when our office in New York called to let us know that someone from TNT was trying to reach us.

DH Ted Turner was then engaged to Jane and he suggested doing a program about her father. The network had already produced a number of movie star profiles, and we were pleased when they offered us the opportunity to do one about Henry Fonda. The fact is that by this time we had a track record for making this kind of show, working with big name stars, and winning a number of prestigious awards. Where the boss's fiancée was concerned, TNT wanted to be on safe ground.

Since Turner's empire was based in Atlanta, Joan and I went to CNN Center there to meet one of the TNT executives. We were told that Jane and her brother, Peter, would co-host the program. We both felt that two hosts might be awkward, but we kept those thoughts to ourselves for the moment.

JK and DH A few weeks later, TNT invited us to LA for meetings with Scott Sassa, the head of Turner Networks, and then with Jane Fonda. Sassa, himself, drove us in the company's SUV to her Santa Monica office. Several other high-level colleagues of his came along too. When we arrived, she looked rather startled to see a large group of people walk in.

She said, "Oh, I thought just Joan and David were coming."

For about an hour, we talked with her about her father, their relationship, his movies, etc. Sassa and the others sat in the room and listened, but had nothing to contribute to the conversation. The hour we spent there must have seemed like four hours to them. We could sense their discomfort at having no role to play. But they obviously felt they had to show up. Perhaps they also wanted to see how we and Jane would relate to each other.

At some point, we said, "We've been told that you and your brother will host the program."

To our relief, she interrupted. "No. That would be rather clumsy. I'll host it and I'll ask Peter and our stepmother, Shirlee, to co-operate."

We asked Jane if we could meet with her again after we'd done more research, and would have more specific questions.

JK Peter was enthusiastic and touchingly candid when I called him at his home in Montana. He told me that he used to open his father's dresser drawers to touch his pajamas, just to feel closer to him. He also said he was in the process of writing a book called *Don't Tell Dad*, which years later was finally published. I came away from that conversation feeling that he was still a young boy in a man's body, still looking for approval and love from his father. At the same time, I was flattered that he was willing to speak so intimately about their relationship.

Shirlee Fonda was in New York when we first met her over lunch. She was polite, but a bit cool. We felt a reluctance on her part to commit to the project and we didn't know why.

Yet, by the end of the lunch, she said, "Let's talk more when I get back to California."

DH Weeks later, Joan and I spent an entire day in the Fonda Bel Air home, where Shirlee still lives. She has an extensive collection of home movies, photographs, letters, etc., much of which was in the basement. So she and I made many trips up and down the stairs. We'd started in the early afternoon and were still there as the sun went down. We ordered pizza for dinner and didn't leave until 11 pm. Early the next morning, she called and told us she hadn't slept all night. She'd continued searching long after we'd left and asked us to come back to see if anything she'd found in the early hours of the morning would be useful.

That's when she admitted that this was very emotional for her. She hadn't looked at any of these things since Henry had died over eight years earlier, and she apologized for appearing reserved at our initial meeting in New York. When she first heard from Jane about the production, she didn't know if she could handle it. She'd given it a great deal of thought since then and decided she had to help in any way she could. As a result, the project was serving as a catharsis for her.

It was also the beginning of a long friendship. Not only did she allow us to film her interview inside the house, but she gave each of us two lithographs of her husband's paintings: one is of the three hats he wore in *On Golden Pond*, including the one that had belonged to Spencer Tracy; the other is a magnified page from the book, *The Grapes of Wrath.*

Henry Fonda lithograph: "The Three Hats."
Courtesy of Shirlee Fonda.

Henry Fonda lithograph: "Grapes of Wrath."
Courtesy of Shirlee Fonda.

Back in New York, Jane and Ted were in town for an event at the United Nations. They were staying at the UN Plaza Hotel and she agreed to set aside some time to talk with us. We took an audiocassette recorder so that we'd be able to craft our script for the show based on her own words.

Betty Cohen was the executive at TNT assigned to the project and she flew to New York from Atlanta to join us at the meeting. The network was still super-sensitive to the fact that we were working with Ted's fiancée, and wanted one of their representatives present whenever we met with her. At one point the doorbell rang. Jane said it must be the valet service delivering Ted's tuxedo, and asked Betty to answer the door, take the tux and hang it in the closet, which was embarrassing, since she was essentially our boss. However, Jane didn't know her and she was busy talking with us. Then Ted came in, and Jane introduced us to him. Betty had to introduce herself. Even though she worked for him, he obviously didn't know who she was[1].

JK and DH Our conversation with Jane lasted about two hours and was very useful. She's forthright and very smart, and was more than willing to talk about her father's weaknesses as well as his strengths. She's also very vulnerable and sensitive, and at times we saw her well up with emotion. She told us her father had always said, "The Fondas cry over a good steak."

JK She talked about how wonderful it was for her and her father to have had the chance to work with Katharine Hepburn. And then she said, "I thought, 'What a shame they hadn't known each other when they were young. Maybe they'd have married and she would have been my mother.'"

I remember saying, "That would have been a disaster. By her own admission, Kate would have been a terrible mother. She felt it was impossible to have a career and raise a family, and her choice was her career. She once told us, 'If I had to give a performance on Broadway,

---

1   It wouldn't be long before Betty Cohen was promoted to head the new Cartoon Network.

and a child of mine was sick, I'd want to strangle that kid.'"

DH We admitted that, after having watched most of Fonda's films, we had trouble locking onto his persona. Unlike Jimmy Stewart, about whom we'd done a profile three years earlier, Fonda wasn't a cozy actor and it took time for us to understand his technique.

Jane said that he always projected the truth in his performances. He just "did it," and because he was such a shy man in real life, he called acting his "mask." He was most comfortable when he could become someone else.

She suggested that we talk to a number of people with whom he had worked and that she'd put us in touch with them. Some of them, she said, adored working with him. Others had a hard time. She wanted us to hear both sides.

JK Among those I called was Anne Bancroft. She and Fonda had worked together on the stage in *Two for the Seesaw* and did not enjoy the experience. Bancroft was trained in "The Method," and Fonda had no patience for the preparation many "Method" actors seemed to need in order to perform. When I explained why I was calling, Bancroft said, "I'd really rather not talk about him. If Jane wants to call me, I'll tell her why, but it's not something I'm willing to discuss with anyone else."

Exactly opposite were the reactions from Paul Newman and Ron Howard. Paul had directed Fonda and found him completely professional. He repeated what Jane had said, "He projected the truth in everything he did." Ron Howard credits him with his decision to become a director. He talked about Fonda's perfectionism, his attention to details and gave as an example how Fonda was always aware of continuity from one take to another. He made sure his cigarette was exactly the same length from shot to shot, and that the water in a glass was at the same level.

DH In the end, we indeed were able to get a full picture of Henry Fonda from a variety of sources. And many of them would probably have agreed to appear on camera for the program. However, we decided that the visual materials were so rich and varied, that the show would be better served by only a few key people. With Jane as host, and Peter and Shirlee already on board, the only other interviews we did were with James Stewart, director Sidney Lumet, and Katharine Hepburn.

Our researcher had discovered an interview with Fonda, himself, in the Oral History Archives of Columbia University. It was an important "find" because it gave us the opportunity to let him tell his own story as much as possible. Thus, the title of the program, *Fonda on Fonda*, reflects the participation of all the Fondas.

JK Through the months of production, occasionally we would get a message from Jane's office asking when she could expect to see a script. However, unlike a dramatic feature film, the script for a documentary evolves out of the interviews, film clips, graphics, etc., and is written as part of the editing process. She eventually received it just a few weeks before we shot her host sequences in Los Angeles.

The date was set, and she suggested the location: the Brentwood home in which the Fonda family had lived until she was six years old. The house had recently been bought by Rob Reiner, but he and his family hadn't yet moved in. Since it was empty and we only needed exterior shots, he allowed us to film there, and to use the empty guest house as Jane's dressing room.

DH We'd received a call from her assistant to say that Jane was happy with the script. However, I knew that her final piece to camera was very emotionally charged. It summed up her father's life and included her reaction to his death. Even though we'd written it using her own words, I knew it would be hard for her. So I asked if we could go over it with her in person. She suggested we meet at her home in Santa Monica the day before the shoot.

Which brings us back to that lunch on her patio.

We arrived just after she and Ted had come in from a jog

around the neighborhood. They were both wearing running suits and baseball caps.

"It's such a nice day. Let's eat outside," she said.

They served lunch themselves, and were gracious hosts. And it was Ted who kept going into the house to get more bread, etc.

Jane repeated that she was satisfied with the script, but I knew that the time for any changes was now, not with an expensive film crew waiting around for us to re-write. It was near the end of the meal when I said, "Would you read through the closing piece for me? I want to be sure you're comfortable with it."

JK At that moment, Ted was on his way to the kitchen for some more butter. He'd left us all laughing and light-hearted. When he came out again, Jane was in tears. He glared at us accusingly, and asked her why she was crying.

She looked up and said, "Darling, sit down and read this." A few seconds later, tears were streaming down his face too. There we were, four people, and two of them, Jane Fonda and Ted Turner, were crying. Neither David nor I knew what to say.

Finally, to break the silence, I said, "Look at this, we just lost our hosts!" I'd accidentally struck the right chord. Both of them started to laugh, and the mood turned light again.

Jane said, "The script is fine. Don't touch it."

DH However my initial instincts turned out to be correct. It was not easy for Jane to say those words when the camera rolled. And as director, I found myself with not only a sobbing actress, but also a political juggling act with the TNT personnel who had shown up on the set, uninvited, just in time to witness the meltdown of their boss's fiancée.

JK A few days before, Betty Cohen told me that several executives were planning to be present. But David and I felt strongly that Jane didn't need an audience. So I called her assistant, Debbie Karolewski, and shared my thoughts with her.

She said, "Let me talk to her about this and we'll take it from there." She called back the next day and said, "Don't worry. Other

David Heeley, Jane Fonda, and crew.
Brentwood, CA, 1991. Authors' collection.

Jane Fonda with David Heeley and Joan Kramer.
Brentwood, CA, 1991. Authors' collection

than Betty Cohen, no one else will show up. I just called all their offices and said to their assistants, 'Jane wants a closed set. No one is to be there except for the producers and the crew.'"

DH Jane arrived at 8 am in her own car, driven by Ted, who parked outside the gates. He went with her to the guest house—now her dressing room—carrying her wardrobe on hangers. There was no entourage, not even their personal assistants.

I was busy working with the crew, and our production manager was already worried that we were hearing nearby power lawn mowers. Her worries were well-founded; she spent a good deal of that day running from house to house, pleading with gardeners, including Julie Andrews', to turn off their mowers, giving each of them a tip in cash to reinforce the request.

JK Soon after they arrived, Jane began showing Ted around. She saw the mulberry bush that her father had planted some fifty years before.

"This is where I learned to sing, '*Here we go round the mulberry bush, the mulberry bush, the mulberry bush...*'" as she and Ted chased each other around it. Both of them were laughing and clearly having a good time. Then she said, "I'd like to take a look inside." A few of us went into the house with her, and she showed us the room that had been her childhood bedroom.

I realized that the tour was not only for Ted, but it was her way of absorbing the setting and thinking about her life at that house; it was indeed part of her "Method" acting training to get ready for the shoot ahead.

She and Ted went back to her makeshift dressing room, where her makeup artist and hairdresser were waiting for her. When she was ready, Ted settled into a folding chair on the lawn with a book and a stack of magazines, looking up whenever she did a take.

DH We broke for lunch at about noon, and Ted and Jane sat at the large table along with us and the crew. He said to her, "Where did all this food come from?"

She replied, "Darling, there's a catering truck in front of the house."

He then added, "We should take the leftovers home with us."

Clearly embarrassed, she said, "No Ted. We don't need the leftovers. Remember we're taking Troy for pizza tonight." (Troy is her son by her second husband, Tom Hayden.)

Rob Reiner and his wife, Michelle, came by to say "Hello," and also joined us for lunch.

While shaking hands with Reiner, Ted said, "I own you now."

Reiner looked rather startled and asked, "What do you mean?"

Ted replied, "I just bought the rights to *All in the Family*."

JK and DH When Ted was out of hearing range, Jane told us, "He employs a lot of people to make television programs and movies, but this is the first time he's ever been on a set. So he doesn't know anything about catering services, or any of the details involved in production."

And then she added rather wistfully, "I just wish my father were alive now so that he could see me this happy for the first time in my life."

JK Obviously word had somehow spread to the offices at TNT that Ted, himself, was on the set. And slowly, one by one, executives from the company began to show up, even though they'd been told not to come. I chatted with them between set-ups, trying my best to keep them busy and away from David and Jane, who didn't need to be distracted by visitors.

DH Based on Jane's reaction the day before, I realized that the end of the script had to be the final set-up of the day. If she was going to cry, no amount of makeup would cover her red eyes. So I juggled the order of the shoot, and we got to that last page at about 4 pm.

I called, "Action."

After about ten words, her voice broke and tears started running down her cheeks.

I said, "Cut," and went to where she was sitting on a bench. "Jane, take your time and think about it. There's no rush. Just tell me when you're ready."

Take two began, and this time she got through the first two sentences before breaking down.

I said, "Cut," and was about to go and talk to her again, when I heard a woman's voice saying, "David, let her take a break. She's obviously upset." It was one of TNT's executives, and she had decided to intervene.

I said, "No, I don't want her to lose the emotion."

The executive insisted, "She's upset. Let her take a break."

"No, she knows what she's doing. If she needs a break she'll ask for one."

I was pretty sure Jane and I were on the same page and I knew I had to hold my ground. She never asked to move out of her position, and a few minutes later, was ready to go again.

She finally made it all the way through, but only just, starting to sob during the last few words.

I said, "Cut. That was terrific. Can you do another one for me as a protection?"

She said, "Yes. But right now."

I called, "Action," and this time she managed to finish again, with as much emotion, but without falling apart at the end.

I said, "Cut. That was perfect. And that's a wrap."

JK David walked with her back to her dressing room. And as the crew was packing up, I looked around and saw that just as they had appeared seemingly out of nowhere, the TNT executives had vanished.

I remember thinking that it was somewhat poetic. The sun was setting as David and Jane were walking away from the camera, and he had prevailed in a sticky situation.

DH We recorded her voice-over narration the following day. She finished the script in no time, with very few second or third takes for any section. But to me it seemed as though she was rushing—a reading that was somewhat dry and lacking in feeling. I told her that all her takes were good, but that the pace felt just a tad fast.

Without any reservations, she said, "You may be right. Let's do it again." This time she took it a little slower, and it definitely felt like a warmer delivery. But when we listened to her various takes later in the editing room, I realized that maybe *she* was the one who was right. We chose from the first reading more often than the second.

After the last shot.
Brentwood, CA, 1991. Authors' collection.

Before she left, I had a favor to ask her. My life-partner, Don, was back in New York recovering from a spell in the Intensive Care Unit of New York's Beth Israel Hospital. He was a great admirer of Jane, so I'd brought a get-well card with me and asked her if she'd be kind enough to sign it for him.

"Of course," she said with a smile. "Let me have it and I'll ask Ted to sign it too."

JK I also heard her say, "Thank you, David. You're a very good director." I know he was pleased.

JK and DH The following evening found us with her and Ted again, this time at a black-tie event in his honor at UCLA. Our friend, Roger Mayer, had invited us not only to attend, but to sit at the same table with him, his wife Pauline, and Ted and Jane. He said, "It will be good for them to have familiar faces around." We joined the Mayers at the pre-dinner cocktail party.

DH A commotion of photographers told us Ted and Jane had arrived. They eventually spotted us and made their way through the crowd. We all embraced, and then she said, "Before I forget," as she reached into the jacket pocket of Ted's tuxedo and pulled out an envelope. It was the card I'd given her the previous day, now signed by both of them and wishing Don well. I thanked her and told her how much he would appreciate it. (He was indeed thrilled when he saw the two signatures.) I repeated how happy I was with the filming and recording she'd done over the last couple of days.

Then, out of the blue:

"Why don't you two do a program about Katharine?" she asked.

"We already did a profile of her about ten years ago," I told her. "That was the first time we met you, right after you made *On Golden Pond.*"

"Well do another one—for us this time—and I'll host it. It can be for TNT, can't it, Ted?"

"Of course, darling," he said with a smile.

JK We all went in to the main room for dinner. Jane looked beautiful in a black silk dress with an overlay of sheer black chiffon. We sat at a round table, and after dessert was served, the band played and people danced. I happened to glance at her during a particularly romantic piece of music and our eyes met. She had a wistful, peaceful look on her face as we continued to smile at each other. Then she began swaying to the music, and I noticed that her eyes were misty. I thought, "She's completely content, not only with

"Get Well" card signed by Jane and Ted.
1991. Authors' collection.

Ted, but also with the events of the last few days."

JK and DH By the time we were back in NY, Ted had already informed his production executives that we were going to produce a new profile of Katharine Hepburn. It was the fastest and easiest commission we ever had.

Of course, nothing is ever that simple. There was a rocky road ahead. But it was the birth of our program, *Katharine Hepburn: All About Me.*

And by the way, Jane was not its host.

Fonda on Fonda "graduation picture."
Brentwood, CA, 1991. Authors' collection.

Katharine Hepburn at her home in Fenwick.
Old Saybrook, CT, 1991. Photograph by John Bryson, courtesy Bryson Photo.

CHAPTER TWENTY FOUR

Kate on Kate

DH "Why do you want to do another show about me?" said Hepburn. "Because I'm so fascinating?"

"Yes, you are fascinating," I said. "But you're also a public figure, so you're fair game—anyone can produce a program about you. If *we* do a new one with you, you can tell your story the way *you* want it to be told."

"You mean, let's do it before I'm dead. But I don't need Jane to host it. I like her, but I'm alive and can speak for myself. Isn't that simpler, less contrived? And how long do you think the thing should be?"

"The show we just did about Henry Fonda is an hour. And so are all the others TNT's done."

"This has to be longer—different from the rest. I don't want to be part of a series."

JK Breaking the news that Hepburn did not want Jane to host the show had to be done with finesse. Our first call could not be to anyone at TNT. Clearly, it had to be to Jane Fonda.

"Katharine hosting her own show is a terrific idea," she said.

"And besides, I'm really busy planning my wedding [to Ted Turner], so I was worried how I'd find the time to do this."

"And she wants it to be longer than an hour."

"She's right. You can't do justice to her amazing life and career in an hour."

"But it'll be breaking TNT's mold," I said.

"Don't worry. Just say you've talked to me and I'll tell Ted."

With Jane's support, it didn't take long for the project to get a green light.

JK and DH We already knew that Hepburn had her own collection of home movies, dating back to the 1920s and 30s. Some of it had been shot by her ex-husband, "Luddy," whose full name was Ludlow Ogden Smith. When they married in 1928, she insisted that he change his name to Ogden Ludlow. She told us, "I never wanted to be Kate Smith." Not only did that sound too ordinary, but it was also the name of a well-known singer.

"I can have all the film sent to you, and you decide if there's anything interesting."

What arrived were cans and cans of 16mm film—most of it unlabeled.

She agreed to watch some of it with us, to help identify where the footage was taken and who was in it, especially the rare shots on the sets of her early RKO pictures.

"There she is with George Cukor when we were doing *Little Women*," she said. "There she is diving off the pier at Fenwick. Not bad. Strong swimmer." It was always "she," and we realized it was as though she were looking at a completely different person. However, she seemed to get bored when she wasn't on the screen, perking up when someone else was behind the camera and she was the main attraction again.

DH We were pleased when she suggested that we shoot at her home in Fenwick, a section of Old Saybrook, CT, which had been the family's private retreat for over sixty years. She had never before allowed anyone to film there.

"Come and take a look," she said.

JK The house was large, and very rustic. It felt more cluttered and eclectic than her townhouse in New York. In the entrance hall was a large wooden barrel containing the family's golf clubs. A couple of old canoes were hanging upside down from the ceiling, tied by ropes to the rafters. Painted wooden birds stood on the mantel over a fireplace, and on the walls were several of Hepburn's own paintings. A few low tribal chairs and small benches, which she'd brought back from Africa after making *The African Queen,* were in the enclosed sun-porch and living room. And throughout the house were embroidered pillows and painted signs that read, *"Listen to the Song of Life,"* which she told us was the motto by which her parents had lived. Her bedroom on the second floor had large windows on three sides, giving her a breathtaking view of the water, and in the corner was a wooden rack holding the various hats she used to protect herself from the sun.

DH We decided to shoot for two days at Fenwick in early November. But the weather reports were ominous. The East Coast was bracing for the biggest Nor'Easter of the year, and it was headed straight for Connecticut. The powerful winds coincided with what were already high tides and brought the Long Island Sound crashing into the Hepburn house—forty-eight hours before we were due to arrive.

She called me before I had a chance to call her. "What do you want to do?" she asked. "You can come and film us bailing out the water. Or you can juggle the schedule and wait until next week. I can drive into the city tonight and we can shoot some of what we want to do in New York."

I was torn. The sight of her and the Fenwick household dealing with a flood would have had its own fascination. However, I realized that the prudent thing to do was to have the crew report to her East 49th Street townhouse the following morning.

Crew and Katharine Hepburn, setting up the first shot.
New York, 1991. Photograph by John Bryson, courtesy Bryson Photo.

JK The first shot had her sitting in her favorite chair and answering the phone. She'd ad-lib a short conversation, turning down an invitation to make a personal appearance. David told Norah, the housekeeper, who was downstairs, that he'd cue her to dial Hepburn's number, using the second line in the kitchen.

DH I called, "Roll film" and "Action," and was about to cue Norah, when the phone rang. Kate picked it up.

"What? When? No I couldn't possibly do that. Sorry. Goodbye."

I said, "Cut," wondering what was wrong with Norah; why hadn't she waited for my cue?

Hepburn started laughing. "That was a friend of mine. He must think I'm gone in the head—feeble-minded. I'd better call back later and explain that we were making a movie here."

JK and DH Early in the planning stages, she'd said, "You have to shoot what goes on every time we leave to go to Fenwick for the weekend. It's like a circus. We take enough stuff for a month—food, clothes, and all the flowers. I never leave the flowers behind."

DH So we shot it that day, and she was right—it was quite a scene. Her assistant, Phyllis, was the first to walk out of the house, carrying a bottle of Scotch, followed by Norah with bundles of clothes, then Jimmy, Kate's driver, with boxes of food he piled into the trunk, and finally Hepburn came out, carrying flowers. She handed them to Phyllis in the back seat, before getting into the car herself next to Jimmy. They went for a short trip around the block, and then came back to do another take.

As they headed into the house, Kate said to me, "When you've finished this shot, don't let me forget to return the plant."

"What plant?" I asked.

"My neighbor's," she said. "All the flowers I have are pink and white—and they'd look rather dull on camera. No contrast. So I picked up this pot of red geraniums from next door. Stephen Sondheim lives there. And his assistant came out and said, 'Why are you stealing our plant?' I said, 'Don't worry. I'll give it back. We're shooting a movie, and I need a bright color.' So, David, make sure I remember."

Three takes later, she did indeed return it.

Katharine Hepburn with Stephen Sondheim's plant.
New York, 1991. Photograph by John Bryson, courtesy Bryson Photo.

JK Our production assistant had made notes of where everything was in the trunk, knowing that when we shot in Fenwick, we'd be filming the *un*packing of the car and all the items had to be in the exact same place for continuity.

The following week, when everyone really *was* taking off for Connecticut, we went to 49th Street to be sure that they hadn't forgotten anything. Once again, Hepburn took Sondheim's plant and, for the second time, his assistant saw her and opened the door.

"Kate, what are you doing now?"

She said, "I'll bring it back next week. I need it for the film when we unpack the car in Fenwick." True to her word, she returned it several days later.

DH We then took off ourselves and checked in to The Old Saybrook Inn, right on the water.

But the next morning when I looked out of the window, I couldn't see a thing. A thick coastal fog obliterated what had once been a beautiful view—and all the scenes we'd planned were exteriors. However, when the crew and I set out to film establishing shots of the house from across the pier, I had a glimmer of hope that the fog might be lifting. And eventually it did, giving us a clear picture by the time the camera rolled.

JK I went directly to Hepburn's house. As usual, she was ready long before she needed to be. I'd been there only a few minutes when her makeup artist, Michal Bigger, came downstairs.

"Kate wants to talk to you."

"Uh-oh," I thought. "Something's wrong."

I climbed the stairs to her room and found her looking out of the window.

"We can't do the first shot of me spreading my laundry on the grass. There's no sun. Idiotic."

I tried to sound reassuring, "Don't worry, we have lights and reflectors. It'll work."

"Where's David?"

"He's out there with the crew," I said, pointing towards the pier.

"Get him," she said.

DH I saw a car heading towards us and realized Hepburn must be ready. "She's probably itchy to start," I thought.

As soon as I walked through the door, I could tell from the look on Joan's face that trouble was brewing.

"David, we have a problem. Kate doesn't want to do the laundry shot because there's no sun."

"Let me go up and talk with her," I said.

JK What felt like a split second later, he came down the stairs, walked straight past me to Michael Barry, our cinematographer, and said, "Let's set up for the laundry shot."

I couldn't believe it.

"What did you say to her?" I asked incredulously.

"I just told her not to worry. It will be fine."

"But that's exactly what I told her."

He shrugged and went outside with the crew. She needed to hear it from the director, not me.

David, Kate, and crew preparing for laundry shot.
Old Saybrook, CT, 1991. Photograph by John Bryson, courtesy Bryson Photo.

DH Hepburn walked out of the house with her arms full of wet sheets, but obviously felt she needed to acknowledge the gray sky.

"I hope it's not going to rain," she ad-libbed, looking upwards, before spreading everything out to dry on the grass.

Then she suddenly shouted, "Norah!" And her housekeeper came running out to help. Now, Kate had never mentioned to me that she wanted Norah to be a part of the scene, but it didn't seem like a bad idea. I'd already learned to roll with the punches, knowing that I would get the best out of her by allowing her plenty of leeway, so I didn't say "Cut." When I finally did, she started to laugh.

"No. Don't come out," she said to a very confused Norah. "I don't need you. I'm just trying to make it more interesting."

We did two more takes; Norah stayed inside; and it didn't rain.

JK and DH She had taken cold showers every day from the time she was a child. Her father, Dr. Thomas Hepburn, told her it was good for her character. For most of her life she also swam daily at Fenwick, even when there was snow on the ground. Maybe she'd built up an immunity to cold water over the years. Or maybe she believed she was still improving her character.

She volunteered to let us film her going in for a swim.

DH Even though the sun was out by late afternoon, all of us still were wearing sweatshirts and jackets.

Kate was on her way upstairs to change into a swimsuit, when Phyllis became very upset. "Miss Hepburn, it's too cold. You shouldn't go into the water today." I knew there had to be a good reason for her concern. But her protest was having no effect. So she took me aside and asked if I would talk Kate out of it. What I only found out later was that, after several bouts with the flu, Hepburn had cut back on her swims, especially in cold weather.

I knocked on her door. "Come in." She was already in her swimsuit, looking out of the window onto Long Island Sound. I knew I couldn't say, "It's too cold to do this today." But suddenly a plausible argument came into my head, although I was not sure she'd buy it.

"Miss Hepburn, the tide is going out. I don't see where we can get a decent shot of you. The water's too shallow."

"Hmmm. Yes, you're probably right," she said. "Let's do it tomorrow. I owe you a shot."

The weather the next day was about the same, perhaps a few degrees warmer. However, no one brought up the idea of the swim. Not even Katharine Hepburn. Perhaps she forgot, or perhaps she thought *we* forgot. My own belief is that she allowed me to let her off the hook gracefully, and once off it, she was happy to stay off—and so were we. An eighty-four-year-old woman swimming in ice cold water was not a good idea, whether or not she was used to it. Had we insisted, undoubtedly she would have done it. And Phyllis would have never forgiven me.

Joan Kramer, Katharine Hepburn and crew. During second day's filming at Fenwick. Old Saybrook, CT, 1991. Photograph by John Bryson, courtesy Bryson Photo.

JK It had turned into a pleasant, sunny afternoon. I suggested to David that he might want to consider filming Hepburn lying on the beach at the back of the house.

DH The light was just right and I could visualize a beautiful image with the lighthouse in the distance. I mentioned it to Kate.

"I don't do that. I'm allergic to the sun. I never lie on the beach. Absolutely not."

Instead we set up for a shot in her canoe. The water was calm, and the results were quite striking, both visually and symbolically. (She'd told us, "I always took charge of my life; always 'paddled my own canoe.'") After we'd finished, and we were walking up the beach together, she said, "Why don't I lie down over there on the sand and read a newspaper. Would that work for you?"

"That's a great idea," I told her. "Let's do it now."

Undoubtedly, she'd needed time to think about it and come up with her own twist: the newspaper as her prop.

JK She still often rode a bicycle, which David and I wanted to include in the program. As she took off on her bike for the starting point he'd chosen, I snapped a picture, which shows him running behind her. He always tells people, "There it is—a perfect example of me directing Katharine Hepburn."

JK and DH After she and Spencer Tracy made the movie, *Pat and Mike,* director George Cukor gave her a golf cart, so we suggested filming her driving it around Fenwick.

"Oh, that was a long time ago. I don't have it anymore," she said. So that was crossed off the list of things to do.

But as we were shooting a scene outside, where she was gathering logs for her fireplace, we heard the sound of crunching gravel on the driveway. Looking up, we saw a man approaching in a golf cart.

"Here it is," he said to her. "Just call me when you're done with it."

David and Kate.
Old Saybrook, CT, 1991. Authors' collection.

Once more, she'd thought about it, and decided it was too good an idea to pass up.

DH I hadn't ordered a dolly or any way to shoot a moving golf cart. It was time for a quick conference with Michael Barry. "We can pan as she passes the camera, but that will be boring. How can we do this?" I asked him.

Mike was calm, as always, and he had a solution. "We can put the camera on baby legs (a very small tripod) in the back of my van with the rear doors open. Just tell her to follow us and let's see what we get."

JK There was no room for me in the van, and the small caravan was gone for almost an hour.

Several days later, when I saw the footage for the first time, I noticed that while she was driving along, she turned her head a few times and waved. I asked David, "Who was she waving at? Did crowds gather along the way?"

"No, there was nobody there," he said. "The place was deserted. So instead of just staring straight ahead, she decided to add a little variety to the scene."

It's no accident that Katharine Hepburn was, and still is, the only four-time winner of the Academy Award for Best Actress[1].

DH We needed one more full day of filming in New York—a single set-up with her sitting in her favorite leather chair in the upstairs living room. However, at around 4 in the afternoon, Joan took me aside and said, "Why don't we shoot her on the stairs? It would be the perfect lead-in to the scene of her packing the car and driving off to Fenwick."

I knew that Kate was getting tired at this point, and she was expecting dinner guests at 6. So I was reluctant to move to another location in the house, but Joan was right.

I said to Hepburn, "We just have one last shot. And I'd like to do it on the stairs, with you putting on your shoes, getting ready to leave for the weekend in Connecticut."

It was a tight space, and she didn't object. But as we were preparing for the first take she said, "David, when we've finished this scene, you're going to tell me why you decided to stage it this way."

I simply nodded, but I knew that she was getting more antsy by the minute.

Then she added, "And this might be the last shot I ever do in my life."

"Well then, we'd better get it right, hadn't we?" I said.

---

1   *Morning Glory* (1933), *Guess Who's Coming To Dinner* (1967), *The Lion In Winter* (1968), *On Golden Pond* (1981).

The words had come out of my mouth before I could stop myself. And suddenly there was a dead silence. No one moved.

Kate burst into laughter—the deep snorting laugh that we'd come to know so well.

"OK, everyone," I said. "Let's do this. Roll film."

We did three takes—each one better than the last.

"That's a wrap. Thank you, everybody."

By the time the crew had packed up it was just after 5:30—a close call, but still time for Hepburn to get ready for her dinner guests.

JK However, as we were about to leave, she said to me, "Go get your cameraman. He's been an angel. I want to talk to him." I found Mike Barry, who was taken aback for a moment, but went upstairs to her living room, where he found her pouring scotch into two glasses.

He recently wrote to us, recalling his memories of that day:

"After a long, hard shoot, I was totally spent. We did not have a large crew; in fact we had no lighting crew at all. My gaffer, Mark Chamberlin, and I did it all ourselves, and we were sweaty and dirty, loading the equipment into the truck, when Joan told me that Miss Hepburn would like to have a few words with me. We had worked her quite hard that day, and she was anxious to get rid of us. I was very nervous. Was she going to take me to task about my lighting? Can you imagine how stressful it was to light the great Katharine Hepburn? I tentatively entered her living room, and she said, 'Come and sit down. Let's have a drink together. We deserve it.' I hate scotch, but I wasn't about to tell her that.

She started off by asking me if I was related to the writer, Philip Barry, who'd been a friend of hers. She then proceeded to compliment me, and tell me what a delight it was to work with me. We had shot with her a number of days in both New York and Connecticut, filming her packing her car, doing her laundry, playing tennis, etc. Then she asked, 'What do you want to do in the future? Make movies?' 'Yes, of course,' I said. 'But those jobs don't come easily.'

*'You can do it. Just keep trying,' she told me. 'You're very talented.'
As I was sipping the scotch (and pretending that I loved it), I was
essentially pinching myself. Was this a dream? Sitting with the great
Katharine Hepburn in her living room, just the two of us! Without
question, that was the highlight of my career."*

JK and DH Throughout the production she never asked us which
film clips, photos, or anything else we planned to use or not use.
So when we screened the finished program for her, we didn't know
what to expect.

"I won't ask you how much they paid you for doing it," she said.
"But I'm sure it wasn't enough. Damn good job."

Katharine Hepburn: All About Me received a tremendous amount
of publicity, including a billboard above Sunset Boulevard in Los
Angeles. There were two invitation-only screenings: one at Lincoln
Center's Walter Reade Theater in New York, and the other at the
Alfred Hitchcock Theatre on the Universal Studios' lot in California,
where Jane Fonda was the host of the evening. Kate turned down
requests to attend either of them, as she always did for such events.

But she had an even more pressing reason than usual. Phyllis
was in the hospital, and she told us, "I can't be out celebrating while
Phyllis is sick." However, she agreed to tape on-camera introduc-
tions, to be shown right before each screening. The two pieces were
similar, telling the audience that the main reason she had agreed to
this project was to talk about her extraordinary parents. But the one
for California also included a personal greeting to Jane.

The program was nominated for an Emmy (TNT's only nomination that year). It didn't win, but was honored with several other
awards including a Telly, a Cine Golden Eagle, and a Chicago
International Film Festival Silver Hugo.

We continued to see Hepburn regularly over the next ten years.
The last time was a few years prior to her death. She was in her
nineties by then, and living full-time at Fenwick, no longer going
back and forth to New York. She was sitting on the sofa in the living

room when we arrived, and greeted us warmly. But it was clear that she didn't have the strength she once had, and was somewhat forgetful about whether people she'd worked with in the past were still alive. However, we had one of our usual spirited discussions, along with tea and her sinfully rich, flourless chocolate brownies.

Katharine Hepburn died in 2003 at the age of ninety-six. At home, on her own terms, just as she had lived.

For us, it was a privilege to have known her and been trusted by her. While she worked with many producers and directors throughout her life, we have to stop and remember that we're in the tiny group of people who produced and directed projects that were personal to her, that she really cared about. And that fills us with pride.

Photograph by John Bryson, courtesy Bryson Photo.

Richard Dreyfuss and "Bruce," the shark from *Jaws*.
Universal City, CA, 1995. Authors' collection.

Glenn Close with "Captain America" bike from *Easy Rider*.
Culver City, CA, 1998. Authors' collection.

CHAPTER TWENTY FIVE

Two Birthdays— Universal and Columbia

Two studio anniversary celebrations, an eightieth for Universal and a seventy-fifth for Columbia, presented unique challenges. How could we make an audience care about corporate entities, albeit entities that glittered with stars and legendary movies? And how could we tell the stories of these two great studios by showing excerpts from the motion pictures they made, when the movies' plots had nothing to do with the tales we were trying to tell? Of course there were powerful behind-the-scenes personalities here— Carl Laemmle, the founder of Universal Pictures, and Harry Cohn, who, with his brother, Jack, created Columbia—but most people had never heard of them. However, having unrestricted access to their libraries, and a free hand to use anything we wanted, must have blinded us. We said "Yes" to both projects—and afterwards vowed we'd never take on anything like this again.

DH One of our first decisions had to do with interviews. There was such a vast amount of visual material available that we decided to record people audio-only. We would show excerpts from the movies themselves, and behind-the-scenes shots, but with no interruptions from "talking heads." It would be much more compelling to hear Arnold Schwarzenegger tell us about the making of *Conan the Barbarian,* and how he was bitten by one of the wild dogs, as we saw the scene play out, than it would have been to stop the scene and cut to Arnold on camera. And this audio-only approach had an additional benefit: we could include archival interviews, most of which were not on film, and these would be on a par with the ones we did ourselves. Thus Lew Ayres, Paul Newman, Mary Tyler Moore, Steven Spielberg, Lupita Tovar, Susan Kohner, Gregory Peck, as well as Arnold, to name a few, could be indistinguishably mixed with stories told by Mary Pickford, Fred Astaire, Boris Karloff, Orson Welles, and others we found in collections.

JK In 1990, Universal City turned seventy-five. But the studio let the milestone go by with virtually no hoopla.

Three years later, Blair Westlake, who headed the Pay Television Division, called to ask if we'd be interested in producing a program in time to celebrate Universal's eightieth birthday. He was upset that its seventy-fifth had been all but overlooked, and was determined not to allow the eightieth to have the same fate.[1] We'd met Blair some seven years earlier, when we shot on the Universal backlot with Johnny Carson and Jimmy Stewart for *James Stewart: A Wonderful Life.* Blair was responsible then for making certain that we had the proper insurance coverage. He came by the set and we struck up a friendship. He subsequently rose through the ranks, eventually holding the title of Chairman of Universal Television.

When we started the project in 1994, the studio was ruled by Lew Wasserman[2] together with his second-in-command, Sidney

---

1   Universal Pictures came into being as The Universal Film Manufacturing Company in 1912, the result of a merger between a number of small independent companies (IMP, Nestor, Rex, Éclair, et al). For some reason, MCA/Universal decided to recognize the 1915 opening of Universal City as the birth of Universal, and created a 75th anniversary logo for its feature films released in 1990.

2   See also "Getting to Know The Last Mogul."

Universal City opening day poster.
March 15, 1915. Authors' collection.

Sheinberg, and it was obvious that we needed them both for the program. However, Wasserman rarely ever agreed to be interviewed;

his policy was to work unseen by the public, to avoid the limelight. We asked Blair to help. He spoke to Sheinberg, who somehow persuaded Wasserman that they should do an interview together. But Sid had misunderstood that we needed voice only, so we found that we had them scheduled for an *on-camera* interview. It would be at 11am on a Thursday morning on the top floor of the corporate building known as the Black Tower, which is near the entrance to Universal City. When we reminded Blair that we only needed their audio, he said, "Let's film them anyway. You can use just their voices for the program, but we'll have a rare interview for the archives."

By an unfortunate coincidence, that same Thursday morning was the only time that Steven Spielberg was available, and we had already scheduled him for 9:30 at the Amblin Entertainment complex, which was also on the Universal City lot, but a good fifteen minutes away from the Black Tower.

DH I had our film crew start setting up for the Wasserman/Sheinberg interview at about 8:30, and when I was satisfied that all was going well, left them to head to Amblin. As Spielberg was to be audio-only, it would not take long to get ready. The receptionist told us that Steven wanted the interview to take place in his screening room, but he was currently in a meeting which was running long, and he would probably be about fifteen minutes late.

Steven Spielberg started his career at Universal, and had played a large role in the studio's success over the last twenty-or-so years. We had a long list of questions for him.

JK At 9:45 there was another message from the receptionist. Steven was still in his meeting, but would be with us as soon as it was finished. David and I were now looking at which questions we could eliminate. We had to be finished at Amblin by 10:30 if we were to get back to the Black Tower in time for the Wasserman/Sheinberg filming. There was no way we could be late for that.

DH At 10 o'clock Steven Spielberg walked into the screening room. He was full of apologies, and suggested that we begin recording immediately. I had in mind a few questions that we could cut, but started at the beginning.

"Can you tell us about the first time you were on the Universal lot?"

It was with his first answer that I realized we had our dream interviewee. His responses were all concise and to the point. There were no rambling stories, no irrelevant asides. This was a filmmaker who knew what it was like to be in an editing room—which answers could make it into the final cut, and he was doing his very best to deliver those answers. For example, when I asked him who the producer was on one of his early films, he gave a name, and then paused momentarily.

"No, that might be wrong," he said. "I'll give you another line and you can edit in whichever is correct."

Despite our many questions, and starting half an hour later than planned, I knew early on that we would not have to eliminate any of them.

JK Near the end, David asked him something that I thought was pushing the envelope too far. We'd read an article about the making of *Schindler's List*, in which Spielberg was quoted as saying that one location was the real site of a Hitler death camp, and he had hired German actors to play the guards, all of them dressed in authentic Nazi uniforms. Between shots, they wanted to chat with him about *Jaws, E.T.*, and his other famous movies, but he found he couldn't deal with them. Even though he knew intellectually that they were actors in costume, all he could see were Nazi officers. He just turned his back and walked away.

I was afraid that bringing this up might cause Steven some embarrassment, but David waited until the end of the interview and went for it. I was holding my breath.

Spielberg said that the story was true, and that we were the first to ask him about it since the article had appeared. He reiterated that he couldn't get past the sight of those actors in those uniforms in that location and what it all represented. However, they were still at that same location at the beginning of Passover, and he decided to hold a Seder for the entire cast and crew. At one point he turned and saw the German actors enter the room, wearing suits and ties, with yarmulkes on their heads. They took seats at the table, held hands with everyone else and bowed their heads, joining in the prayers. Steven said he sat at the head of the table and began to weep. And at that moment he knew he would never again judge a man by his forefathers.

I had tears in my eyes too.

As we were about to leave, I said to him, "What's interesting to me is that after all the films you've done, you don't seem to have lost the 'wonder.'"

"It's true," he replied. "I get that from my mother. She's always been filled with 'wonder' and still is."

DH Looking back, it's perhaps one of the best interviews anyone ever gave us.

But now there were only twenty-five minutes to wrap up, get to the Black Tower—running was the only option—and check that everything was ready for Lew Wasserman and Sid Sheinberg. When we arrived, I had one small adjustment I wanted the crew to make, and as it was completed, the two of them walked through the door. It was exactly 11 am.

Wasserman began with, "You know, we have final cut on this." I reminded him that the studio had final cut on the entire program. He wasn't an easy interviewee, warming to some questions, but giving only brief replies to others. Sheinberg was more forthcoming. But by the end, both of them were comfortable and Sheinberg joked, "Now we'd like to turn the camera around so we can ask *you* some questions."

JK and DH Like all studios, Universal has its hierarchy, and there's a pecking order for getting things done. We knew that as outsiders, we needed some top-flight muscle to cut through the red tape, otherwise, requests for screening cassettes, photos, research files, etc. would take months. We couldn't afford any delays since we were on a budget and a strict timetable.

Sid Sheinberg sent out a memo to the ten thousand department heads at Universal Studios in California, Florida, Europe, and New York, directing them to inform their staffs that this project was to be given priority status. It worked like a charm.

However, that wasn't the only perk that came with having the highest-level executives as allies. Towards the end of one of our trips to Los Angeles, Universal Television Chairman, Tom Wertheimer, offered us a rare opportunity: to be flown back to New York on the studio's private jet. Never before or since have we had that experience. We were picked up at our hotel and taken to the Burbank airport where the twin-jet Gulfstream IV was waiting on the tarmac. The aircraft's tail number was N315MC, and we discovered that it was more than just coincidence that Lew Wasserman's birthday was March 15th (and, oddly enough, Universal's founder, Carl Laemmle, had opened the gates to Universal City on March 15th, 1915).

David and Joan on steps of Universal's corporate jet. Burbank Airport, CA, 1995. Authors' collection.

DH The interior of the plane was furnished with sofas and plush chairs, and in addition to the pilot and co-pilot, there was another engineer who also served as the steward, looking after our every need. We were on board with some studio executives who had to stop in San Jose for a meeting before going on to New York. When we landed in San Jose, two limos were waiting: one took the executives to their meeting and the other took us sightseeing. We stopped at a few shops and bought souvenirs and, about ninety minutes later, headed back to the airport.

The pilot invited me to sit in the cockpit during take-off, and it was thrilling. And several hours later, when we were about to land at Teterboro Airport in New Jersey, Joan was equally as thrilled when she was asked to be in the cockpit for the descent and landing. Once again, two limousines were waiting on the tarmac: one to take the executives to their hotel, and the other to take us to our respective homes.

I told Joan, "Let's not get too used to all this pampering, or we'll never be able to fly coach again."

JK *The Universal Story* was hosted by Richard Dreyfuss. Sheinberg chose him from a list I discussed with him in a phone conversation that lasted about twenty-five minutes. When Blair heard about it, he said, "You talked for twenty-five minutes? Sid is known for thirty-second calls. He's not a guy who chats on the telephone."

"Well, he did with me. And his choice was Dreyfuss. He said, 'Go with Ricky. He's smart; he's in one of our most important movies, *Jaws*, among others; and he cares about Hollywood history.'"

Fortunately, Richard was our first choice too. We'd met him when he agreed to be interviewed for the show about James Stewart. Back then he had impressed us with his detailed knowledge of films and the motion picture business. He is a true movie buff.

I called his assistant, Audrey Bamber, and told her we were inviting him to host and narrate the program about Universal, and that he was not only our choice, but Sid Sheinberg's as well. We'd need him for four days of shooting on the Universal lot plus two days of narration. And we'd like to meet and talk with him before the shoot to go over the script. He called the next day and accepted the offer.

I asked him, "Do you prefer to be called Ricky?"

"Why?"

"Because that's the name Sid Sheinberg used."

"He probably called me that because Steven Spielberg does, and they're good friends. But everyone else calls me Richard."

Richard Dreyfuss filming introduction to *Jurassic Park* sequence for *The Universal Story*. Universal City, CA, 1995. Authors' collection.

JK and DH The story of Universal was right up his alley. He relished learning about its founder, Carl Laemmle, and how Laemmle eventually lost the studio when he borrowed money to finance a sound version of *Show Boat*. He was so sure the picture would be a hit that he put up his studio as collateral for the loan. As luck would have it, the production fell badly behind schedule, and when the loan repayment became due, Laemmle lost his gamble—and Universal Pictures. When *Show Boat* was finished and released, it was indeed a big hit, but it was too late. By then, the film—and Universal—belonged to a bank, Standard Capital.

But there were portions of the script to which Richard objected. He felt that some of it, especially the more recent history, sounded too promotional and he said, "I don't want to be part of just a puff piece." Neither did we, so his comments were particularly helpful. And he kept reminding us to include phrases about the studio being "big business," with its eye always on how much money their films, the tour, etc. were making.

DH One of the locations we used was Stage 28, the oldest on the lot. It was built in 1924 for the original *The Phantom of the Opera* and contains an exact replica of the interior of the Paris Opera House, which has also been used as a "theater set" for many films since. We arranged to have Richard wear a tux and sit in one of the boxes as he talked about *Phantom*.

The day before the shoot, our production manager came to me with a problem. "We have to re-arrange our schedule. The studio's cleaning crew found fleas in the curtains of the opera house boxes, so the stage has to be fumigated."

We all agreed that it was best not to mention the problem to Richard—and we almost got away with it.

Unfortunately, as a studio car was bringing him there the next day, the driver said, "I hope they got rid of all the fleas."

Richard turned to Joan. "Fleas? What fleas?" he said.

When we arrived, there was a slight smell of mustiness and extermination fumes, but no sign of the fleas.

Stage 28, by the way, has always been rumored to be haunted.

JK Each day we had a catered lunch on tables near our "home base." All of us, including Richard, sat and ate together, with him telling stories about the making of *Jaws,* and many of his other films. The crew later told us that this job was one of the best experiences they'd had. It's more usual for a star to have lunch in his dressing trailer,

Richard Dreyfuss on the Phantom Stage.
Universal City, CA, 1995. Authors' collection.

rather than socializing with the members of the crew.

Our last location was at "Jaws Lake," where we'd been asked to set up and get our shot quickly, so that the Universal City tour bus didn't have to be diverted any longer than absolutely necessary. The shark was a main attraction, and people would be very annoyed if they weren't able to see it.

The studio's engineers had agreed to adjust the computer that controlled "Bruce" (the fake shark), so that it would rise up out of the water directly behind Richard at the right point in the script. It turned out to be more complicated than we had imagined, and in take after take, "Bruce" bopped up in the wrong place or at the wrong time.

Richard turned around and said, "Some nightmares never end," a reference to the fact that the original mechanical shark used in the making of *Jaws* was famously temperamental too.

JK and DH We had planned to send a limo to bring Dreyfuss to the set every morning, but he insisted on driving himself. At the end of each day, we asked him again, and again he turned us down.

Finally his assistant, Audrey, said, "Richard, do you know why they keep offering to send a car and driver for you? They're worried about you."

The truth was that we were, indeed, worried. He had had a well-publicized problem with substance abuse and had once driven his Mercedes into a tree. He was seriously injured and is lucky to have survived. He checked into a rehab facility and has been clean ever since.

JK He told me, "If you're afraid that you're going to lose your host in a ditch, I'll make a deal with you. I still want to drive myself, but I'll arrive fifteen minutes early just to reassure you." True to his word, he drove onto the lot at 7:45 am each day, parked his car, and when he saw me, did a little dance with arms opened wide, saying, "Ta-dah—I'm here."

DH After our four days of shooting at Universal, we started the two days of narration. We played back the rough-cut of the show, which had my voice as a "scratch track" on it, so that Richard could see the visuals as he read his lines. But some of them had to fit in very tight spaces, and when he had trouble speaking fast enough, he took it as a challenge.

He said, "David, if you can do it, so can I. Let me hear your scratch track in my headphones." I had never seen anyone do that before. But it worked. He succeeded in reading the script with the exact timings we needed, sounding completely natural and not at all strained or mechanical. However I decided not to tell him that my speed had been faked. Our editor, Scott Doniger (who edited almost every program Joan and I did), had cut out breaths between words, in order to make my narration fit.

JK and DH By the time the show was finished, we were exhausted. The research had been exciting, even thrilling at times, when we uncovered elusive footage or stumbled across forgotten events. But it had been a very big undertaking, and just getting to the end felt like an achievement.

Joan and Richard discussing script.
Universal City, CA, 1995. Authors' collection.

Universal was very happy with the program, as was the Starz network, on which it premiered. *The Universal Story* vividly shows how a second tier Hollywood studio[3] survived against the odds, and eventually became one of the most powerful in the industry.

---

3   In the 1930s the leaders were MGM, Paramount, 20th Century Fox, and Warner Bros, with RKO close behind.

***

Glenn Close on the original Columbia Pictures lot.
Sunset-Gower Studios, Los Angeles, CA, 1998. Authors' collection.

Somehow the agonies of production are overshadowed, and all but forgotten, if the show turns out to be a success. *The Universal Story* was well-received, and we soon recovered from the feeling of being knee-deep in quicksand.

In the fall of 1996, we received a phone call from our friend, Su Lesser, a vice president at Columbia Pictures. She had licensed clips to us for our first two Astaire shows, and we met soon after while she was on a business trip to New York. When the shows were nominated for Emmy Awards, she volunteered to throw a party at her apartment in LA and invited those from other studios who had also helped us. Su is a friend to this day.

She was calling about Columbia Pictures' birthday. "The studio will turn seventy-five in January, 1999, and I think we should be celebrating with a documentary like the one you did for Universal. Would you be interested? I've already mentioned it to Jeff Sagansky[4], and told him about you, and he was enthusiastic about the idea."

Without too much hesitation—actually none at all—we said, "We'd love to do it." We didn't even pause to think about the magnitude of taking on another studio's story.

JK On the day after Christmas, I happened to be in the office alone, cleaning up some paperwork, when the phone rang.

The voice on the other end said, "Hi. This is Jeff Sagansky at Columbia Pictures. Is Joan there?"

Somehow I recovered quickly enough. "Yes, this is Joan."

"Su Lesser gave me your number. As you probably know, she's suggested that you and your partner produce a seventy-fifth anniversary special about the studio. Are you still interested and do you have the time? I confess I haven't seen the show you did about Universal. Could you send me a cassette? Su told me it's terrific."

"I think she's a bit prejudiced, since we're old friends, but yes, we have the time and we'd be happy to do it. By the way, Merry Christmas and Happy New Year."

"The same to you. I'll be in touch again after the holidays."

However, January came and went with no further word. We asked Su what was going on, but she didn't know, so we decided to take the lead. We called for an appointment to meet Sagansky, and booked a trip to Los Angeles.

JK and DH Sony Pictures was, and still is, based in Culver City on the old MGM lot, which we knew well from the shows we'd done on Spencer Tracy and James Stewart. Jeff Sagansky's office was in the legendary Thalberg building. He shook hands and introduced

---

4   Sagansky was Co-President of Sony Pictures Entertainment, which owns Columbia Pictures.

us to Andy Kaplan, head of Columbia Television. Andy was cordial, but not particularly friendly. We wondered if his coolness was because he was being handed a project that he hadn't initiated, basically being assigned to oversee it by his boss. However, Jeff said that he wanted to make this program a reality and it was up to Andy to find the money for it. By now both of them had seen *The Universal Story,* and had been impressed by it.

The meeting ended with a short discussion about who might host the show, and we were told, "Don't worry about that. We have relationships with many stars that we can approach and we won't have to pay them a lot of money."

JK Our contract negotiations were not easy. In fact, at one point, Andy Kaplan told me that he was getting a "visceral" feeling that this project wouldn't happen. I then called Jeff Sagansky and asked if the studio had changed its mind. He assured me it hadn't. After that, our lawyer, Anita Shapiro, ironed out the rest of the deal with Michael Viebrock, the attorney at Columbia.

We were beginning to wonder if our relationship with Andy, to whom we were reporting, would be fraught with tension. As it turned out, we needn't have worried. He was very supportive, always helpful, and always available.

JK and DH Columbia had a close relationship with HBO and Andy saw the possibility of them financing the project. He asked us to go with him to a meeting in Los Angeles with Chris Albrecht, HBO's Chairman and CEO. We were flown out first class and put up at the Peninsula Hotel in Beverly Hills—very different from the way that documentary producers usually travel.

The meeting with Albrecht seemed to go well. He knew of our *Universal Story,* which had been broadcast by HBO's competitor, Starz. But when we told him that Universal had been pretty much hands-off editorially, he said, "You won't find it like that here."

A few days later we were in Andy Kaplan's office to get the

bad news that HBO was not interested. But in the conversation he mentioned a new deal that Columbia now had to supply Starz/Encore with product, and we reminded him that Starz had been very pleased with *The Universal Story*. Maybe they would want this new program about Columbia. Within a week he'd made the sale, and we had the money to produce the show.

DH In order to get a full picture of the business side of the studio, Jeff Sagansky arranged for us to meet the renowned corporate investment banker, Herbert Allen, Jr. We spent an entire morning with him in his New York office, and were fascinated by the behind-the-scenes power that he wielded when he was instrumental in rescuing Columbia from the brink of bankruptcy a number of years back.

In fact, during Harry Cohn's reign, while often tumultuous, the studio never was in the red. Only after he died, when top management seemed to change every few years, was the financial stability of the company on a roller coaster, several times plummeting to near-disaster. Herb Allen was able to give us the details that led to the downfalls and how he and producer, Ray Stark, managed to put the studio back on a sound financial foundation.

And then we lost our most powerful ally. In a typical Hollywood upheaval, Jeff Sagansky resigned. We were stunned; even though we had a contract and were in production, Jeff wouldn't be there to see the project through to completion.

Fortunately Su was still there. We spoke with her every day, sometimes more than once. She made the vital process of getting screening cassettes of movies as easy as possible. And we soon became friends with Maria Blanco, who was responsible for making and sending us the tapes, often a dozen or more at a time. Su also pushed all the right buttons in all the necessary departments to get us through the maze of legal clearances. She was essentially one of our executive producers, along with Andy Kaplan. Unfortunately though, when it came time to finalize the on-screen credits, Columbia took the same position as Universal: no credits for any studio employees. Su was disappointed, but she could hardly argue the point when Andy, himself, was not getting a credit.

But we're leaping too far ahead here.

JK It didn't take long for us to remember how daunting it can be to tell the story of a studio, and how we needed to find a way to make an audience care about a corporation, however glamorous the business. Again, we felt as though we were drowning in a surplus of riches. Here was a producer's dream of having access to all the material in the archives—thousands of feature films, television series, cartoons, shorts, serials, plus photos, posters, contracts, scripts, memos, etc.—offset by the nightmare of having to look at and analyze as many as possible, and then decide what should be used to move the story along.

DH Columbia started out in 1924 as a "Poverty Row" studio, with its headquarters on the notoriously low-rent Gower Street. At the other end of the spectrum, also founded in 1924, was the star-studded MGM, located on a luxurious lot in Culver City. They couldn't have been further apart in all respects.

One of Columbia's most colorful characters was its founder, Harry Cohn. He was known to have been rude, ruthless and vulgar. None of the Hollywood moguls was especially beloved, but Harry Cohn was probably the bottom of the heap. When he died in 1958, huge crowds turned out for his funeral, about which Red Skelton famously quipped, "You give the public what they want, and they'll show up."

But Cohn had a remarkable eye for talent, nurturing actors such as Jean Arthur, Rita Hayworth, Glenn Ford, Jack Lemmon, Judy Holliday and Kim Novak, and—perhaps most importantly—director Frank Capra, who put Columbia on the map with *It Happened One Night*, which swept the Oscars for 1934. But Cohn also made blunders. After Marilyn Monroe appeared in a film for him, he decided not to sign her to a contract. "She can't act," he said.

JK and DH We found that one of the ways to grapple with telling this story was to do what we had done with Universal and create segments focusing on several stars and directors who made their marks while working at the studio. An obvious one was Margarita Cansino. She became one of Harry Cohn's most famous "creations." He changed the color of her hair, and her hairline, as well as her name—to Rita Hayworth. And he cast her opposite Cary Grant, Glenn Ford, Gene Kelly, and Fred Astaire, to name a few. With her smoldering sexuality, she became Columbia's biggest moneymaker in films such as *Gilda*, *Miss Sadie Thompson, Only Angels Have Wings,* and *Cover Girl.* And the public was just as captivated by her off-screen life. Her marriage to Prince Aly Khan caused ripples around the world, and a tidal wave in the office of Harry Cohn when she announced she was giving up Hollywood for the life of a princess. Four years later, she and the Prince were divorced, and Cohn not only welcomed her back, but reveled in the publicity generated by her return.

It was fairly well known that Rita Hayworth lip-synched her musical numbers to other voices, such as Anita Ellis's. But there had long been a rumor that in one scene in *Gilda*, Rita had done her own singing while strumming a guitar. We wanted to either confirm or deny the rumor. So we sent a cassette of the film to her daughter, Princess Yasmin Aga Khan, who lives in New York. She called back a few days later to say that the voice was not her mother's.

DH Soon after we were hired to produce the program, we had dinner in Los Angeles with our friend, Roger Mayer and his wife, Pauline. They both had worked at Columbia years before, and he told us about an ill-fated project called *Joseph and His Brethren.*

He said, "It was at a time when Hollywood was captivated by Biblical epics, and Harry Cohn wanted one of his own. Rita Hayworth was set to play the lead, and while work was being done on the script, director William Dieterle took a second unit film crew to Egypt and shot hours of footage of camels in the desert. But the project was bogged down with one problem after another. I wonder if any of that footage still exists."

What actually happened was that by then Rita was married to singer Dick Haymes, and the last straw was when he decided he wanted to play Joseph. That's when Harry Cohn threw in the towel and finally abandoned the film. It had cost him over two years and close to two million dollars.

A few months later, when we interviewed Jack Lemmon, he said that while he was a contract player at the studio, often butting heads with Cohn, he was tested for the part of Joseph.

"But I told Harry, 'I'm not Joseph, for God's sake. Find someone else.' And Harry said, 'Okay, you don't have to play Joseph, but if you give me any more trouble, I'll show that test all over the Bel Air circuit.'"

I had asked both Su Lesser and the studio's head of Asset Management and Film Restoration, Grover Crisp, about both the footage from Egypt and also Jack Lemmon's screen test. They couldn't find any trace of either.

Then, just before I was leaving for a trip to Los Angeles, I received a call from Grover. He suggested I spend a morning with him looking at some film he'd found.

"What is it?" I asked.

"You'll see. It's a surprise."

I always tell people that Grover is one of the "good guys" in Hollywood. He cares deeply about the Columbia film library and maintains and restores its pictures with a meticulous attention to detail. And indeed, he had "surprises" for me. He'd found costume, hair and makeup tests of Rita Hayworth doing a scene for *Joseph and His Brethren,* as well as Jack Lemmon's test for it. And there were also screen tests of Harrison Ford, Warren Beatty, Kim Novak with Tyrone Power, Barbara Streisand with Omar Sharif, and Joan Perry, Harry Cohn's wife-to-be. And finally, two shots of camels walking in the desert—all that was left of the twenty-seven-thousand feet Dieterle had filmed in Egypt. It was a treasure trove, all of which we used in the program.

JK Another of Harry Cohn's "creations" was Kim Novak, who was groomed to replace Rita Hayworth as she grew older and her star began to fade. Cohn carefully crafted Novak's sex-goddess image in *Phffft* with Jack Lemmon, and in *Picnic,* when she slow-danced in the moonlight with William Holden. Then, to make it absolutely clear that she had reached that lofty goddess position, Cohn cast both her and Rita Hayworth opposite Frank Sinatra in *Pal Joey.* Only one of them "gets the guy." Of course, it's the young, blond Kim Novak.

We tried to reach her, but she never responded to our letter. However, in addition to Jack Lemmon, we did interviews with Dustin Hoffman, Dennis Hopper, Evelyn Keyes, Richard Dreyfuss, Gregory Peck, Anthony Quinn, Barbra Streisand, and producer Ray Stark; and we found archival recordings of Clark Gable, Jean Arthur, Irene Dunne, and directors Frank Capra, Orson Welles, and David Lean. I also attempted to convince socialite, Leonore Annenberg (wife of former US Ambassador to Great Britain, and philanthropist, Walter Annenberg) to participate in the program. She was Harry Cohn's niece, and was raised by him from an early age after her mother died. I found a number for Mrs. Annenberg and she answered the phone herself. When I told her why I was calling, her response was immediate and abrupt. "I don't discuss the Cohn family," she said, and hung up.

However, we were able to get a glimpse into Cohn's personal life thanks to some home movie footage of him, his second wife, Joan Perry, and their children. Our associate producer, Mary Bell Painten, tracked down his daughter-in-law, who not only had that footage, but also Cohn's personal scrapbooks filled with news clippings and photographs.

JK and DH As with *The Universal Story,* the right host was crucial. And even though the studio had told us that they'd be able to find someone for not a lot of money, they discovered that it wasn't all that easy. We wanted a big star who'd made a number of films there. Our top choice was Glenn Close, and fortunately everyone agreed.

DH The narration session was in New York at Sony's Columbia Records on Manhattan's West Side[5], prior to the on-camera shoot in California. We were given a studio that had been built for Mariah Carey's recording sessions; it was elaborate and comfortable. Glenn came in from Bedford Hills, just north of the city. She was not steeped in Columbia's history, but was fascinated by the story and eager to learn more about it. We worked together well, and the day felt very relaxed.

Understandably, the shoot in California was less easygoing, mainly because it was more involved on many levels. Glenn had

David and Glenn Close on the Sony lot.
Culver City, CA, 1998. Authors' collection.

chosen the hairdresser and makeup artists she wanted, and they sometimes acted as though they were the stars. However, they did their jobs well. The hairdresser cut Glenn's hair that morning; it was

---

5   On 10th Avenue, at 54th Street, the building was once the home of Fox Movietone newsreels, as well as where *On the Waterfront*, *Fail Safe*, *Sophie's Choice* and *Kramer vs. Kramer* were filmed, before it was turned into recording studios.

much shorter than before and suited her perfectly. And the makeup was commendably subtle. Glenn Close has a natural luminous quality, and her skin looked flawless.

She had told us that Giorgio Armani would provide her with either a pink or light blue suit. She arrived with dark taupe pants, a slightly lighter, striped jacket, and a choice of two shirts—both in the beige family. I was concerned that her clothes would blend in with the overall color of the studio buildings, but the right lighting solved that problem.

An additional "extra" was that I had persuaded Columbia to let us produce the program in High Definition. Although it added more than a few complications, it seemed appropriate, as Sony not only owned Columbia Pictures, but was poised to become a major supplier of HD equipment to broadcasters. However in 1996, shooting in HD was cumbersome. For example, each camera came attached to its own small truck full of equipment. Then I remembered reading that Sony in Japan had developed a much smaller camera which did not need to be tethered to a truck. When I asked if we could get hold of one for this project, I was told that only two existed, both of which were being used at the Winter Olympic Games in Japan. If we could schedule our shoot late enough, one could be made available. I was hoping that going HD was not going to result in unexpected delays. I had asked for this, and I would bear the brunt of any problems it caused.

Fortunately there were none. The results were better than I could have hoped. When Glenn Close saw herself in the finished show, she said, "How did you make me look so good?" In part, that was simply a polite compliment; in part, it was because she is a beautiful woman and was in the hands of makeup and hairdressing experts; but it was also because she was lit and photographed so well.

JK Glenn's daughter, Annie, had come with her to California and was with us on location at Columbia's original Gower Street lot (now known as the Sunset-Gower Studios). The lot has a number of stages, and our crew was not the only one shooting there. During a break, a group of people, including the singer, Brandy, came out of an adjoining soundstage where they were making a music video. Annie was excited when she spotted them, and told her mother.

Glenn walked over and said, "You're Brandy, aren't you?"

Brandy replied, "Oh my gosh. You're Glenn Close."

Later, I noticed some rap singers come out of another nearby stage and introduce themselves to Glenn. As I walked by, I heard her telling them the story of Columbia Pictures, about Harry Cohn, and his "little studio that could."

Glenn with rap singers.
Sunset-Gower Studios, Los Angeles, CA, 1998. Authors' collection.

JK and DH   In December, 1998, we were invited to attend the Sony Christmas party, where the theme was the upcoming seventy-fifth anniversary of Columbia Pictures. The centerpiece was an enormous model of the torch lady logo made out of ice. Then a month later, we went back to California to introduce *The Lady With the Torch* at a special preview screening. It was in the Kim Novak Theater on the lot, and the studio spared no expense. It felt like a true Hollywood premiere, complete with a red carpet leading all the way from the front gate. Afterwards, there was a reception in the Rita Hayworth Dining Room. We were struck that all these festivities were taking place on the former MGM lot, which had always been the envy of Harry Cohn, and which was now the home of his Columbia Pictures.

On the way back to our hotel that night, we breathed a great sigh of relief. The show was finished; it was attracting a great deal of good publicity; and we were still standing. But we said, "If anyone ever asks us to do another story of a studio, please let us have the strength of character to turn it down."

The Lady With the Torch "graduation picture."
Culver City, CA, 1998. Authors' collection.

Lobby of the Lew R. Wasserman building.
Universal City, CA, 2002. Authors' collection.

CHAPTER TWENTY SIX

Getting to Know The Last Mogul

He was known as "The King of Hollywood." Following in the footsteps of the famous moguls who were the founding fathers of the motion picture industry, Lew R. Wasserman loomed as large as any of them. In his dark suit, white shirt and black tie—the dress code for all MCA/Universal executives—he was both feared and revered. His temper was as legendary as were his relationships with stars, directors, unions, United States Presidents, and the Pope. And he wielded his power shrewdly, staying away from reporters, microphones and cameras. He'd first built his reputation as a super-agent at MCA, which represented almost every big name in the entertainment business. When the agency's founder, Dr. Jules Stein, decided to relinquish the day-to-day running of the company, Wasserman became its president, and expanded it into a production center for television and movies. Eventually, the government mandated that MCA couldn't represent talent and also be producers, so he gave up the agency and bought Universal. Coincidentally, he was born on March 15th, 1913, two years to the day before the studio opened its doors.

By the time we met him, his title was Chairman of MCA/Universal, the oldest movie studio in Hollywood, based in Universal

City. His office was on the fifteenth floor of the Black Tower (now named the Lew R. Wasserman building). At the other end of the hall was President Sidney Sheinberg. Together they ran the company with an iron hand.

When we started producing *The Universal Story,* the first person we asked to meet was Lew Wasserman. Frankly, we were rather surprised he agreed. But Blair Westlake, who had initiated the project, and was among his protégés, asked him to talk with us and accompanied us to the meeting. When we thanked Wasserman for seeing us, he glanced at Blair and said, with a dry humor we would come to know well, "He made me."

Blair Westlake with Lew Wasserman.
Beverly Hills, CA, 1999. Blair M. Westlake collection.

JK We spent ninety minutes with him and I found him absolutely fascinating—and subtly flirtatious. He was full of stories about Hollywood and the history of the studio. He spoke in an almost monotone voice, rarely smiling, except for an occasional glint in his eye, although many of his stories were funny.

When we left, I said to Blair, "He's adorable."

Blair replied, "Believe me, Joan, that's not the word most people use to describe Lew Wasserman."

DH Our next meeting was with Sid Sheinberg, a few offices away. We were half an hour late and Sheinberg's reputation as a tough, no-nonsense executive was well-known. If the delay had been caused by anyone other than Wasserman, I'm sure we would have had an earful.

As it was, we heard this: "If I'd known about this project before, I'd have killed it. I don't like looking back. My focus is on the present and the future."

Not exactly the most welcoming of opening lines. But to this day, we wonder if it was a test to see if we'd flinch. We didn't.

Once we got over that bump, Sheinberg said, "I hope this program will tell the truth. The studio has had its ups and downs, and the movies weren't always wonderful. Don't do a puff piece on us. Make it honest." It was a mandate that we knew was unusual. Most studios want to shine only a positive light on themselves.

It had been an extraordinary morning. We couldn't have asked for a more successful start. It was followed by over a year of very hard work.

JK Every time we were in Los Angeles from then on, we visited Lew Wasserman, either in his office or at home. Sometimes he invited us to have lunch with him at his reserved table in the studio commissary, or if he already had a lunch date, he'd escort us downstairs and see that we were given a choice table. We always had one of his reserved parking spaces behind the Black Tower, and he used to say to David, "Drive carefully. You're carrying precious cargo."

He told us story after story: about his friendship with Pope John Paul; how he helped Bill Clinton get elected; how his house and grounds were permanently wired by the Secret Service.

I once asked him, "When you were an agent, did you ever drop a client from your roster of talent?"

He said, "Just two. Bette Davis and Frank Sinatra. Bad boy, Frank. He lives right next door."

"Why Bette Davis? I would have guessed Joan Crawford."

"No, Joan Crawford could swear like a truck driver, but she would take career advice. Bette Davis was impossible to please. No deal was ever good enough for her."

"And Sinatra?"

"Well, I made a deal for him to do seven pictures for MGM, and while he was making his first color film, he asked the producer, Arthur Freed, if he could see the dailies. Freed said, 'I never let actors see the rushes.'

"Frank kept insisting, and Freed kept saying 'No.' So Frank went to Louis B. Mayer, who told him, 'I don't override my producers. If Freed doesn't want you to see the rushes, then you can't.'

"Frank said, 'Fine. Then I'm leaving.'

"It was 8:30 in the morning and I was getting dressed to go to work when my phone began to ring off the hook. The studio's head of production screamed, 'Sinatra just walked out. You'd better get him back here in a hurry. We're halfway through the picture and he's in almost every shot. Now he's costing us thousands of dollars while a full cast and crew are just sitting around. Get him back on this set or he'll never work in this town again.'

"I said to my wife, 'I'll be back in forty-five minutes. I'm going to the beach.'

"She said, 'What? Why?'

"'I'll tell you later.'

"I drove to Malibu and saw Sinatra lying on the sand, smoking and slugging from a bottle of liquor. When he noticed two shiny black shoes next to him, he looked up and said, 'Lew! What are you doing here?'"

Wasserman then interjected, "As you can imagine, I looked like the last guy you'd see on a beach, dressed like that.

"I said, 'Well, Frank, I came to talk about some offers I've had for you.'

"Yeah, what d'ya got?'

"There's two weeks in concert in Cincinnati, a week in Cleveland, another two weeks in Paramus, New Jersey...'

"And then he interrupted me: 'Wait a minute, Lew; I don't have time for those concerts. I've got seven pictures to make back to back.'

"'Well, you're never going to work in this town again, so I've got two weeks in Cincinnati, a week in Cleveland....'

"In one second he was on his feet and heading for his car. He was back at Metro in twenty minutes and I was home drinking coffee with Edie before 9:30.

"You see, you have to know your customers. If I had said, 'Look Frank, you'd better get your ass back on that set or else...' it wouldn't have worked. I knew I had to go in the back door."

DH He had some iconic photos in his office. Among them was one of him with Pope John Paul II. I asked where it was taken.

"The Pope invited me to sit in his box when he spoke at The Hollywood Bowl. His security detail said to me, 'When he finishes the speech, try to get him to exit towards the left because we have more coverage on that side.'

"Well, after he finished, he saw someone he knew on the right and began heading in that direction. I suddenly felt someone grabbing the back of my neck and whispering in a seething tone of voice, 'We told you to get him off to the left.'

"I said, 'Listen you guys. First of all, take your hands off me. And secondly, even *I* don't tell the Holy Father what to do.'"

"Mr. Wasserman," I said, "I think I saw that picture of you and the Pope in the papers at the time. You know, of course, what most people said when they saw it, don't you?"

"No, what?"

"Everyone wants to know who that guy is with Lew Wasserman."

He said innocently, "Really?"

I have no doubt that he'd heard that before.

JK On another visit, this time to his home in Beverly Hills, we were standing in the large forecourt, when he said to me, "It was your sex that found the flaw."

"Excuse me?"

"Your sex found the flaw. I was about to give a fundraiser for Bill Clinton and even though the house and property have been wired by the Secret Service for many years, since I've had almost every President here, an advance team always comes to check that the security is still in place. So a female agent was here and she said, 'Mr. Wasserman, what's up there?' as she pointed up that hill in front of us.

"'It's a house; what does it look like?'

"Now as you probably can guess, Secret Service agents aren't known for having a sense of humor. Through clenched teeth, she said, 'I know it's a house. Whose house it that?'

"I told her that a singer lived there, and she said, 'It's a straight shot from that house into this forecourt. And we're not covered.'

"Within minutes, the Secret Service was installing wiring. But do you know how many presidents and world leaders could have been assassinated right where we're standing?"

And then, again, this time with just a hint of a smile, he said to me, "And it was your sex that found the flaw."

DH While we were in his office one morning, his secretary buzzed him. That was unusual since she usually didn't interrupt when he had visitors.

He said to us, "Sorry, but I have to take this. I'll just be a second."

We asked if he wanted us to leave the room, but he motioned for us to stay where we were.

"Rupert. I'm throwing a fundraiser next month for Clinton and the plan is for you to sit next to Hillary and your wife to sit next to the President. So can I count on you to be there? Good. See you then."

The conversation lasted no more than a few seconds, and as he put the phone down, he said, "I just raised another $10,000 from

Rupert Murdoch. When you tell someone he's sitting next to the First Lady and his wife will be next to the Commander-in-Chief, you can't lose. It's foolproof."

What may be more surprising is that Murdoch is a Republican. But obviously, no one turned down an invitation from Lew Wasserman.

He then told us about his long relationship with Bill Clinton.

JK "If it weren't for me, he still would have been on the bus," he said.

His opening lines were always perfect teasers.

I laughed and asked, "What happened?"

"I've been to many Governors Balls in Washington, so I'd probably met Clinton when he was still Governor of Arkansas, but I certainly didn't know him well. And when he was running for the Presidency, even after he'd won the New Hampshire Democratic Primary, he still didn't have a high profile. The fundraisers he was doing were from hunger. They charged about $50 a plate and if they made a few thousand dollars, they were thrilled.

"One day, my secretary buzzed me and said, 'I have Governor Clinton on the line and he says he's on a bus.'

"I picked up the phone. 'Governor, this is Lew Wasserman. What can I do for you?'

· "In his southern drawl, he said, 'Well, Mr. Wasserman, Hillary and I and Al and Tipper are on a cross-country bus tour meeting folks and we're heading for LA. We're throwing a small fundraiser at the Beverly Hilton Hotel, and since you're such a famous Democratic supporter, I wonder if we could come to your house for dessert.'

"I said, 'When is the fundraiser?'

"He said, 'In thirteen days.'

"'Let me ask you a few questions. What time is the event?'

"He said, 'Oh, I guess drinks will be about 7:30 and then dinner and a couple of speeches.'

"'And so what time do you think you'd be here for dessert?'"

Wasserman said to us, "Now remember, back then no one knew that Bill Clinton was seldom on time. But even if he was, this wasn't going to work.

"I said, 'Look, Governor, Edie and I go to bed by 9:30, so I don't want a few hundred people showing up for ice cream and cookies at 10 or 10:30. Why don't you let me throw the entire fundraiser? We'll start at 7 and everyone will be home in bed by 9:30.'

"Clinton said, 'Mr. Wasserman, do you really want to do that? I'd be honored.'

"I said, 'Yes, Governor, I'm happy to. Have one of your guys call me.'

"As I put down the phone, the light was blinking again. My secretary said, 'There's a gentleman here to see you. He says he's from the Clinton campaign.'

"Now I've been around a long time, but that really threw me off my pins. Clinton knew exactly what he was doing. He led me right to the trough and I jumped in head-first.

"'Send him in.'

"The guy was wearing plaid pants, a matching jacket, some strange-colored shoes and was holding a cap. I thought he looked like a country bumpkin.

"'Sit down,' I said.

"He began, 'Well, I know you're doing a fundraiser for the Governor, and he wants me to get the details. How many people are you thinking of inviting? And how much are you charging each person?'

"'Listen. I've got a lot to do,' I told him. 'I have to print invitations, order food and liquor, and start calling people. So I'm throwing you out. Tell the Governor that I'm inviting about two hundred and fifty people at $5,000 a plate. I guess about a hundred and fifty will actually show up. And I'm calling Barbra Streisand, Steven Spielberg, Tom Hanks, a few studio heads, and corporate business leaders to be there.' He was speechless as I ushered him out of my office.

"The next morning, my secretary buzzed: 'Governor Clinton is calling.'

"'Hello, Governor.'

'Mr. Wasserman. You can't invite that many people. Hardly anyone knows me. And you can't charge so much money. And are you kidding? Barbra Streisand? Steven Spielberg? They won't come.'

"I said, 'Governor, I don't mean to be rude, but the event is now twelve days away and I'm busy. I've got a lot to do. So I can't stay on the line. Have your guy call me if you need anything else. Otherwise leave it to me. Have a nice trip, enjoy the scenery and I'll see you in LA.'

"My phone was buzzing again. And again, that same guy was outside my door. I said, 'Get in here. I just spoke to the Governor so I don't have anything to say to you. Don't come back here. I'm busy.'"

And then Wasserman interjected, "And by the way, this time his outfit was a little better, but not by much. Clinton called once or twice more, but his guy never showed up again, thank goodness."

He paused for a few seconds, and then said to us, "Eleven days later, the fundraiser made 1.7 million dollars.

"So, as I said at the beginning, if it wasn't for me, he'd still be on the bus."

DH He obviously loved telling stories and we were an enthusiastic audience. It wasn't an act. We found him captivating.

He almost never consented to on-camera interviews, so we were surprised when he agreed to do the one for *The Universal Story*[1]. And then a few years later, for another project[2], he allowed us to record a long audio interview with him. In short, he was clearly comfortable with us.

JK It was during our very first meeting that he told us about his personal collection of Universal memorabilia, which he kept at home.

---

1   See "Two Birthdays—Universal and Columbia."

2   It was a profile of Alfred Hitchcock, which we started, but didn't finish because of some insurmountable problems.

That was all I had to hear. I must have asked him at least three times, "Mr. Wasserman, can we come and rummage in your closet?"

"Sure," he said. "Let me know when you're ready."

We were more than ready, and soon were spending hours in his screening room/den as he pulled scrapbooks from the shelves, including one of a stag party he threw for Jimmy Stewart right before Stewart's marriage.

DH A few weeks later, we returned to photograph the parts of the collection we needed for the show. This time he wasn't there. It was his wife, Edie, who let us in, and I realized immediately that she expected us to be there for about fifteen to twenty minutes. I knew it would take me at least an hour, so it became Joan's job to keep her occupied while I set up lights and took pictures. Fortunately Edie was happy to give Joan a tour of the house, showing her paintings, hand-written notes by John F. Kennedy outlining the plans for what would become The Kennedy Center in Washington, DC, etc. Joan kept asking questions to divert her from checking her watch. I think she also enjoyed the tour.

JK The last time we saw Lew Wasserman was on May 10th, 2002. It had been three years since our last visit. When we walked into his office that morning, he said, "Where the hell have you two been? I thought you'd forgotten me."

I said, "My mother's been ill and I couldn't travel."

"Don't blame your mother. You're probably the one who made her sick."

We were there about forty-five minutes and it was getting close to noon.

He said, "I have to throw you out now. I have a lunch date. Do you want a table in the commissary?"

For some reason, I chose that moment to make a request. "Mr. Wasserman, I've never asked you this before. But I have a camera in my bag. Would you let us have a picture with you?"

He pushed his intercom button, "Get in here. You're going to take a photo."

His assistant, Melody, said, "I'm terrible with cameras. Let the driver do it." (Wasserman was showing his age by then. He had a chronic knee problem, and used a driver to bring him to the studio and back home.)

I said, "We can't use the flash with that big window behind you. Would you please swivel your chair so we can have a different angle?"

David and I then stood on either side of him and the driver took two pictures. One is better than the other.

Twenty-four days later, Lew Wasserman died. We believe those are the last photographs ever taken of him.

The final speaker at his memorial service was Bill Clinton, who told the mourners, "If it weren't for Lew Wasserman, I never would have been elected President of the United States."

David, Lew Wasserman, and Joan.
Universal City, CA, 2002. Authors' collection.

The John Garfield Story narration session. Recording engineer John Heffernan, Julie Garfield, Joan, and David.
New York, 2002. Authors' collection.

CHAPTER TWENTY SEVEN

Garfield–The Good Die Young

His rise to fame in Hollywood and eventual crash-landing was a compelling story. However, the idea for a program about John Garfield wasn't ours. The head of Turner Classic Movies, Tom Karsch, proposed it. And the initial idea wasn't his either. Garfield's daughter, Julie, had written and suggested it to him. Tom admitted to us later that his mother had always loved Garfield and his films. She wasn't alone. Many women used to say, "He can put his shoes under my bed any time." And men admired him too. He was handsome without being pretty, rugged without being brutish, and vulnerable without being soppy.

We met Julie Garfield in her apartment in New York. She is an actress, acting teacher, and painter. She looks very much like her father, and is the only one of his three children still alive. Her older sister, Katherine, died at the age of six, and her brother, David, died when he was in his early forties. We felt an instant connection to Julie and apparently she felt the same towards us.

John Garfield made an immediate impact when he appeared on screen in his first film, *Four Daughters,* winning an Academy Award nomination as Best Supporting Actor. But his life was a roller-coaster, and it ended when he was just thirty-nine years old.

JK His story is well-known among actors and many of them are passionate about his films, his performances, and his personal code of ethics. During the communist "witch hunts" of the 1950s, he became a victim of the House Un-American Activities Committee (HUAC), when he was summoned to testify. He refused to "name names" and particularly wanted to protect his wife, Robbe, who had once been a member of the Communist Party, as he knew that the Committee was in possession of her expired Party membership card. As Richard Dreyfuss said, "By taking that position, he must have known he was committing professional suicide." Indeed *He Ran All the Way,* which was released the same year that he testified, was Garfield's last film.

It was not unexpected that almost everyone we asked to participate in the program willingly agreed. Among them were—in addition to Dreyfuss—Joanne Woodward, Danny Glover, James Cromwell, Ellen Adler, Phoebe Brand, Patricia Neal, Harvey Keitel,

Danny Glover said of John Garfield, "You watched him mold the internal life of his characters through the silences, through the moments."
New York, 2002. Authors' collection.

Norman Lloyd, Hume Cronyn (his last interview before his death at the age of ninety-one), Joseph Bernard, Lee Grant, and a class-mate of Garfield named Michael Coppolo. They each had a unique perspective on either his acting or his personal life—and sometimes both. Some had known him for many years; some had been his co-stars; and some, unfortunately, had been blacklisted.

JK and DH We weren't too far into production before we realized that the host for this show should be Julie. Tom Karsch gave his approval with the proviso that the script be written to avoid any over-the-top sentimentality. Julie completely understood that and struck just the right balance.

She was also an invaluable colleague. Not only did she let us borrow her personal collection of photos, news clippings, etc., but she also pitched in to help us find materials that were hard to come by. Among them was footage of her father's funeral.

When he died, she was only six-and-a-half, and she remembers being surprised that her mother didn't cry. She said, "I knew she was strong, but wondered how she could keep herself from falling apart, and thought that it must have been to protect my brother and me. But the night of his funeral, after I'd been put to bed, I couldn't sleep, so I sneaked out of my bedroom and into a corner near the living room. That's when I saw my mother crying. She was sobbing on the shoulder of a friend as news film of the funeral was playing on television."

DH Obviously Julie had been profoundly affected by the scene she'd witnessed, and hearing her tell it affected me too. I then realized that incidentally there was an additional nugget of information here: that there had been news coverage of the funeral. I had already seen a *New York Times* headline saying that the turnout had been the largest in the city since Rudolph Valentino died back in 1926. Garfield's death must have had a visceral impact on many people. We needed to find that film.

Since Julie's mother had been watching television late in the evening, she had to have been tuned to a local news broadcast. So Joan and I called all the New York area television stations, only to be told that none of them had any record of the film in their files. I was stumped, but decided to ask our researcher in Washington, DC, Cindy Mitchell, to check the National Archives to see whether any of the national newsreels had shot the funeral. They hadn't. However, digging further, Cindy found a card indicating that WPIX, Channel 11 in New York, had donated some of its news film collection to the Archives, but that access to it was restricted. The card suggested that the footage we were looking for might be there, but Cindy was not even allowed to screen it. We discovered that Tribune Entertainment had bought WPIX some years earlier, so Joan called the main office in Chicago. No one there knew anything about the collection in the National Archives, but told her to contact a WPIX lawyer in New York.

JK Roger Goodspeed confirmed that the station had indeed deposited much of its news film with the National Archives. However he reiterated that the no-access policy was still in place. I had a feeling that there might be room to maneuver, so I told him more about John Garfield's story, Julie's involvement, and how everyone we had contacted was being very co-operative. Eventually he said, "Why don't you have Julie herself write a letter to me telling about how she saw the news coverage when she was a child? And also say who else is letting you have footage."

We helped her compose the letter and she concluded it with a plea to reconsider our request. It went immediately to WPIX by messenger. The next day, Julie came to our office and called Mr. Goodspeed. She said, "I'll get down on my knees and beg if I have to." He replied, "That won't be necessary. We've decided to let you use the film."

It is this funeral footage that opens the program.

DH Another hard-to-find piece of film was related to *Humoresque,* about a violin virtuoso. John Garfield had never played a note on the violin in his life, but wanted to immerse himself in the character, so he asked the studio for help. Warner Bros. had already hired

Isaac Stern to perform the soundtrack, and shot special footage of him playing so that Garfield could study an accomplished violinist, especially his arm and finger movements. Warners and Turner Entertainment Co. searched their libraries, but neither could find any reference to it.

I asked Julie if her father had had the film. She'd never seen it, but told me she'd donated his entire collection of 16mm movies to New York University's film department. Fortunately NYU had made an inventory—and it included one unlabeled can. It was a long-shot, but I decided it was worth going to screen it. And there it was—the footage of Isaac Stern that Garfield had used to prepare for his performance. Stern's widow gave us permission to use it in the program, and we sent her a cassette for her own archives.

JK We also enlisted Julie's help in asking Harvey Keitel for an interview. She had appeared with him in a stage production of *Death of a Salesman* and, more recently, in the film, *Mortal Thoughts*. Even though he usually turned down such requests, he agreed as a favor to her. He lived in New York, but was going to be in Los Angeles at the same time that we would be there, so we arranged to tape him at the home of one of his business associates. He was delayed, and by the time he arrived, was obviously pre-occupied. For some reason he was testy and irritated by almost every question. It was one of the most difficult interviews I've ever done. He refused to sign the release we needed, and for quite some time, it looked as though we wouldn't be able to use any of his comments.

Once we returned to New York, he asked to look at the footage we'd shot of him, and David went with Julie to his office. After another special request from her, he did agree to let us use one—and only one—of his on-camera statements. In it, he explains Garfield's audience appeal: a combination of tough and vulnerable. It's succinct and to the point, and while quite short, we were happy to have those few seconds in the show.

Richard Dreyfuss, Joanne Woodward, and Julie Garfield.
New York, 2002. Authors' collection.

Completely opposite were our experiences with Joanne Woodward and Richard Dreyfuss, whom we scheduled to be taped on the same day. Both of them were able to tell us why they felt so strongly about John Garfield as an actor.

Joanne described his performances as "subtle; whatever he chose as the inner life of his characters we'll never know. But in each one of his films, he had an 'interior dialogue' that he used to inform every nuance of his performance." Like him, she was trained in "The Method." But as a young student, she told her acting teacher, Sanford Meisner, that she didn't understand it and therefore didn't know how to use it. He replied, "Joanne, 'The Method' is whatever works for you." She said, "Garfield certainly had a method, and whatever it was, it worked for him."

Richard Dreyfuss arrived just as Joanne was about to leave. They knew each other slightly, but hadn't seen each other in many years. At the time, she was the Artistic Director of the Westport Country Playhouse. When Richard embraced her, he said, "I'd love to do a play for you."

She said, "Terrific. I'll be in touch." Indeed, the following summer he starred in *All My Sons* there.

Dreyfuss was in the midst of filming his television series, *The Education of Max Bickford*, frequently working fourteen-hour days, when I contacted his assistant, Audrey, and told her we'd love to have his "take" on John Garfield. But she said he'd told her he couldn't do anything else because he was just drained by the end of each day. The next morning she called me back. Apparently Richard had said, "If it's for Joan and David, I'll be there." He was indeed, and gave us an insightful interview.

He'd spent many late nights as a kid watching Garfield's movies on television, and knew every one of them. His ability to recall the plots and then analyze specific scenes was extraordinary. And he pointed out a quality not just in Garfield, but in many actors who play romantic leads.

He said, "They all have an off-stage wound. And it may not ever be explained to the audience, but you just know that something in the character's back-story causes him to act and react to the circumstances in the film the way he does. Often the wound is caused by a lost love; other times it's because of racism or war or some other traumatic event. But all the great actors—Brando, Bogart, Tracy, Stewart, Fonda, Flynn, and Garfield—have a wound. For instance, just look at Humphrey Bogart when you first see him in *Casablanca*. His wound is all over his face, and it's irresistible. And when Garfield encounters an anti-Semitic drunk in a restaurant in *Gentleman's Agreement,* he has a knee-jerk reaction. In one second, he goes from having a light-hearted conversation during dinner with some friends, to an enraged victim of racism. And it's because he has that 'wound' that he's in that guy's face faster than you can spit."

The following week, Audrey called again. Richard was in the hospital, being treated for exhaustion. Not, by the way, as a result of the interview he did for us.

DH Most of our New York filming was in my loft. Although I have a fairly large space, we needed almost all of it for the camera set-ups, so I had to clear away all my personal belongings, and the only place to pile everything was the bedroom, which started to look like a disheveled storage warehouse.

Signing her interview release, Patricia Neal with Joan.
New York, 2002. Authors' collection.

Patricia Neal, who had played opposite Garfield in *The Breaking Point,* arrived early and was fascinated by the loft, insisting on a complete tour. When we came to the doors that lead into the bedroom she asked, "What's in there?" "It's my bedroom," I told her. "But it's a terrible mess right now." However, try as I might, nothing I said would deter her; she had to see inside. When I reluctantly opened the door, she realized my description was no exaggeration. I was embarrassed, but she didn't seem to care.

JK After the interview, she admired the blouse I was wearing and asked where I'd bought it. When I told her it was from a neighborhood store not far from David's loft, she said, "See if you can find another one for me." I indeed did find it and brought it to her apartment overlooking the East River.

"How much do I owe you?" she asked.

"It's a present to thank you for participating in our program."

"Stay right there," she said, and went into another room. When she returned, she handed me a first edition of her autobiography, *As I Am,* which she inscribed for me.

"Now perhaps we're even," she said.

"I think I've wound up with the better end of the deal," I replied.

JK and DH John Garfield had been a member of The Group Theatre in the 1930s, so we knew about his acting training, thanks to the five years we spent producing *Broadway's Dreamers: The Legacy of the Group Theatre*[1]. Although a number of the original members we'd interviewed during the 1980s had died in the years since, a few were still alive and living in New York. Among them was Phoebe Brand, who came in her wheelchair and gave us a first-hand account of working with Garfield in several Group Theatre productions.

Phoebe Brand and Joanne Woodward, together for the first time since our Group Theatre show.
New York, 2002. Authors' collection.

---

1   See "Joanne and The Group."

"A scrappy kid, who was perfect for those plays at that time, during the Depression," she said. "He was sweet and tough."

Lee Grant added, "He had a smoldering, somber, troubled, street guy kind of presence that was incredibly attractive."

"In some way," said Danny Glover, "you felt that his story was your story."

DH Everyone talked about Garfield's natural talent. He'd grown up on the streets of New York, fighting with other kids who, like him, had little-to-no interest in going to school. But one of his teachers at P.S. 45 in the Bronx decided to put him on the debating team. And that was a turning point. Garfield found another way to channel his energy—through his voice. Not long after that, he joined the school's drama class and performed in several plays.

Joan and I went to P.S. 45 to take photos of the school and see whether its archives included anything related to Garfield. While we were there, the principal said, "There's an elderly man, a former student, who appeared in a few plays with John Garfield here. His name is Mike Coppolo. Are you interested in contacting him?"

A week or so later, Julie went back with us to the Bronx, where we interviewed Coppolo in the school auditorium. There was still plenty of the actor in him. He volunteered to go on the stage, and performed some of Garfield's lines from *The Vision of Sir Launfal*, a play they'd done together. It was a gem, and the earliest recollection we had of Garfield's budding talent, many years before he went to Hollywood and became famous.

JK and DH And it was his fame that made him so attractive to HUAC. By 1951 the hearings had been going on for some six years, and the Committee was losing its mandate. It needed to make a splash with a star victim, and Garfield fit the bill perfectly. As John Cromwell stated, "It was an attempt at self-aggrandizement to generate publicity, so that the members of the Committee would have a job." Perversely, John Garfield's interrogators, who attacked him during the hearings, would gather at the end of the day to have their pictures taken with him.

In a final statement to the Committee he said, "I have nothing to be ashamed of and nothing to hide. My life is an open book. I am no Red. I am no 'pink.' I am no fellow traveler. I am a Democrat by politics, a liberal by inclination, and a loyal citizen of this country by every act of my life."

However, the pressure took its toll, and in the opinion of many, ultimately destroyed him.

Among HUAC's other victims was Lee Grant, who told us, "John Garfield dying at thirty-nine was a casualty of the blacklist." His friend Joe Bernard went even further. "The Committee did kill him," he said. "They were murderers."

JK *The John Garfield Story* premiered on February 3rd, 2003. He was TCM's *Star of the Month*, and Julie appeared with the network's host, Robert Osborne, to introduce several of her father's movies.

A few months later, she received a call from a man who'd seen the program. He told her that he had found her father's wallet many years before, but hadn't known how to reach her. He was coming to New York on a business trip and wanted to give her the wallet. Julie was skeptical. She had no way of knowing whether or not he was telling the truth, or whether he was just another of those fans—as in "fanatics"—that bask in the glow of movie stars. Understandably, she didn't want to meet him by herself, so her fiancé (now her husband), Charles, went with her. To her astonishment, the man handed her a well-worn leather wallet with her father's name embossed on it in gold. Inside were childhood photos of Julie, her brother, David, and late sister, Katherine; scraps of paper with phone numbers for Lee Strasberg, Harold Clurman, Elia Kazan, Zero Mostel, Joe Bernard, among others; business cards, including that of the lawyer who defended him during the HUAC period; and a card with the name of the FBI agent who'd been tracking him. It was a snapshot of John Garfield's last few days, and for his daughter, a treasure from the past.

JK and DH We asked everyone who participated in the program to sign the book, *The Films of John Garfield.* Julie wrote on the title page:

"My Dearest Joan and David,

As you continue to spend your lives illuminating history to others, you have certainly illuminated mine to me. You, more than anyone I know, have explained my past to me, so that I can be released from it at last.

With Great Love,

With Great Respect.

Julie Garfield

6/10/02."

At premiere screening of *The John Garfield Story*, three descendants of Hollywood legends: Julie Garfield, Lorna Luft, and Susie Tracy.
Burbank, CA, 2003. Authors' collection.

Errol Flynn, Patrice Wymore Flynn, and their baby Arnella.
1955. Authors' collection.

CHAPTER TWENTY EIGHT

Life Was a Series of Adventures; Acting Was Just One of Them

Stories swirled around Errol Flynn in the 1930s and 40s, when he was one of Warner Bros. hottest stars. The young, handsome Australian lived a life of adventure that rivaled in excitement—some would say recklessness—the fictional parts he played. When TCM and Warners asked if we'd be interested in producing a profile of him, we accepted immediately. But we had no idea how little we knew about him, and how our opinion of him would change.

JK I confess that I wasn't a fan, perhaps because I knew virtually nothing about his life or career. I'd always considered his movies to be for boys, and hadn't gone out of my way to see them when I was younger. Over the next few months I came to realize what I'd been missing.

The first person I tracked down was one of Errol Flynn's daughters, Rory, who explained that she wasn't on speaking terms with either her sister, Deirdre, or their stepmother—Flynn's widow—Patrice Wymore Flynn, who lived in Jamaica.

DH Errol Flynn had always been an avid yachtsman, and was once caught in a life-threatening hurricane while sailing in the Caribbean. Somehow his beloved yacht, *Zaca*, withstood the onslaught and deposited him and his crew on the northeast coast of Jamaica, where they limped into the harbor at Port Antonio. Knowing that the repairs were going to take a number of weeks, Flynn went exploring and fell in love with the island and its people—so much so that he bought a hotel that was for sale, as well as many acres of land. Eventually Jamaica became his refuge, and he developed that land as a coconut farm and cattle ranch, where he built a house on a high bluff overlooking the ocean. Several years after his death, Pat Flynn moved there permanently, where she remained for the rest of her life.

JK Rory told me that her stepmother was somewhat reclusive, and always turned down invitations to talk about her famous husband. She did not have a phone number for the ranch, but when I pressed her further, she said that Pat was friendly with the owners of the Trident Hotel in Port Antonio, and would sometimes spend a part of her afternoons there.

I called the hotel, and the receptionist told me that Mrs. Flynn had just left. So I decided to push my luck and ask whether she had the number at the ranch. Without hesitating, she gave it to me. I waited another twenty minutes or so to give Pat time to get home, and then called.

She was cordial, but wary. I told her about the other shows we had done, and that Turner Classic Movies wanted us now to produce a profile of her late husband. Luckily she was a big fan of Fred Astaire and asked if we could send her copies of our shows. She explained that previous programs about Errol were less about his acting than his exploits off screen—he had loved women, liquor and drugs, but was also a serious actor who was never given his due. We must have been talking for almost half an hour when I said we'd like to come to Jamaica to meet her. She agreed, and offered to ask her friends at the Trident Hotel to give us a good deal on rooms there. She also told me that her stepdaughter, Deirdre, was a very private person, but maybe she could persuade her to speak with me.

DH The Trident Hotel was on the water's edge, overlooking the Caribbean, and each of us had our own villa, complete with patio, kitchen, ceiling fans, and a large living room and bedroom. Peacocks lived on the property and treated us to many displays of their iridescent plumage. It was March, and a welcome relief from the chill of New York. The temperature in Jamaica was in the eighties.

We had flown into Kingston and, at Pat's suggestion, hired a car service and driver for the two-hour trip to Port Antonio.

"You don't want to make that drive yourselves," she advised us. We saw donkeys, chickens, and thatched-roof huts, as well as many beautiful homes along the way. The contrast was often stark and stunning.

JK Pat met us at the hotel the next morning. An elegant woman, she was thin, statuesque and beautiful. Her gray hair was pulled back and secured with a bandana; she wore jeans with a long-sleeved t-shirt, and was very tanned from being in the sun for so many years. Her voice was deep and husky, possibly because she was a chain-smoker.

We had brought her cassettes of our shows about Fred Astaire and Katharine Hepburn, which she said she was eager to watch. The three of us sat on my patio and talked for about an hour before going for lunch at the outdoor dining area of the hotel. She was gracious and very eager to tell us about her late husband. By the time she left, we felt as though we were old friends, and she had asked us to have dinner with her that evening near the Marina, which has since been named for Errol Flynn. She not only agreed to appear on the program, but also to be its consultant.

DH The following day she took us on a tour of the town of Port Antonio, about ten minutes away. We strolled by stalls where local merchants sold jewelry, Blue Mountain coffee, and clothing. It was clear that she was a well-known figure there; many people acknowl-edged her with a look or a nod.

Later we drove to her house high above the coast road, along a path with what looked like scorched coconut trees everywhere. I asked her how big the property was. She said, "It would take several days to circle it on a horse."

Errol had chosen the spot well; the view was spectacular—and easy to take in because the windows of the living room were gone. I remember sitting near an opening where a window should have been, and Pat said, "If you look down, you can see the swimming pool. But be careful not to fall because there's no water in it. The windows blew out in the hurricane, and made a mess of everything. The house needs some major repairs, but I haven't been able to do them yet."

I realized that the hurricane to which she was referring had occurred some ten years earlier, and wondered what happens when it rains.

She had pulled out many photos, documents and newspaper clippings, including pictures of Errol as a child and teenager in Tas-mania, where he was born. We spent about an hour going through them, putting aside those we wanted to photograph for the show.

JK While David was still organizing the memorabilia, Pat showed me around the rest of the house.

"I think Errol must have been drunk when he built this place," she said. "Because to get to the bedrooms, we have to go outside and down this path." We passed several closed and locked doors, before reaching her room, which was at the end of what must have been intended as a group of guest rooms. It was large, and its windows were intact, with the bed at floor level, and opposite it I saw what looked to be at least a few dozen sneakers underneath a dresser. She pulled out a pair, took off the shoes she had on, tossed them into the pile, and put on the newer ones.

DH That evening, she invited us to a dinner party being given by some of her friends. Their house was on a beautiful sheltered bay with a large deck at the water's edge. Rum flowed freely and the food was delicious. Our hosts, many years younger than Pat, had been friends of Arnella Flynn, Pat and Errol's only daughter together.

JK and DH   Errol Flynn was married three times and had four children. His only son, Sean, by his first wife, Lili Damita, was a photojournalist, who shared his father's love of adventure. While on assignment for *Time* magazine in 1970, Sean disappeared in Cambodia, and is believed to have been killed by the Khmer Rouge the following year. His body was never found.

Deirdre and Rory are Errol's daughters by his second wife, Nora Eddington.

His youngest child, Arnella, by Patrice Wymore, was born on Christmas Day, 1953, and died of a drug overdose in 1998, when she was only forty-four years old. Arnella's son, Luke, uses the surname Flynn, and has inherited his grandparents' looks.

JK As promised, Pat paved the way for us to talk with Deirdre Flynn, who was more than happy to participate in the program. But her sister, Rory, said she wanted to see a finished script before she'd agree. I explained that was impossible, since the script for a documentary doesn't exist until all interviews have been done, because unlike a feature film, the interviews are used to tell the story. Unfortunately she decided not to take part. But after the show aired, she called and said, "I made a mistake. The program was terrific and I should have been in it."

DH The interview with Deirdre did not have an auspicious beginning. We rented a conference space at the Los Angeles hotel where we were staying and set up to film a number of people there. We finished shooting Burt Reynolds late in the afternoon, and had about an hour before Deirdre was scheduled to arrive, so I went back to my room to freshen up. As I was getting out of the shower, I heard a banging on my door. Clad only in a towel, I went to answer and found an upset and angry Deirdre standing in the hallway. Somehow there had been a miscommunication because she was thirty minutes early. Expecting someone to meet her in the lobby, she had waited about ten minutes and then come to my room. I think we were both shocked.

Fortunately my semi-naked mishap was soon put behind us. I grabbed some clothes, summoned the crew, who had also taken a break, and we were soon ready to shoot the interview.

Deirdre had many stories to tell from the perspective of a daughter—about how attentive her father was as she was growing up; how he gave her a horse and taught her to ride it; and then about his steady decline due to his addiction to alcohol and drugs. She also explained how she learned the news that that he had died: a reporter rang her doorbell and asked if she would like to make a statement. She was only fourteen years old at the time, and has been wary of the press ever since.

JK We also interviewed Richard Dreyfuss and Joanne Woodward. Both of them had almost become repertory players for us because they had a vast knowledge of movie history. And they'd each seen almost all of Flynn's films. But perhaps more important was that they were able to analyze his abilities as an actor.

As time went by, I began to understand the Flynn appeal. Not just in his looks, but also his talent. He was completely believable in all those swashbuckler movies and, as Dreyfuss pointed out, some of the lines he had to deliver would have been laughable coming from an inferior actor. He played in everything from adventures to war stories to comedies to serious drama, and he made all those parts his own. It was a revelation for me. Dreyfuss also told me that Flynn, like John Garfield, had an "off-stage wound."

"But it was harder to notice," said Richard. "Because he had such a sense of grace and irony. Eventually, you can see the wound—but he was *filled* with irony."

Which brings us to Olivia de Havilland.

DH She had co-starred with Errol Flynn in more films than any other actress, and their on-screen chemistry was obvious. There had been rumors that they'd also been off-screen lovers, although she adamantly denied that.

Convincing her to take part in this program was a feat unto itself. And once again, it was Roger Mayer who helped make it all come together. He contacted de Havilland at her home in Paris, telling her about our program, and also about the plans for a new release on DVD and BluRay of *Gone With The Wind*, to mark its fiftieth anniversary. She was the only one of its four main stars still alive, and Roger asked if she'd agree to do interviews for the DVD extra features as well as for our Flynn profile. He offered her any location she would like: Los Angeles, New York, or Paris. We thought that if she consented, she would have chosen to remain at home in Paris, since she was eighty-seven at the time. We were wrong.

Roger suggested we write a letter to her explaining the focus of our program and who else had agreed to be on it, especially Pat Flynn and Deirdre. She gave it a great deal of thought, and asked a lot of questions about the production.

Finally she said, "Yes."

Her choice of location? New York City.

JK Roger and George Feltenstein, who was in charge of the new home-video release of *Gone With The Wind*, were as pleased as we were. And Roger met all of Olivia's requirements, which were in keeping with the big star she was: first-class round trip air travel; her favorite suite at the Hotel Pierre on Fifth Avenue; a limousine at her disposal during the days she would be there; a new wardrobe for each interview, bought with the help of a personal shopper at Bergdorf Goodman; all meals; and a separate suite for the filming. Roger also asked if she'd like to bring someone with her, but she chose to travel by herself. We have no idea what the total costs were, but they must have been substantial. Fortunately they were picked up by the *Gone With The Wind* budget—not ours.

DH It was late on a Saturday afternoon not long after she arrived that we met her at the Pierre. She was dressed beautifully, her hair was gray, and her brown eyes sparkled as she spoke about Flynn. We talked for hours—or, to be more accurate, she talked and we listened. At about 8 pm she decided that we should call room service and order dinner. I think we left some time after 10.

JK and DH This elegant, well-spoken woman surprised us with stories of her personal feelings for Flynn, as well as their working relationship in the eight films they had made together some sixty years earlier. We came away believing that, despite her marriages, Errol Flynn might have been the love of her life.

She asked to see the questions we'd be asking in the interview. So the following day we delivered them by messenger to her hotel. That was also the day she went shopping for her new wardrobes.

Then, a curve ball was thrown at us. On Monday morning, Roger called to say that she was upset by the questions we'd sent. We explained that we had based them on the stories she had told us, and so didn't understand her reaction. Suddenly, it looked as though all the arrangements, which had taken so long to put together, were now falling apart, and this interview might not happen. Our guess is that she had a case of nerves, realizing she was about to go public with her long-held feelings about Errol Flynn. We don't quite remember how it was smoothed over, but it was, and the shoot was that same afternoon.

DH It had been agreed that the Warner Home Video director would use our camera crew to film the *Gone With The Wind* piece in the morning. Then we'd do our interview after the lunch break. I had already discussed with the cinematographer what would be the best locations to use in the hotel suite, which had a large living room, a small bedroom, a foyer and, of course, a bathroom. We found two areas in the living room that could be made to look different, and would not be too cramped. So when I arrived that afternoon, I was taken aback to find the crew setting up in the bedroom. Even with the bed pushed to one side, there was hardly room for lights and a camera position. The cinematographer told me that de Havilland had insisted that the interview be done in a different room from the piece for *Gone With The Wind*, and this was the only space left. (She later denied having any involvement in choosing the bedroom.)

Knowing that she was already unhappy with us because of the questions we had sent, I knew we had to make this work somehow. We did it by bringing the camera and some of the lights out into the foyer, and shooting through the open bedroom door from as far away as we could get. This allowed us to use a more flattering lens, and also prevented the room from looking cramped on camera (although in reality it was very tight).

JK When she arrived, whatever had been bothering her had been put aside. She was dressed in a pale blue suit, and appeared calm and confident. We had already decided that David would ask the questions.

However, with her first answer, we had another surprise: a completely different Olivia de Havilland. The relaxed, engaging woman with whom we had spent much of Saturday was not there. Instead she had decided to give more of a performance. At first we were disappointed, but then realized it was more in keeping with her image as a "grande dame," and it did work. The fact is that what she had to say was marvelous. It added a new dimension to the program, because she was honest about her feelings for Errol Flynn, from the first time she met the "handsomest, most charming, most magnetic, most virile young man in the entire world," until the time she heard about his death in 1959.

DH She told us that he had expressed his love for her around the time they were filming *The Adventures of Robin Hood.* But he was still married to Lili Damita, and Olivia had made it clear to him that he had to sort out his marital situation before she would begin a personal relationship with him, and he agreed. However, when he showed up on the set with Lili, it became clear to Olivia that he wasn't keeping his promise. So when they had to shoot a kissing scene, she decided to get her revenge.

She told us that she deliberately blew every take. "So we had to kiss all over again. And Errol Flynn, if I may say so, had a little trouble with his tights."

I couldn't quite believe what I'd just heard. And neither could everyone else in the room. Because the camera was rolling, none of us could laugh out loud, but it was hard not to. It's the last thing I expected from this perfectly coiffed, beautifully dressed, refined lady. Of course, we used that comment in the show and it's the one that audiences remember most.

JK After the interview was over, Olivia asked me if I knew Flynn's daughters. She said she'd recently received a letter from Rory, but wondered about Deirdre. I told her that while I'd spoken to Rory on the phone, I'd never met her, but that we'd filmed Deirdre for the program when we were in Los Angeles. I explained that the two sisters weren't on speaking terms. She put her arm around my shoulder and said in a conspiratorial tone of voice, "My dear, I know about sisters who don't speak." (She was referring, of course, to the fact that she and her sister, Joan Fontaine, hadn't spoken to each other in many years either. As far as we know, they never did make up before Fontaine died in 2013.)

DH A few weeks later, I flew back to Jamaica for the shoot with Patrice Wymore Flynn. She wore a red silk shirt and simple jewelry, with her gray hair pulled back. She lit up when she spoke about meeting Errol Flynn when they co-starred in the 1950 film, *Rocky*

Mountain. They fell in love and he formally asked her parents for her hand in marriage. He was forty-one years old; she was twenty-three. The ceremony was meant to be a small private gathering in Monte Carlo, but the press got wind of it and the crowd outside the church grew so large that the local police had to be called in to control the frenzy.

I asked whether she had had any doubts about marrying a man who had such a famous reputation as a womanizer. She said, "I know there was a big to-do over it, but I felt that the love between us was strong enough."

However, Flynn's wandering eye was built into his character. And so were his addictions to drugs and liquor. While he was making *Too Much, Too Soon* on the Warner Bros. lot, he met fifteen-year-old Beverly Aadland. It was at a time when Pat was "getting rather impatient with his daily injections of morphine," and had revived her own career as a stage performer. He was meant to meet her in Las Vegas after one of her club dates, but he never showed up.

"So I called the hotel where he'd been staying," she said. "And was told he'd checked out. I asked, 'Did he leave a forwarding address?' 'No,' said the receptionist.

"So he just walked out."

JK According to her, they remained in contact over the next couple of years, and were planning to give their marriage another chance. In October, 1959, almost exactly nine years after their wedding, she came offstage at the end of a performance, and the manager of the club handed her a drink, suggesting she sit down. He then broke the news to her that Flynn had died a few hours earlier. Strapped for money, he had gone to Canada with Beverly Aadland to sell his yacht, *Zaca.* His life of self-destruction had taken its toll. He was fifty years old.

Pat decided that he should be buried at Forest Lawn in California, even though others thought he should be laid to rest in Jamaica. But she felt that if his children wanted to visit his gravesite, it would be more convenient for them if it were in Los Angeles.

After a few years, she went to live permanently on the Flynn property in Jamaica, where she died in March, 2014, at the age of eighty-seven. She asked to be buried next to her husband in California.

JK and DH So it seems that none of the women in his life were ever able to get over their love for Errol Flynn. His first wife, Lili Damita, hounded him for money and apparently even stalked him; his second wife, Nora Eddington, remarried several times, but did many interviews about their relationship prior to her death in 2001; Patrice Wymore Flynn, his widow, never remarried, but lived the life he loved on their ranch in the Caribbean. And Olivia de Havilland still admits to her love for one of the most profligate and exhilarating of all Hollywood stars.

We gave a premiere party for the TCM broadcast of *The Adventures of Errol Flynn* in April, 2005, and Pat Flynn flew in from Jamaica to watch it on the air with us.

When it was over, she said, "Thank you. Errol would be so proud that finally he's being taken seriously as an actor." Of all the reviews the show received, that one from Pat was perhaps the most meaningful.

It was the last profile we produced, and it may be one of our best.

David, Pat Flynn, and Joan.
Jamaica, 2004. Authors' collection.

Authors' collection.

CHAPTER TWENTY NINE

A Few That Got Away

It has to be obvious by now that every production had its bumps in the road. We usually overcame the obstacles that were thrown in our way, but not always—twice we were fired. There were also those projects that came tantalizingly close to actually happening, but not close enough.

We spoke to Cary Grant, who gave us a somewhat back-handed blessing to produce a profile of him, but made it clear he wouldn't appear in it. "I never do television," he said. "But I can't stop you."

We replied, "We think you know that you control the use of clips from many of your films. So you actually *can* stop us."

"That won't be a problem," he said. "I know you won't choose any that make me look silly. Call me any time. Here's my home number." Then, to our dismay, PBS would not fund the project.

Marlene Dietrich was living as a recluse in Paris when we approached her. Her response was terse—and unprintable. We also pursued shows about Gene Kelly, Rita Hayworth, Esther Williams, Jack Benny, George Burns, Johnny Cash, Sol Hurok, and Irving Berlin, but could not get over the final hurdle with any of them. A profile of George and Ira Gershwin, to coincide with George's 100th birthday, had the full co-operation of their estates, but fell apart when the owner of their music publishing rights, Warner/Chappell, would not even consider negotiating an affordable deal. Barbra Streisand requested copies of every show we did; we met with her manager and then with her. She's well-known for taking years to decide on a project—and we're still waiting. Dick Cavett agreed to let us do a retrospective of *The Dick Cavett Show*, and narrated a sample reel we'd put together, but the residual payments to the guests, directors, writers, and musicians, made the budget prohibitive.

While we made a name for ourselves in the non-fiction world of television, we always wanted to produce a feature film. Michelle Pfeiffer became our partner to produce, and play the lead in, an adaptation of Edith Wharton's *The Custom of the Country*, with a script by Academy Award-winning writer, Christopher Hampton. We had it set up at TriStar, but "development hell" and the ever-changing powers at the studio put an end to that. And Pulitzer Prize-winner, Charles Fuller, wrote a script for us based on Paula Fox's book, *The Slave Dancer*, which had been the recipient of the Newberry Prize. We had a deal for it at Disney, but eventually that too collapsed. Joanne Woodward agreed to co-produce and star in several dramatizations of novels we all thought could be turned into movies for television, including *Kinds of Love* by May Sarton, and three mysteries that Gore Vidal had written under the pseudonym Edgar Box. Vidal was an old friend of Joanne's and the agreement she made with him was that we'd produce them as a trilogy. A&E was interested in the concept, but refused to commit to all three up-front, and that became the stumbling block that derailed the entire project.

In the documentary arena, the list of those we did work with still astounds us. Most belong to the era in Hollywood that blossomed after the introduction of "the talkies," when the industry was reinventing itself. They were products of the studio system, which closely protected its most valuable assets by controlling every ounce of publicity about them and the pictures they made. Little was known about the stars' real lives, and many of the stories released about them were manufactured to nurture their public images. As a result, there was a mystique and mystery surrounding them. They existed on the big silver screen in movie palaces, and not in our living rooms, which is perhaps what gave them a special aura—the feeling that they were just out of reach. And even though there was no shortage of fan magazines, there wasn't the daily barrage that feeds today's celebrity-obsessed culture, in which we're told more than we really need to know about everyone from performers to politicians.

Some thirty years ago, we brought back to life a dormant form of programming and perhaps can take credit—or blame—for the abundance of movie star profiles that have sprung up as a result. When we happened to luck into this niche that others were ignoring, the field was wide open, so we had our choice of the biggest and the best. By establishing relationships with these icons from the "Golden Age of Hollywood" and their families, we had the chance to shine a new spotlight on them. Or did we? After all, they were damn good actors.

In retrospect, we realize that each of our shows was a stepping stone to the next; each star who allowed us to pierce his or her wall of privacy effectively told the next ones that we could be trusted, that we wouldn't hurt or exploit them, that our goal was to present their stories as accurately and completely as we could.

So who do we want to do next?

After we completed our profile of Errol Flynn, we felt that the time had come to stop. We met some remarkable people, and we'll never see their likes again.

Now it's time for new challenges. Writing this book is one of them.

Authors' collection.

ACKNOWLEDGMENTS

In putting together this book, we would have been lost without the help and support of many people. They include our literary agent, Doug Grad; Eric Kampmann and Megan Trank of Beaufort Books; Brian T. Whitehill for his beautiful cover design; Mark Karis for the interior design; and Felicia Minerva at Midpoint Trade Books, and Jeff Abraham at Jonas Public Relations for getting the word out.

We subjected many of our friends to early drafts of chapters and received valuable comments. From some we requested advice on clearances and ownership, and from others we were given support and encouragement. In alphabetical order, they include Rick Amon, Mark Bagang, Pamela Becker, Albert Bellas, John Berendt, Sherry Buch, Dick Cavett, Jean Cohen-Neiditch, James Curtis, Richard Dreyfuss, Shirlee Fonda, Julie Garfield, Maria Cooper Janis, Peter Kane, Carol Katzka, Sherri Kramer, Su Lesser, Bette LeVine, the late Don Lynn, Roger L. Mayer, Kay Mazzo, Dennis Millay, John L. Miller, Charles Mintz, Michael Mowatt-Wynn, Arnold Neiditch, Bonnie Nelson, Robert Osborne, Scott Rodman, Hazel Rudeis, Ann Rundio, Renee Russell, Bess Schenkier, Carol Schneider, Lynda Sheldon, Lillian Smith, Golf Srithamrong, the late Edward Summer,

Charles Tabesh, Susie Tracy, Blair M. Westlake, Robert Wolders, and Joanne Woodward.

The majority of the photographs are from the authors' personal collections. However a number of photographers have generously allowed us to use their pictures here, and we are especially grateful to them: Scott Bryson (on behalf of his father, the late John Bryson), Ken Diego, John Haggerty, Brownie Harris, Don Perdue, the late Len Tavares, and Mitzi Trumbo. We also want to thank Shirlee Fonda, Susie Tracy, and Blair M. Westlake for allowing us to use images from their collections.

Films and television programs are essentially collaborative efforts, and we will be forever indebted to all those who contributed to the ones we produced. A comprehensive credit list would overwhelm this book, so will not be attempted here, although many key people are identified in the relevant chapters.

Not least, we want to thank all those who let us tell their stories, as well as their families and friends, and the many others who participated in our programs. Without them, this book would be filled with only blank pages.

APPENDIX

Productions referenced:

Skyline and *Skyline with Beverly Sills (WNET)*	1978-80
Fred Astaire: Puttin' On His Top Hat (WNET)	1980
Fred Astaire: Change Partners and Dance (WNET)	1980
Starring Katharine Hepburn (WNET)	1981
Paul Newman and Joanne Woodward (ABC News *20/20*)	1984
Judy Garland: The Concert Years (WNET/Sid Luft)	1985
The Spencer Tracy Legacy: A Tribute by Katharine Hepburn (WNET/MGM)	1986
James Stewart: A Wonderful Life (WNET/MGM)	1987
Bacall on Bogart (WNET/Turner Entertainment Co.)	1988
Broadway's Dreamers: The Legacy of The Group Theatre (WNET)	1989
The Perfect Tribute (Proctor & Gamble Productions)	1991
The Fred Astaire Songbook (WNET/Turner Entertainment Co.)	1991
Fonda on Fonda (Top Hat Productions/Turner Pictures)	1992
Katharine Hepburn: All About Me (Top Hat Productions/Turner Pictures)	1993
The Universal Story (Top Hat Productions/Universal Television)	1996
The Lady With the Torch (Top Hat Productions/Sony Pictures Entertainment)	1999
The John Garfield Story (Top Hat Productions/Turner Entertainment Co./TCM)	2003
The Adventures of Errol Flynn (Top Hat Productions/Turner Entertainment Co./TCM)	2005

INDEX

NOTE: Page numbers in *italics* indicate a photograph. Page numbers followed by an *"n"* indicate a footnote.